WITHDRAWN

Harvard English Studies 3

Veins of Humor

HARVARD ENGLISH STUDIES   3

Veins of Humor

Edited by Harry Levin

Harvard University Press, Cambridge, Massachusetts   1972

Publication of this volume has been aided by a grant from the Hyder
Edward Rollins Fund
Library of Congress Catalog Card Number 72–78425
Printed in the United States of America

Editorial Note

The fourth volume in this series, *The Uses of Literature in the United States,* will be edited by Monroe Engel; the fifth, *Chaucer,* by Larry D. Benson.

W. Jackson Bate
Morton W. Bloomfield
Reuben A. Brower
Harry Levin

— *Editorial Board*

Contents

Veins of Humor

Introduction

The unifying theme of the present volume might have lent itself more easily to an illustrative anthology than to an extremely miscellaneous collection of critical essays. Inherent in its pleasurable nature is a tendency to ward off serious treatment, to fight shy of interpretation, and consequently to defy analysis. There does exist a two-volume *History of English Humour,* published by the Reverend A. G. L'Estrange in 1877, and it is almost as desultory as *Tristram Shandy.* Qualified exponents of the subject — Harold Nicolson, J. B. Priestley, Stephen Potter — have rambled on about it pleasantly. But, in view of the unending and inconclusive effort of theorizing that has been expended on comedy, or more precisely the comic, we may well be surprised that so little of it has come to grips with the humorous. A persistent if not always consistent awareness of the expanding position that this peculiar element has occupied within the wider domain, from Ben Jonson to George Meredith, has been amply documented in *The Idea of Comedy,* a recent compilation of the most relevant texts from English criticism, edited with an illuminating commentary by W. K. Wimsatt. Perhaps it will suggest a continuity, or facilitate an access to some of the varied problems raised and exemplified in the miscellany before us, if I begin by sketching a rough outline of what our key-word has meant to many of those who have conjured with it.

Some of them have shied away from definition, in the obscurantist fear lest we murder to dissect. Others, more fortunately for our purpose, have shown a Houdini-like compulsion to disentangle the mystery they profess. One of the anti-definers, S. J. Perelman, puts us in our academic place by remarking that "Humour is purely a point of view, and only the pedants try to classify it." Mr. Perelman's vein is truly one which challenges classification, depending as it does on an inimitable style and even more upon a point of view toward the multiplicity of pre-existing styles. Yet it exudes a pedantry of its own, which invites a more meticulous scrutiny. Some of his writing, indeed, may already be needing footnotes. In contrast to the ironic naiveté of earlier American humorists, Mr. Perelman displays a parodic savoir faire. Lately, by shifting his residence to England, he has attested its traditional claims as the homeland of humor, where a richer backlog of conventions and clichés should continue to offer him laughing matter. On the negative side, his gesture seems to confirm the earlier impression of Charles Dickens that the Americans are not really a humorous people; certainly there is not much Dickensian jollity in the harsh transatlantic derision of *Martin Chuzzlewit*. On the other hand, it will be remembered that Americans have many jokes about the Englishman who misses the point of a joke.

The notion that humor ought somehow to be treated as an undefinable *je-ne-sais-quoi* has a tradition behind it which is ballasted by the skeptical authority of Swift:

> What Humor is, not all the Tribe
> Of Logick-mongers can describe.

Nonetheless Swift, being neither a logic-monger nor a pedant, went so far as to link the phenomenon at hand with the larger inscrutability of life itself. Here, as contrasted with those collateral gifts of conversation, wit and raillery,

> Here, onely Nature acts her Part,
> Unhelpt by Practice, Books, or Art.

This conversational gift is not only odd and grotesque; it is also wild — a natural and spontaneous growth which therefore cannot be cultivated and would merely be spoiled by the joyless exercises of affectation.

> Tis never by Invention got,
> Men have it when they know it not.

Henry Fielding would differ markedly in his fiction, insofar as he would view affectation as "the only Source of the true Ridiculous." But when he explicitly addressed himself to the concept of humor, in *The Covent-Garden Journal,* he would emphasize the vagueness of the word and the variety of opinions about it. And yet for all the pluralism and skepticism that have beclouded its ultimate signification, one aspect of it seems to have been clearly and widely understood: whatever humor might or might not be, it was thoroughly English. Thus incidentally, in the course of his ode "The Manners," William Collins paused to tender a patriotic tribute:

> O *Humour,* Thou whose Name is known
> To *Britain's* favor'd Isle alone . . .

Alone? Is humor, then, to be regarded as the exclusive property of the English? The name itself, which Charles Baudelaire linked pertinently with *spleen,* was exported to other languages as a conscious Anglicism. A notable example is furnished by Luigi Pirandello's monograph *L'Umorismo,* but Pirandello himself is an eloquent witness to the fact that humor could speak other tongues. The standard English spelling, ending in -*our,* interestingly enough, has been affected by the French. American usage favors the Latin suffix -*or* — which, as it happens, was used both by Jonson, in one of his quartos, and by Dickens, in his manuscripts. Fernand Baldensperger has surveyed the semantic history of the term and registered some of the intercultural reactions. He informs us, among other matters, that Montesquieu distinguished between *l'humeur des Anglais* and the Gallic *esprit,* that Voltaire found a closer translation in *chagrin* and Lessing a German counterpart in *Laune.*

Traditionally the Frenchman has looked upon the Englishman as an individual who takes his pleasures sadly — more given to morosity than gaiety, according to Madame de Staël, and hence better typified by Swiftian misanthropy than by Molieresque sociability. She concludes, without much concern for the evidence, that English literature is lacking in good comedies. An actual witness during the Restoration, the Seigneur de Saint-Evremond, had praised English comedy for its naturalness, though later critics have been more struck by the comparative artificiality of the plays he must have seen.

The capacity for laughter is doubtless a universal quality, one of the few that differentiates human beings from beasts. But the mode whereby it manifests itself and the objects that stimulate it seem to be capable of multiform variation: national, regional, social, sexual, cultural, ethnic. Such variations have a good deal to tell us, both about the laughers and about those who are not amused, the agelasts. Although many of Britain's greatest wits have been Irishmen, Englishmen have customarily taken a condescending view of Hibernian humor, sometimes equating it with the type of non sequitur known as a bull. It is reported of the early Sorbonne that one of the scholastic theses disputed there was whether or not a German could have wit. Yet *Galgenhumor* is not a uniquely British commodity, and the Nonsense Rhymes of Edward Lear have something in common with the *Unsinnspoesie* of Christian Morgenstern. One of the sexes has been charged by the other with a lack of humor — despite the sparkling instance of Mistress Millamant, "A Woman, and a kind of Humorist." That charge, we may suspect, goes back to the days when it would have been considered unladylike to appreciate Rabelais. George Lyman Kittredge was fond of maintaining that Jews, though often witty, were basically humorless. This assumption may simply have been a confession of insensibility to a wry *Weltanschauung* more widely shared today than a generation ago.

"The stroke of the great humorist is world-wide, with lights of Tragedy in his laughter," wrote Meredith in his lecture-essay *On Comedy and on the Uses of the Comic Spirit*. He was speaking contextually of Cervantes — whose quintessential Spanishness, to the contrary notwithstanding, has been underlined by many another commentator. Meredith's theories, particularly with regard to the civilizing influence of women, seem to have weathered better than most of his novels, where the Comic Spirit all too frequently seems to be laughing up her diaphanous sleeve. His impressionistic rhapsodizing tells us little about "the spirit of Humour," except to stress its rough-and-tumble heterogeneity. He is mainly concerned with a highly rarefied comedy of manners, which envisions its prototype in the lost works of Menander and discerns its masterpiece in the atypical *Misanthrope* of Molière. On most other comic writers he sounds unconvincing, since he is less interested in drawing concrete distinctions than in building up a sort of composite paradigm. Now, granted the argument of Joseph Addison that the test of true wit is translation, that genuine humor ought not to be bounded by frontiers, still there is much to be learned from the untranslatable or from a foreign perspective. Mr. Punch may embody the typically English figure of fun, yet he was born in Naples, and acquired his beak and hump in France. It would be instructive to contrast him with his semblances in other cultures: Guignol, Kasperl, Karaghiosis.

The particularity of English humor seems, at all events, to have been universally acknowledged. Locally it was a matter of self-recognition — and of self-congratulation, too, for John Ruskin. Some drawings in an exhibition at Oxford by one of *Punch*'s most popular illustrators, John Leech, led Ruskin to speculate on "a moral and metaphysical question, to determine the share which English humour has in completing our courage and affection, in enabling us to bear hardship with a smile and convey reproof in play." So heroic a virtue is bound to have its invidious defect, since it invites a Podsnappian comparison with the lesser breeds: "I believe the total want of this faculty in the Italian mind to be at the root of much of its cruelty, and to give more dangerous languor to its vices." Ruskin himself was obviously no humorist, although the unconscious irony of such a passage is not without its humorous overtones. Broaderminded critics, like Meredith, managed to give the English humorists a cosmopolitan tinge by making honorary Englishmen out of Cervantes and even Rabelais and Aristophanes. Among continental observers Hippolyte Taine, past master of

French generalizations about England, summed up by alluding to the bitter taste of its humor. Though he was not familiar with the useful American compound *deadpan,* that was the very feature he singled out: "la plaisanterie d'un homme qui en plaisantant garde une mine grave."

Observation at the international level generally reflects the observer as well as the observed. If a certain nation tends to jest with staid and sober mien even to the point of melancholia, another nation may elude high seriousness by grimaces, gesticulations, and frivolous habits. Such, at any rate, has vulgarly been the English stereotype for the French. From first to last, the British Channel has offered a two-way thoroughfare for historical interaction and mutual appraisal. French Anglicists, among whom the late Louis Cazamian held a respected place, have contributed special insights to the appreciation of English culture. They were especially fascinated by *The Development of English Humour* — to cite the title of a small book brought out by Cazamian in 1930 and much revised and augmented in 1952. Therein he does not deny the British their birthright, but he propounds his own thesis about its provenance. His starting-point is the relative paucity of humor in Anglo-Saxon literature, a circumstance which has seldom been questioned though variously explained. Thence he moves on quickly to the period of Chaucer, and to a humorous flowering which can be readily illustrated. What has happened meanwhile? The Norman Conquest, of course. Mirth has come to Merry England largely as an importation from the Continent, personified by that gifted woman of letters, Marie de France. The catalyst for English humor has been the *esprit gaulois.*

We are reinforced in the tentative conclusion that humor is not an instinctive racial trait, though there are solidly circumstantial reasons for the local habitation with which it has repeatedly been associated; and likewise that, since different races have differed in their expression of it, it had best be studied in the widest possible context. However, if we are curious why the English presented themselves to the world — in Oliver Goldsmith's phrase — as "a nation of humourists," we must further inquire why they found it necessary to supplement the more usual conception of wit with the idea of humor. The dichotomy between them has its locus classicus in the spirited essay "On Wit and Humour" that introduces William Hazlitt's *Lectures on the English Comic Writers* (1819). Those two terms had traveled far together since the seventeenth century, now loosely synonymous and again in polar opposition. Etymology reveals a kind of paradox, since — while *humor* comes intact from the Latin — *wit* has an Anglo-Saxon origin. Deriving from the verb *witan,* "to know," it may boast a historical kinship with wisdom. Its Greek equivalent was *Euphues,* literally an able or clever person, a designation borrowed by John Lyly from Roger Ascham, for whom it signified a good mind. Other Elizabethans employed it to mean imagination — or else what Samuel Taylor Coleridge might have called fancy. Its shades and shifts of meaning form the basis of a pyrotechnical sequence in Alexander Pope's *Essay on Criticism.*

A similar ambiguity is conveyed by the French *esprit,* which seems less wholeheartedly committed to spirituality than its portentous German synonym, *Geist.* The striking distinction is that, in comparison with the intellectualistic connotations of wit, the reverberations of *humor* are corporeal, not to say materialistic or earthbound. The first of nine definitions listed in Dr. Johnson's *Dictionary* is quite literally "moisture." More specifically, according to ancient and medieval physiology, this denoted the four fluids of the human body — choler (or bile), melancholy, phlegm, and blood — which in turn had been determined by the four elements. During the Renaissance a growing emphasis was placed upon the psychological consequences of these physical attributes. Ideally, it was thought, they should commingle in due proportion, originally designated as *temperament.* In practice, one of the humors usually predominated over the others, thereby determining whether the individual *disposition* — another technical term — would be choleric (or bilious), melancholic, phlegmatic, or sanguine. An ingenious Spanish physician, Juan Huarte, even published a treatise in 1575, *Examen de ingenios para les ciencias,* suggesting that all infants be examined at birth and assigned to their subsequent careers in accordance with their temperamental predispositions. That deterministic program came under the strictures of the Inquisition for its implicit challenge to the freedom of the will. But it was translated and circulated in England, where it was undoubtedly read by Ben Jonson.

More casually, humor could be conceived as a person's state of mind at the moment: a mood, a caprice, a whim, an inclination to be indulged — or humored (Shakespeare was apparently the first to use the verbal form). Persons subject to such passing states — moody, capricious, whimsical — were said to be humorous. But this is at the other extreme from a psychic condition rigidly predetermined by a predominant humor or ruling passion, a master faculty or *idée fixe*. It is the latter which animates the stock figures of the comic stage, as they have been fixed by convention and stiffened by decorum. And it was Jonson who took the critical step of transposing the category of humor from the plane of physiognomy to the sphere of comedy. Actually, his first great theatrical success, *Every Man in his Humour* (1598), was preceded one year before by George Chapman's play, *An Humorous Day's Mirth*. The catchword seems to have accorded with certain movements in the direction of satire and the fashionable humor of melancholy. With Corporal Nym it gathered a Shakespearean resonance: "And that's the humour of it." Jonson's original version of *Every Man in his Humour* was a conventionally Italianate piece of work, whose happy title was hardly more than a quasi-proverbial phrase. It was in the programmatic Induction to *Every Man out of his Humour* (1599) that Jonson fully asserted his individuality and formally announced a new comic dispensation.

This dialogue allows his angry spokesman Asper to be drawn out by two judicious interlocutors into a psychophysical description of humor, which he thereupon brings into the playhouse:

> It may, by *Metaphore,* apply it selfe
> Unto the generall disposition:
> As when some one peculiar quality
> Doth so possesse a man, that it doth draw
> All his affects, his spirits, and his powers,
> In their confluctions, all to runne one way,
> This may be truly said to be a Humour.

Jonson goes on to insist, like Swift, that humor is ingrained and not to be achieved by affectation, although one can think of Jonsonian characters who come closer to Fielding's in that respect. The additional metaphors that here come into play are the standard properties of the didactic satirist: mirror, scourge, anatomy. *Every Man out of his Humour* marks the first stage of an experimental trilogy described as "Comicall Satyre." These were failures as comedies, nor did they succeed in the reforming endeavor to which they were dedicated. Asper, under the guise of Macilente, enters the drama itself, seeking to castigate and cure the distempered dramatis personae. But if men are so physically conditioned as the theory maintains, can a mere reflection of their behavior move them to change their motives? The stage would seem less suitable than the judge's bench or the psychoanalyst's couch for putting men out of their humors. Jonson evades the dilemma in his maturest plays by again permitting every man to enact his humor freely, for better or worse. We speak broadly of the genre he devised as the comedy of humors; yet his ripest characters are by no means monomaniacal; Volpone is not a hedgehog but a fox. The asperities of Asper seem to have been closely parodied by the punitive language of Jaques in *As You Like It,* whose talk about flaying and purging may be interpreted as Shakespeare's genial burlesque of the stern Jonsonian attempt to impose poetic justice upon a fallible humanity.

The melancholy Jaques is cast in that role which Hamlet, while enumerating the members of a repertory troop, terms "the humourous man." The principal characteristic of this personage, moodiness, stems from a fundamental dissatisfaction with the world which is not unlike that of the tragic malcontent. Hamlet, who combines both parts, is deliberately — if grimly — comic when he assumes his "antic disposition." But the adjective *humorous,* for Shakespeare, indicates a potential subject for fun and not a funster. Bardolph and the other followers of Falstaff are denominated "irregular humourists" in the Folio list of actors' names for *The Second Part of Henry IV* (the noun itself does not appear in Shakespeare's text). The title page of the Quarto promises to include "the humours of sir Iohn Falstaffe." Note the plural: the Prince has previously labeled his companion "that trunk of humours," and John Dryden will echo the epithet in hailing him as "a miscellany of humours."

Falstaff thus transcends the single-humored type by his sheer diversity and flexibility. He himself is his best interpreter when, after having somewhat unexpectedly run away with the show in Part I, he makes his self-heralding entrance into Part II: "Men of all sorts take a pride to gird at me. The brain of this foolish-compounded clay, man, is not able to invent anything that intends to laughter, more than I invent or is invented on me. I am not only witty in myself, but the cause that wit is in other men."

Falstaff has been discoursing about wit; but, as its sentient object, he stands in a strategic position to formulate its relationship with humor. For he is not only a butt, a figure of fun, a cause that wit is in other men; he is moreover witty in himself, a laughing-stock who can join in the laugh and end by ironically turning it against his would-be mockers, as in the mock-epic of Gadshill. Compare him with Bardolph and observe the difference. Except for his gruff objurgations, Bardolph has no defense against jokes about his nose; Falstaff has endless ripostes to the gibes against his belly, and excels the others in the inventiveness of his self-mockery — an imaginative flow which, as he later soliloquizes, has its unbounded source of inspiration in sherry. Inasmuch as bellies and noses are bodily rather than mental, and natural rather than artificial, they are the stuff of humor; and once set forth, it becomes the task of wit, as Hazlitt would argue, to perceive and expose such exaggerated appurtenances. By the same token it follows that wit is impersonal, in the Coleridgean sense that it could be remarked by any observer, whereas humor — Coleridge maintains — "always more or less partakes of the character of the speaker." Where the wits are bland suitors, walking gentlemen, and men about town, whose urbane repartee is more or less interchangeable, humorous characters always have idiosyncratic voices of their own; and Falstaff plays the dual personality of the Erasmian fool who brings out the follies of other men.

Falstaff's statement about his role-playing helps to explain the central figure he is destined to cut in any discussion of English comedy. Furthermore, it has far-reaching implications which can illustrate and interrelate much of the esthetic theory that has attempted to analyze the comic. Most of the theorists have had something in their grasp, like the blind men with the elephant; what still needs to be shown is the connection between the parts. By and large, their views can be boiled down to two schools of thought. One of these, following Thomas Hobbes, emphasizes superiority; the other, with Immanuel Kant, stresses incongruity. In other words, the first concentrates on the witty viewpoint, the second on the humorous situation. Among the moderns, Sigmund Freud aligns himself with the first by focusing on self-expression and personal animus (*Witz* meaning both wit and joke). What he dismisses as harmless wit can be looked on as playful humor, whose protagonist is *homo ludens,* the hero of Johan Huizinga's brilliant treatise on play as a component of civilization. The same word, *ridicule,* was utilized by both Stendhal and Lord Kames as a touchstone for wit. The playfulness of humor is characterized by Stendhal as *le plaisant* and by Kames as risibility. These terminological variances might be reconciled by speaking normatively of the ridiculous, on the one hand, and of the ludicrous on the other. Laughter is the common denominator between *laughing at* and *laughing with,* and Falstaff is our agent in both camps.

However, prompted by Falstaffian instinct perhaps, we anticipate. Historically, the explicit antithesis between wit and humor seems to have emerged from the hard-hitting controversy between Dryden and Thomas Shadwell. Jonson's most faithful disciple, Shadwell was trying to revive the older comedy of humors, while Dryden inclined toward a newer, French-inspired, more elegant comedy of manners. In his preface to *An Evening's Love* (1671), disclaiming humor on his own part, he declared that Jonson had been the only playwright who practiced it — probably in order to compensate for his deficiency in wit. But meanwhile humor had been acquiring a broader and more positive significance, and could not so tartly be put down. Sir William Temple paid especial attention to it in his important essay *On Poetry* (1690), wherein it is traced to Shakespeare rather than Jonson. Pointing to the essential Englishness of both the word and the vein, Temple attributes this favorable outgrowth to the native soil, the changeable climate, and above all a government which tolerates free opinion and speech. The environment fosters an individualism which brings out eccentricities to a degree not paralleled elsewhere. Where the conformities of the Continent are expressed through the same old typical characters, England glories in its Originals, whose variety is mirrored in the theater. "We are not only more unlike one another than any Nation I know, but we are more unlike our selves too at several times."

William Congreve, though he claimed novelty for his subject, amplified a number of Temple's points in his letter to John Dennis *Concerning Humour in Comedy* (1695): the predominance of the English, their singularity as individuals, and "the great Freedom, Privilege, and Liberty which the Common People of *England* enjoy." Rather a wit than a humorist, as Samuel Johnson would testify, Congreve vaguely undertook to synthesize the two categories; but it was rather inconsistent of him, as the creator of Millamant, to question women's humor. Dennis himself, an austere and blunt neoclassicist, advocated humor at the expense of wit because he felt that characters of lower rank were more appropriate to comedy. Addison expectably proposed a compromise (in *Spectator* 35) through one of his allegorical pedigrees, where Humour was the offspring of Wit and Mirth. In *Sensus Communis: An Essay on the Freedom of Wit and Humour* (1709), the Earl of Shaftesbury posed the highminded argument that truth and justice could not be vulnerable to ridicule (yet Socrates himself had, after all, been injuriously ridiculed by Aristophanes). A social conflict between the aristocracy and the bourgeoisie was implied by George Farquhar's *Discourse on Comedy*: "The Courtier crys out for *Wit* and *Purity of Stile*; the Citizen for *Humour* and *Ridicule*." The ideological tension was confirmed by Goldsmith, in terms which would soon be reversed: "Wit raises human nature above its level; humour acts a contrary part, and equally depresses it."

But Goldsmith was engaged in a rear-guard action on behalf of superior wit, and so was the third edition of the *Encyclopaedia Britannica* (1788–1797) when it stated that humor might not be "perfectly consistent with true politeness." Vocal laughter, which Lord Chesterfield had condemned for its democratic vulgarity, would ring loud in the nineteenth century. When Johnson was depicted by Sir John Hawkins as "the most humourous man I ever saw," and likened to the old comedians, the reference was not to his fits of depression but to his bouts of jocularity. To be sure, he offered a fine illustration for Temple's and Congreve's point that English culture fostered originality of character. Further illustrations are abundant in such books as Edith Sitwell's *English Eccentrics* — a publication which might have been subtitled, like Thackeray's *Book of Snobs, By One of Themselves*. As we may have noticed, the appellation of *humorist* was initially applied to an eccentric, rather than to a writer who pointed out the eccentricity. Gradually it shifted from the objective to the subjective mood, and from the passive to the active sense. Samuel Butler is said to have marked the transition, very likely because he was identified with his humoristic creation, Hudibras. Yet when Corbyn Morris brought forth his *Essay towards Fixing the True Standards of Wit, Humour, Raillery, Satire, and Ridicule* in 1744, he took the earlier attitude: *To Which is Added, an Analysis of the Characters of an Humourist, Sir John Falstaff, Sir Roger de Coverly, and Don Quixote.*

As the focus of humor is shifted from actor to spectator, from the individual whose oddities are noted to the writer who is taking note, a more sympathetic relation seems to develop between the two. Ridicule gives way to empathy; the characterization becomes the author's mouthpiece, not his victim; and the author himself becomes a role-player, a practical joker, a collector of hobby-horses. Laurence Sterne is omnipresent — and very far from invisible — throughout *Tristram Shandy*. Edward Lear is the moonstruck protagonist of his own limericks, and Lewis Carroll's nonsense is the looking-glass image of his Oxonian logic. Dickens was notoriously implicated in acting out the lives of his characters through his public readings. Typically, the American humorist has been a monologuist, drawling or misspelling a rustic dialect under a facetious pseudonym. His performance is that of an *eiron,* a self-ironist who dissembles his wit — like Socrates himself, or like Will Rogers saying "All I know is what I read in the papers," or like the accident-prone anecdotists in the *New Yorker*. (The related case of Falstaff is complicated, in this respect as in so many others. He comes on as an *alazon,* the *eiron's* opposite, the eternal braggart whose boasts will be duly exposed, and hence the cause that wit is in other men. But, being wittier in himself than they are in themselves, he rises above his temporary discomfiture and contrives to outwit them. He is an *eiron* masking as an *alazon*.)

The extraordinary softening that English humor underwent during the eighteenth century and the Romantic period has been chronicled step by step in an excellent study by Stuart M. Tave, *The Amiable Humorist.* The reservations voiced in Sir Richard Blackmore's *Essay upon Wit* (1716) are among the indications of a collective change from satirical raillery to cheerful benevolence. Socially this can be correlated with the increasing pervasion of middle-class sentimentality. "Between Swift and Sterne," as E. N. Hooker has written, "a mighty chasm occurs." Out of that chasm arise the mollifying concepts of good humor, good nature, innocent mirth, sweet philanthropy, and pathos. Andrew Lang would retrospectively comment that the old-fashioned humor had gone out of English life together with its old-fashioned cruelty. The transformation is graphic when we turn from Hogarth and Gillray to Cruikshank and Phiz. The leveling process had so repressed the originals, and thereby so impoverished the theater, that Hazlitt could believe: "We are deficient in comedy because we are without character in real life." He underestimated the extent to which comedy and character would stage their resurgence in the Dickensian novel; and Dickens, with all his sentimental Victorianism, could draw upon a counterbalancing strain which was pungently Jonsonian. Amiable humor had its heyday in the essays of Charles Lamb, where the writer struck up an intimacy with the reader, to whom he confided his nostalgias and whimsies.

It was William Makepeace Thackeray, in a lecture entitled "Charity and Humour," who expounded what could be taken as the official Victorian formulation. Thackeray's professions of worldly cynicism and his fondness for Augustan pastiche hint that he might have been more at ease among the coffee-house wits in the age of Queen Anne; but his *Lectures on the English Humourists of the Eighteenth Century,* aimed at a nineteenth-century audience, are biographical, moralistic, and by no means nostalgic. An assignment coupling humor with charity would inevitably subjoin other qualities, notably tears, and would indulge the lecturer's penchant for sermonizing. Humorists are "weekday preachers"; Mr. Punch himself "preaches from his booth"; and "was there ever a better charity sermon preached in the world than Dickens's 'Christmas Carol'?" Thackeray's tone sounds forced whenever he speaks of Dickens, and he must surely do so on this occasion: "What a humour! and what a good humour!" To sum it all up in two monosyllables, "humour is wit and love" — a recipe which Thackeray interjected into the much less charitable context of *Mr. Brown's Letters to his Nephew*. As for the humorist:

> A literary man of the humoristic turn is pretty sure to be of a philanthropic nature, to have a great sensibility, to be easily moved to pain or pleasure, keenly to appreciate the varieties of temper of people round about him, and sympathize in their laughter, love, amusement, tears. Such a man is philanthropic, man-loving by nature, as another is irascible, or red-haired, or six feet high.

If this be a portrait of Dickens — and it is manifestly not a self-portrait — we should have to add that irascibility is as much a part of his humor as philanthropy. But the propensity to overflow the normal limits of definition, and to blur the picture by throwing in extraneous matter, is habitual with our subject, as should by now be evident. It reaches its most transcendent heights when Thomas Carlyle, that virtuoso of overstatement, undertakes to describe the indescribable humor of Jean-Paul Richter:

> . . . it is vast, rude, irregular; often perhaps overstrained and extravagant; yet fundamentally it is genuine humour, the humour of Cervantes and Sterne, and product not of Contempt but Love, not of superficial distortion of natural forms, but of deep and playful sympathy with all forms. It springs not less from the heart than from the head; its result is not laughter, but something far kindlier and better; at it were, the balm which a generous spirit pours over the wounds of life, and which none but a generous spirit can give forth. Such humour is compatible with tenderest and sublimest feelings, or rather it is incompatible with the want of them.

Joe Miller, the name of a long defunct comedian, has survived among his compatriots as a byword for the unblinking fact that jokes get stale. Jean-Paul no longer seems quite so cosmic a genius, and Carlyle has all but dropped out of the syllabus. The tenderness he lovingly dwelt upon has given way to a resurgence of toughness during our more violent century; and the wheel has come full circle, revolving back from amiability to aggressiveness, to a more sharply satirical frame of mind. George Bernard Shaw, though both a wit and a humanitarian, would not have been numbered by Thackeray among "the kind English humourists." Comedy, with Bertolt Brecht or Samuel Beckett or Eugène Ionesco or Harold Pinter, has moved from sympathy to alienation. Absurdity is treated seriously, as indeed it must be when it breaks in on us from all directions and unsettles the presuppositions of daily living. Grotesquery has come into its own. André Breton, a generation ago, rediscovered the roots of Surrealism in *l'humour noir*; and if the English have not figured prominently among its current exponents, they were its pioneers and Swift was its "veritable initiator," in the testimonial of Breton. Black humor too confronts us literally, as the power of Afro-American blackness asserts itself in our time. The struggle has not abated as the protean challenger has continued to change his shape. "Trying to define humor," said that dazzling artist Saul Steinberg, in a recent interview with Pierre Schneider, "is one of the definitions of humor."

On Pirandello's Humorism

The events that brought Luigi Pirandello to write his essay
"L'Umorismo" in 1908 are on the whole well known. After
fifteen years of a career reluctantly spent teaching stylistics in a
girls' college in Rome, he needed a solid publication in order to
convince his judging peers of the seriousness of his academic
involvement.[1] And indeed, the essay that enabled him to earn a
tenured position in his school has all the connotations of a
scholarly endeavor. By calling to task the authorities on humorism — D'Ancona, Bonghi, and Nencioni for Italy, Taine for
France, and his own former teacher in Bonn, Theodor Lipps,

1. For the essay "L'Umorismo" I have followed the M. Lo Vecchio-
Musti edition included in L. Pirandello, *Saggi, poesie, scritti varii*,
Milan, 1960, pp. 17–160. This edition reproduces the 2nd ed. of the
essay (Florence, Luigi Battistelli, 1920). In the same volume, pp. 1245–
1248, Pirandello's "Lettera autobiografica" (first published in the Roman periodical *Le lettere* in 1924) is reproduced; but for a clear state-
ment of the reasons why Pirandello wrote "L'Umorismo" see also
Corrado Alvaro's "Cronologia della vita e delle opere di L. Pirandello,"
in L. Pirandello, *Novelle per un anno*, Milan, 1956, I, 43–54, esp. 46.
Among the critics of Pirandello who have attached great importance
to the essay "L'Umorismo" see especially Ulrich Leo, "Pirandellos
Kunsttheorie und Maskensymbol," in *Deutsche Vierteljahrsschrift für
Literaturwissenschaft und Geistesgeschichte*, 11 (1933), 94–124; and
J. Chaix-Ruy, *Pirandello: Humour et poésie*, Paris, 1967.

for Germany — Pirandello in fact shows an impeccable knowledge of the discussions on the subject; by differentiating his point of view from the opinions of others with the caution of a self-restrained scholar, he indicates that he knows how to avoid the risk of transforming his intellectual assets, of which his colleagues in Italy were certainly well aware, into a professional liability.

As is all too obvious, however, if the academic pressure could in a certain way condition the length of the essay, or the thickness of its erudite apparatus, it nevertheless appears immaterial or bears only marginal significance when we come to explain the deep motivation of Pirandello's undertaking. Even the dedication, to "the late Mattia Pascal, librarian" — that is, to a figment of Pirandello's imagination, to the most eloquent fictional mouthpiece of his relativism — strikes a dissonant note irrelevant to and contrasting with the erudite purpose of the essay.

A careful look at the material that constitutes the bulk of the essay shows, furthermore, that Pirandello's reading in the works of literature related to humorism only represents a frame of reference called upon to support a highly personal order of values toward which the critical discourse is impatiently gravitating. The works of Pulci, Rabelais, Ariosto, and Cervantes — unavoidable topics for an essay on humorism — act as an impressive reservoir of learned examples and constitute above all a vehicle of clarification for a theoretical issue that bears particular force for Pirandello the artist. In fact, while preparing his essay, Pirandello had already ceased to believe in knowledge as a goal to be reached through daily efforts, a goal having in itself its torments and its rewards. Rather, he considered it a heritage to be absorbed in the focus of a vision eternally present for the spirit of the artist, in an all-consuming act of creation. As early as the beginning of the century, Pirandello's culture was fixed and crystallized: a product of an enthusiastic experience to be placed in his German years, when he considered himself basically a linguist and a romance philologist, hence in the past.[2] Thus in a sense in the essay on humorism, not only

2. In his years of great reading and scholarly pride Pirandello liked to express himself on the question of learning with unusual enthusiasm.

the exemplifications, but the images themselves — even the most striking ones, in spite of their appearance of genial improvisation — are recurrent experiences returning to the page with almost formulaic value to prove what has already been proven, to underline the *déjà vu*: at once focus of repose and obsessive fixity.

It is the merit of one of the first reviewers of Pirandello's essay, Benedetto Croce, to have realized the marginality of its erudite apparatus and to have discarded that altogether from his critical considerations.[3] By showing little or no concern for the diachronical disposition of Pirandello's material, Croce at first seems inclined to emphasize that in the matter of humorism only theoretical assumptions have the right to be considered relevant, and that Pirandello's conceptualization of art should not so much be judged in its historical application to authors whom he happens to call humorists as it should be evaluated in itself, by going at the very roots of its esthetic relevance. No wonder then if, in agreement with a monistic conception of art that allows no classification of sentiments, no reflective mood capable of defeating the free expansion of the artist's imagination, Croce dismisses Pirandello's effort as theoretically unsound. The counteracting reflexes of Pirandello's humorist, always looking at the other side of the coin, freezing his initial thrust for life or reversing it in negation of life, could only appear to Croce as the product of a sincerely tormented but chaotic mind, and at best as the offspring of the moody improvisation of a philosophizing dilettante.

It should however be added that — since for Croce an erroneous ideology of knowledge does not necessarily create a

---

"I study Romance philology," he wrote in 1890, "with deep love and assiduous care, and the opinion I follow is the one of the science I have dedicated myself to" ("Per la solita questione della lingua," in *Saggi, poesie, scritti varii*, p. 858). For the years of Pirandello's formation see Gösta Andersson, *Arte e teoria: Studi sulla poetica del giovane Pirandello*, Stockholm, 1966.

3. Croce, "A proposito della dottrina dell'Umorismo di L. Pirandello," in *La critica* (1909), pp. 219–223; also in *Conversazioni critiche*, Bari, 1939, I, 44–48. See also Croce, "Luigi Pirandello" in *La letteratura della nuova Italia*, Bari, 1940, VI, 359–377. On the Croce-Pirandello relation see A. Piromalli, "Pirandello e Croce," in *Atti del congresso internazionale di studi pirandelliani*, Florence, 1967, pp. 863–875.

false form of art, the creating artist in the depths of his imagination being able to reach for compensating resources unknown to the artist as a theoretician and unforeseen by him—it may well happen that in the matter of Pirandello's humorism Croce's primary target is not necessarily what it appears to be. In fact his opposition to the cognitive effort of Pirandello's mind ought to be definitely placed within the framework of his inborn distrust of any artistic vision of the world, from Leopardi's *Operette morali* to Pirandello's theater, that is imbued with an irredeemably pessimistic outlook.

As for Pirandello, though in disagreement with Croce on practically everything, he accepts the assumption that the source of art is imaginative and not conceptual. Paradoxically, however, humorism, the only form of art in which he is truly interested, is also to him the only one ready to open the door of the creative process to reflection. All his efforts, when talking of humorism, are therefore turned to justifying that exceptional experience which humorism underlines, without denying the truth of the above-mentioned statement concerning the imaginative nature of artistic expression.

Pirandello's definition of humorism as *sentimento del contrario* indicates a dilemma at the core of his aesthetic convictions. If *sentimento del contrario* does not mean, as in my opinion it does not, the objective manifestation of a challenging emotion, counteracting from the opposite pole the expansion of another emotion obstructing its path — if it is not the vectorial force carrying the rights of an emotion well into the alien territory of an opposite emotion which has acquired undue prominence — it could only indicate the presence of a subjective "feeling" that somewhere in the stratified world of our affections there is an emotional explosion that shakes our privileged heritage of sentiments, refusing to accept them as the only ones which really "are." This "feeling," however, is not really a kind of seismograph limiting itself to measuring the waves of an emotional earthquake, in spite of the qualifications attributed to it by Pirandello; it is not a sentiment at all, since its activity is overwhelmingly critical, analytical, and rational. By trying to give another name to a cognitive activity Pirandello, instead of making his dilemma inconspicuous, as he would have liked, ends up by giving the limelight, unwittingly but revealingly, to an all-encompassing and proliferating imagery suggested by the intrusive concept of reflection.

In order to qualify better the issue of reflection versus sentiment, I shall quote a few examples of what I would like to call the metamorphic presence of reflection in the core of Pirandello's essay on humorism. Reflection appears at first in the guise of a judge who calls the artist to duty and meanwhile helps him to decompose a given sentiment. It may well be that by analyzing and decomposing a sentiment or its image, this demiurgic and personified reflection literally creates the counteracting sentiment, which freezes the expansion of the previous one or at least erodes its territory. There is of course a significant difference between "creating" an emotion almost *ex nihilo,* or at least unpredictably through the manipulation of another emotion, and acknowledging its presence in the bulk of reality, or detecting its objective right to exist as a negation and reversal of the truths more obviously established. The dividing line between idealistic subjectivism — also in its relativistic impact — and positivistic objectivism is, in Pirandello, far from easy to trace. A connotative sign of the detachment and objectivity in the judging role attributed to reflection can be detected in the emphasis Pirandello gives to a kind of philosophical remoteness attainable by looking through turned-around binoculars at the surrounding human landscape.

Reflection also appears in the deceitful form of a mirror composed of iced waters in which the flame of the sentiment dives to extinction. The fizzling of the water and the steam coming from the liquid surface become, for Pirandello, alluring symbols for the laugh aroused by the humorist and for his somewhat smoky imagination. This is the point at which Pirandello comes closest to an imagistic definition of humorism. The same result is envisioned when Pirandello rather obscurely underlines the equivalence of reflection and a malignant wild plant: the mistletoe, which grows about the seed of a pre-existing sentiment in order to awaken ideas and images in contrast with it, thus transforming it.

The laboriously analogical equivalents for humorism — strident laugh, aerial trace of smoke, and malignant wild mistletoe provoking the metamorphosis of a seed — succeed better in describing the erosive power of reflection over a given sentiment than in helping us figure out its activity in positively creating antagonistic and challenging images (the so-called *sentimenti del contrario*) in the humoristic work of art. Such a function is more efficiently taken up by a different set of statements through which Pirandello, though initially seduced by the usual complicated series of analogies, finally abandons his camouflage of metaphors and reaches the ground of historical reality.

"The spider of experience," Pirandello writes in "L'Umorismo" (pp. 146–147), "abstracts from social life the silk floss in order to compose in the individual the web of opinions in which the moral sense often lies enveloped. Since social relations are often nothing but a calculation in which morality is sacrificed, the task of humorism is that of discovering, through a laugh and without indignation, hypocrisy behind morality."

A close analysis of the preceding paragraph, if we are able to elude the pitfalls created by overstretched metaphors and syntactic intricacies, could lead us to see more clearly the link existing between Pirandello's theoretical statements on humorism and his concrete experimentations as an artist.

It is, for instance, to be noted that on the one hand the individual, almost surreptitiously introduced into the core of the sentence, does not act but is acted upon; on the other hand the spider of experience — the grammatical subject — in spite of its obtrusiveness, remains as abstract as its already discussed vegetal equivalent, the mistletoe of reflection. We have thus — in its full expansion, but completely disembodied from its human support — an idea that, having acquired an abnormal body, moves to entangle the individual in its web.[4]

---

4. One is reminded of a writer much closer to us in time, Jean-Paul Sartre, who in *L'Etre et le néant* (Paris, Gallimard, 1943, pp. 145, 152) translates the imagery of his novels and short stories into philosophical ideograms conveying an unusual set of metaphors inspired by repellent insects. Taking to task the concept of intrastructural protensions present in Husserl, Sartre, for instance, first compares the behavior of the phenomenological protensions to that of flies blindly beating at the glass; then, stepping up the process of passage from comparison to metaphor, he speaks simply of "les protensions [qui] se cognent en vain aux vitres du présent sans pouvoir les briser."

Sartre's protension-flies are a metaphoric vehicle of which the experi-

But in Pirandello the silk thread is a material the spider of experience derives from society. What we have here, carried through the ambiguous byways of metaphor expressing a kind of physiological repulsion on the part of the author, is the paradigm of a basic conflict between society, with its rituals of oppression and hypocrisy, and the individual trapped in them to his own detriment and destruction. Before reaching the elusive but real ground of this uneven struggle, the humorist instinctively establishes an ambivalent link with the conflict he is denouncing. The ingredients of this relationship are manifold: at the level of the subconscious we have already acknowledged the writer's repulsion for the omnivorous spider abstracting its web from society to suffocate the individual's freedom to act. On a more conscious and evident level, the writer's laugh reveals the many degrees of his participation in the drama of human existence. By expressing awareness of foul play hidden behind dissimulation and hypocrisy it shows, according to rules established by Thomas Hobbes in his essay on human nature, the writer's superiority over the terms of the conflict.[5] By denying him any room for indignation, this very laugh paves the way for an all-encompassing and equidistant understanding involving the victim with his hypocritical oppressor. And still — putting aside the very special issues discussed later in this paper in which the author, through his mouthpiece, takes a privileged

---

ence-spider in Pirandello's essay is a rudimentary ancestor. Sartre, the more careful philosopher, basically preoccupied with the exactitude of his correspondences, manages to establish a continuous identity between the idea as a whole and the repellent insects — its concrete equivalent into which the idea is transformed. Pirandello's metaphor appears much more unbalanced because experience, among other things — unlike the self-sufficient spider with which it is identified, who derives everything from itself — abstracts its material from a completely alien ground: society.

For an analysis of the quoted paragraph of *L'Etre et le néant,* see my essay "Jean-Paul Sartre," in *Belfagor,* 31 July 1952.

5. According to Hobbes, laughter takes place when a person confronts himself favorably with the being who becomes the object of his laugh. "The passion of laughter is nothing else but sudden glory arising from some sudden conception of some eminency in ourselves, by comparison with the infirmity of others, or with our own formerly." See "Human Nature: Or the Fundamental Elements of Policie etc.," *English Works of Thomas Hobbes of Malmesbury,* coll. and ed. Sir William Molesworth, London, 1840, vol. IV, chap. ix, pp. 45–49.

role in the fiction or play — in most cases Pirandello as a writer never stands above or aside from the conflict as a detached witness. Rather, he works from within, demiurgically precipitating a confrontation deprived of intermediaries between the oppressing society and the undaunted individual.

At the end of these remarks on the essay on humorism, it should be asked how the narrative theory such an essay espouses, which is based on the demiurgic interference of the writer with the false rationale of human motivations, could be preceded by the period of naturalistic impersonality presumably represented by Pirandello's early narrative writings.

The assumption of a naturalistic heritage in the Pirandellian novel stems presumably from the reader's feeling of the importance acquired by the narrative material per se. Such an assumption is soon rectified by the counteracting thought that Pirandello's intervention in the core of the novel is felt in the unusual, and to a naturalist writer inconceivable, violence by which his cases explode, submitting the shape of his stories to a tremendous, almost unbearable pressure from within.

From this point of view, Pirandello's initiation as a narrator, which took place well before his essay on humorism was written, is telling. Apparently the plot which brings Marta Ajala of *L'Esclusa* to the verge of self-destruction obeys the rules of a naive, overwhelmingly sentimental story.[6] A faithful wife, Marta, married to one Rocco Pentagora is courted by a verbose, middle-aged politician, Gregorio Alvignani; a frustrated epistolographer, he floods her with endless love letters. Marta is compromised by them, becomes a calumniated wife, and then in obedience to the implacably hypocritical rules of a provincial Southern town is expelled from her husband's house and returned to her paternal home. Here her father, deeply wounded by the offense, sacrifices his life on the altar of the infringed laws of honor. He virtually locks himself in his room, never appearing in public again, lets his business go to ruin in the hands of an incompetent and dishonest nephew, and inevitably dies of a stroke. The spell over, the house of Ajala endures. The sister of the unjustly accused Marta cannot find a husband,

6. Pirandello, *L'Esclusa,* Rome, 1901. (Serialized in *La tribuna* (Rome), June–August 1901.)

since offended society prohibits its members from knocking on the door of a family which has betrayed its rules. So Marta is literally compelled to become Alvignani's mistress for good. At this point however, her jealous husband, feeling his solitude and the unjust treatment to which he has submitted his wife, repents and approaches her again with peaceful intentions. The rather corny scene of reconciliation takes place near the bed of Marta's dying mother-in-law — who, by the way, had during her younger years deserted husband and children for a life of adventure, creating a particular sensitivity to waywardness in the vengeful Pentagora family.

The real interest of the story lies beyond the disconcerting plot, in the attention the writer pays to the absurd rules of society and to the reaction of the victimized individual. There is a possible alternative given to human behavior: Francesco Ajala, coherently and uncompromisingly accepting social rules whatever the consequences, chooses the first of the two solutions; his daughter Marta, who rebels against the cruelty of these rules, chooses the second. There is grandeur in Ajala's absurd conformity to the letter of an artificial moral code, as there is courage in Marta's rebellion. But Pirandello's interest does not lie particularly in showing the idiosyncratic aspects of the Ajala family's behavior. Francesco's and Marta's attitudes, so forcefully underlined, appear relevant insofar as they reveal the true laws of life: society cannot afford to forgive a sin which has never been really committed; only when society through its cruel suspicion compels the individual to go astray can a compromise of some sort be reached.

Close in time to the essay on humorism is Pirandello's rather lengthy novel *I vecchi e i giovani* (*The Old and the Young*).[7] This novel is interesting mainly because it touches on the territory explored by "L'Umorismo," written the previous year, and is strongly influenced by it. The obstacle to a reading of the novel's

7. L. Pirandello, *I vecchi e i giovani*, Milan, Mondadori, 1967. The first edition is of 1913, but the novel had already appeared in the *Rassegna contemporanea*, January–November 1909. The English translation by C. K. Scott Moncrieff was published in London in 1928. Intelligent remarks on this novel can be found in M. Baratto, "Le théâtre de Pirandello," in *Présences contemporaines,* Paris, 1957; and L. Lugnani, *Pirandello: Letteratura e teatro,* Florence, 1970, esp. pp. 18–19.

plot in a key close to the setting established in the essay is created by the thick wall of historical conventions which the author must dismantle in order to find his way toward the naked truths of life. The operation that becomes quintessential, burning and abrasive in Pirandello's theater, so universal in its typology, loses itself here in a web of episodes all too plausible because they reproduce historical patterns directly witnessed by Pirandello and Pirandello's generation. Benedetto Croce himself, in his *History of Italy from 1871 to 1915,* has spoken of the crisis of a generation which, having been involved in the heroic deeds that brought about the unification of Italy, found itself unable to cope with the daily routine of administering a very composite state, the end result of different economies and diversified cultural traditions.[8] Furthermore, the moral decay of the leading class in Italy had been the object of the fictional inquiry of novelists of the naturalistic school as well, vividly interested in reproducing the experience of the former conspirators — who, having deprived themselves of every pleasure during a youth spent in jail and in exile, turned politicians, then became in their late years involved in the corruption of power.[9] "Corruptio optimi pessima": in *I vecchi e i giovani* the elderly prime minister, Francesco d'Atri, overburdened by his own past as a national hero, betrayed by a wife young enough to be his daughter and by his political allies, who face great financial scandal, confronts the destruction of his political career with a sort of paralysis of the will, an absolute incapability to act.

But if the character of Francesco d'Atri, a cross between two prime ministers who really existed, is on the whole plausibly shaped according to the rules of the naturalistic novel searching for a political *tranche de vie,* then the annihilation of his will to act shows a sharp experimental interference on Pirandello's part that is strictly linked to basic distrust of the objectivity of his characters' motivations. In *I vecchi e i giovani* there are too many people who do not know what they are doing, who even do not do what the circumstances ask them to do. Donna

8. B. Croce, *Storia d'Italia dal 1871 al 1915,* Bari, 1929. See especially the chapter "Polemiche politiche in Italia dopo il 1870 e realtà storica," pp. 1–26.

9. See Matilde Serao, *La conquista di Roma,* Florence, 1885.

Caterina Auriti and her son Roberto, and even Gerlando Laurentano, the aristocrat who unpredictably takes the side of the Sicilian miners against the government, appear crystallized in their refusal of life in its becoming — prisoners of their past, of "life as form," as the later, philosophical Pirandello would eloquently put it.

Why does all this happen? Why does Pirandello freeze so many characters, extracting them from the stream of the historical narration? In the struggle between the poor *carusi*, relentlessly and hopelessly working in the Sicilian sulphur mines, and the mine owners, the exploiters, represented in the novel by Flaminio Salvo, Pirandello stands aloof in a position of "humoristic" equidistance. This does not necessarily mean that his sympathy for the revolutionary movement of the Sicilian Fasces is to be categorically denied, against the agreement of his biographers. Rather, it could be said that Pirandello's allegiances appear from the beginning sharply divided. There is on the one hand his moderate heritage according to which any rebellious activity is always an assault against the mystic idea of fatherland, a way of debasing the unity of Italy, so painfully achieved through the sacrifices of a generation. On the other there is his awareness of the social injustices this very unity has brought about.

Were Pirandello only on the side of rebellion, we would not understand why he mobilizes the hero of one of his early poems, Pier Gudrò[10] (a peasant who has fought the wars of the Risorgimento and gives lessons of patriotism to the indifferent and cynical bourgeois), changes his name to Mauro Mortara, and brings him to die at the very end of the novel. Pier Gudrò-Mortara sees in the rebellious miners the enemies of the unified Italy for which he has fought many a battle, therefore he goes against them in fighting trim. Mortara, it is true, happens to be killed by the same Italian troops he is trying to help, and his ultimate fate is to lie dead with the miners he wanted to punish so badly. But all this is brought about by the author, who seems to be interested in confusing the issue on purpose. It is in fact from the ideological chaos involving the events that the humoristic distance of the writer truly stems. In the very heart of the

10. L. Pirandello, *Pier Gudrò*, Rome, 1894.

novel a space of reflection is created, a kind of strategic no-man's-land from which the author disembodies and dismantles human emotions, reducing them to their most schematic essence. Pirandello's chosen mouthpiece in the novel, Cosimo Lauren-tano, dismisses with a tired gesture the story of horror and blood the four young revolutionaries are telling him. "Looking at what happened as if already far away in time," Pirandello explains, "don Cosimo could not see either the sense or the purpose of it. His aspect expressed the same feeling of detach-ment that emanates from objects which impassibly witness the fleeting passing of human events" (*I vecchi e i giovani,* p. 439).

Pirandello's attitude of extracting the characters of his novel from the flux of history shows how profound is his reservation toward any harmony artificially created between thoughts and events, between the world and the human mind. The ever-changing rhythm of life destroys ideals we try to formulize and basically modifies the assumptions on which we build what we pretentiously call our personality. Things do not mean, they are: the meaning we attribute to them is an arbitrary construc-tion, an illusion to be dismantled by the humoristic writer. There are, on the one hand, the subjective illusions and affec-tions which would like to give a direction to the world; on the other there is the world, which stands indifferent and unmodi-fiable. Nothing is true except the sea, the mountain, the rock, the blade of grass; man cannot be true to himself because he continuously changes, cannot be true to the world because he can neither know nor modify it.

The task of attempting in an ever-renewed act of heroic de-spair to bridge the gap between the unknown, unpredictable self and the mystery of the universe is entrusted to the character, which Pirandello calls *personaggio,*[11] while the humoristic re-establishment of the implacable truth comes occasionally from a zone of wisdom inhabited by a demiurgic wizard who is Pirandello's mouthpiece. Although this character, observing the plot from the outside, represents a rather archaic tool that will

11. For the problem of the *personaggio* see A. Leone-De Castris, *Storia di Pirandello,* Bari, 1962, especially the chapter "Dalla narrativa al teatro: la nascita del personaggio," pp. 111–144.

eventually be discarded in the great theatrical works such as
To Clothe the Naked, Henry IV, and *Six Characters in Search
of an Author,* the function of clarification attributed to him in
Pirandello's art is not to be underestimated. The role represented in *I vecchi e i giovani* by Cosimo Laurentano is taken
over by Serafino Gubbio in *Shoot (Si gira)* — a novel which
in 1925, ten years after its first publication in the *Nuova antologia,* appeared under the title *Quaderni di Serafino Gubbio
operatore.* Pirandello, who disliked the walking shadows of the
talking movies and dreamed of movies made of pure music and
pure vision (*cinemelografia*), was in his early years particularly interested in the function of the camera.[12] In the novel
Shoot, the camera becomes the impassible eye through which
all the events are observed; but Gubbio, who operates the
camera, becomes the supreme verifier, the one who reads the
events, underlining their complexities and their ambiguities. The
camera only seizes what happens; the human eye goes deeper
into the ambivalence of human actions, detects the ever-changing moods of characters who never are what they were. The
heavy burden of this complicated mechanism (camera plus human eye) was eventually simplified in the profoundly modified
theatrical version of *Shoot,* entitled *Ciascuno a suo modo (Each
in His Own Way).*[13] Here the demiurgic role of Pirandello's
mouthpiece shrinks considerably; and although a character,
Diego, is called on to interfere dialectically and to extricate his
fellow humans from the web of contradictions in which they
involve themselves, his reduced role paves the way for a theatrical solution according to which each character agrees to confront the other and erode the other's thesis without intermediaries.

The role of the intermediary still appears decisive in *Cosi è
(se vi pare) (It Is So [If You Think So]),* where Laudisi not
only leads the story toward its surprising solution, but helps us
to discover the laws of hypocrisy and false morality which un-

12. L. Pirandello, "Se il film parlante abolirà il teatro," in *Corriere
della sera,* 16 June 1929, and in L. Pirandello, *Saggi, poésie, scritti varii,*
pp. 996–1002.
13. L. Pirandello, *Ciascuno a suo modo,* Florence, 1924.

dermine the "respectable" society of a provincial town, in Italy as elsewhere.[14] The final appearance of Signora Ponza, and her confusing, noncommittal statements about her identity, by its humoristic overtones bewilders the spectator in search of a theatrical shock of recognition, defeating his impatience to go home fully reconciled with himself and with the meaning of the story he has been told. Laudisi, though not necessarily identifiable with Pirandello, appears more than anyone else to have grasped the author's awareness that the objective identity of Mrs. Ponza is beyond human reach, a myth of the mind, not a reality.

As far as the artistic destiny of the *personaggio* is concerned, Pirandello goes well beyond the theoretical approach he advocated in "L'Umorismo." While in the essay the character's affirmative striving was counteracted and suffocated by an overpowering reflection, in the works of fiction (novels, short stories, theater alike) the character wants the limelight. He tries hard to achieve an *espace vitale* for his suffering, and finally in spite of everything succeeds at least in presenting his case with eloquent despair. In his long-lasting struggle for survival he shouts his truths against the equally vital counterthrusts continuously voiced around him. Henry IV in order to remove the obstacles to his survival artificially avoids any confrontation, finding in the complete isolation of his pretended madness the necessary space for a self-fulfilling statement of his own identity; of course his illusion is destroyed as soon as he is reintegrated into the realm inhabited by his fellow humans. The father and the daughter of *Six Characters in Search of an Author* vehemently defend the truthfulness of their suffering life as characters against the theatrical artifices imposed on them by the Manager. Of course, the truth of each character is challenged and necessarily eroded by the countertruth expressed by his fellow character.

Pirandello's *personaggio* appears to be born under the sign of an everlasting illusion of survival. The more his power of reflection interferes with his illusions, the less willing he is to give them up, the readier to give them another chance. The plots woven around a series of mirages would be very tenuous indeed,

14. L. Pirandello, *Cosi è (se vi pare)*, Florence, 1925. The "parable" first appeared in the periodical *Nuova antologia* in 1918.

were the resistance of the character to annihilation not so incoherently heroic and vital. It could be said that the humoristic technique used by Pirandello, in revealing the truth of the game underneath the illusion, ends by vigorously underlining the pathetic consistency of this very illusion, its power of survival.

The proof of the self-asserting vitality of the illusions can be easily found in the endless drive for narrative experimentation to which Pirandello submits the otherwise one-sided and irreversible statements of his essay on humorism. Let us take, for instance, the assertion that the world — sea, mountains, rocks, blades of grass — exists but does not mean. Pirandello, who knows that human illusion continuously builds bridges to reach the world, to make it meaningful to us, tells the touching story of the love and care displayed by a poor unfrocked deacon, nicknamed Canta l'Epistola, for a blade of grass valiantly resisting the adverse surroundings. When a lady thoughtlessly steps on it, putting an end to its struggle for survival, Canta l'Epistola insults her, provokes her lover, an expert pistoleer, to a duel, and eventually gets killed.[15]

In concluding, we are duly brought to the *vexata quaestio* of the polymorphic aspect of Pirandello's art. Was he an eminent story-teller turned dramatist? Or was his theater on the contrary the late revelation of a genius that long narrative practice had repressed and undermined? If we were to take at face value Pirandello's statement of indifference toward the theater in an unpublished letter to Mario Puccini written as late as 1912, we would be rather puzzled.[16] Was Pirandello's conversion to the theater really by pure chance? A careful reading of his work helps us to state the problem in sounder methodological terms. In analyzing the essay "L'Umorismo" in its 1920 edition, we realize that the theoretical approach it advocates is the result of the superimposition of experiences belonging to

15. L. Pirandello, "Canta l'Epistola," in *Corriere della sera,* 31 December 1911, and in L. Pirandello, *Novelle per un anno,* I, pp. 444–450.

16. Puccini had written to Pirandello asking permission to use *Lumie di Sicilia* in an anthology he was preparing. Pirandello replied that he certainly had his permission to do so, but that as far as he was concerned his theatrical work was irrelevant and he attributed no importance to it whatsoever.

I am indebted to my friend Dario Puccini for the chance to read this letter, which he inherited from his father.

the large spectrum of Pirandello's literary career. There are statements directly derived from another essay, of 1905, in which the principles of humorism are already formulated; there is also the interpolation of a discussion with Croce which can only follow the first edition of "L'Umorismo," reviewed by Croce in 1909. There is even a prelude to the theory of the contrast between life and form that is the belated result of philosopher Adriano Tilgher's bad influence on Pirandello's theater. I could go on, adding other cases such as the incorporation of the episode of *Pier Gudrò,* written in 1894, in the novel *I vecchi e i giovani* of 1909; or the presence of concepts already well known to Pirandello's readers in a lecture on Verga in 1931.[17]

Furthermore, the article "L'Azione parlata," which appeared in the Florentine periodical *Marzocco* as early as 1899, greatly anticipates Pirandello's involvement in the theater and a painstakingly Pirandellian theory of the stage.[18] Pirandello confines, for instance, the function of the author to the architecture of the plot; the characters are declared free and independent in expressing their drama. While in D'Annunzio, Pirandello states, all the characters speak the eloquent language of their author and therefore are always D'Annunzio, the author of the new theater ought to be able to multiply himself, complying with the rules of the individualities he is representing. This atomistic theory of the theater, so radically formulated, finds in its extremism the limit and the obstacle to prompt scenic actualization. And it is perhaps in this precocious theoretical radicalism that the reason for Pirandello's belated conversion to the theater lies.

The reading of the essay on humorism, understood as a point of convergence of Pirandello's meditation on art, and the perusal of the article "L'Azione parlata," the short story "La tragedia d'un personaggio," and the preface to *Six Characters*

17. L. Pirandello, "Giovanni Verga," in *Saggi, poesie, scritti varii,* pp. 391–407. Pirandello literally repeats long passages from another lecture on Verga of eleven years before. Some ideas on Italian literature present in both lectures appear identical to those expressed in the essay "L'Umorismo."

18. L. Pirandello, "L'Azione parlata," in *Saggi, poesie, scritti varii,* pp. 982–984.

in Search of an Author help us to realize at once the early formulation of Pirandello's artistic ideology and his aspiration toward a synchronic interchange of all his literary experiences. The youthful discovery of the theory of humorism, and its application for years to a whole extended range of novels and short stories, contains in its seed the decisive advocacy of open theatrical forms that we know is posterior to 1916. But why does Pirandello come to the theater as late as 1916? The moment of theatrical truth is reached when the scheme of the novel appears obsolete in its traditional structures of evasion; when even the rhythm of the short story becomes prejudicial to the basic confrontations of the human instincts the writer is advocating, and another "tempo" is needed for Pirandello's art, in which the spoken word becomes the character's last frontier of self-defense, his only possible action.

JOHN V. KELLEHER

Humor in the Ulster Saga

Anyone reading *Lebor Gabála Érenn* (The Book of Invasions) for the first time, and there are probably few who have read it a second time, might well feel that it furnishes many examples of naive, unconscious humor.[1] *Lebor Gabála,* which exists in four recensions dating from the eleventh or the twelfth century, and which is reflected in a number of short protoversions and in scattered early references, is an elaborate pseudo-historical account of the origins and early vicissitudes of the Gaels and of the various peoples who are imagined as having occupied Ireland before them. There is a good deal of disharmony among the recensions on matters of detail and the sequence of events, but all agree that the Gaels originated in Scythia (compare Scotia), were for a while in Egypt where they were on very good terms with the Hebrews at the time of Exodus, and having left Egypt or been run out came at last by long wanderings to Spain which they conquered. Here all the recensions converge, and we are told in wordings so closely alike as to show a common source that at Brigantia in Spain Bregon mac Bratha built a great tower, Túir Bregoin, and that from it, one winter

1. R. A. S. Macalister, ed., *Lebor Gabála Érenn,* Irish Texts Society, 5 vols. (Dublin, 1938–1956).

evening, his son Ith saw Ireland. Ith then went to Ireland where
he was killed by the Tuatha Dé Danann, who had recently conquered the island from the Fir Bolg. To avenge him the Gaels
invaded in force, landing at Inber Scéne, the estuary of the
River Scéne. In all this it is to be understood that their coming
was fated, for the Gaels, by broadest implication, are presented
in *Lebor Gabála* as the second Chosen People and Ireland as the
second Promised Land.

The notion of anyone seeing Ireland from Spain might seem
rather absurd. It certainly did to me for a while, the more since
I knew that the Irish had a fairly constant trade with Spain
and must have been well aware of the distances involved. Some
years ago, however, I happened to look at a reproduction of
the Ebsdorf map (circa 1235), a medieval *mappa mundi* of
the sort that in one degree of elaboration or another was standard for centuries. Sure enough, there in the northwestern corner
of Spain was Brigantia with its tower, and very close by to the
north was Ireland. I then examined other such maps and for
the first time saw that in terms of the world geography depicted
on them the various long voyages of the Gaels in *Lebor Gabála,*
which I had assumed were the products of half-ignorant fancy,
were for the most part quite practicable.

The maps are based chiefly on the geographical treatise in
Book I, chapter 2, of Orosius' *Historiarum contra paganos libri
septem,* written in 418. In discussing *Lebor Gabála,* Eoin Mac-
Neill long ago called attention to the mention by Orosius of the
great Roman pharos at Brigantia, which he regarded as one
of the few notable structures in the world, and to another statement which seems to imply that Brigantia could be seen from
Scenae fluminis ostium in southern Ireland.[2] And MacNeill remarked that it had been natural enough to draw the reverse
conclusion, that Inber Scéne could be seen from Brigantia.

As long as I had thought this just an isolated fragment of
Latin learning seized on by some susceptible Irishman in the

---

2. *Phases of Irish History* (Dublin, 1919), p. 98. The tower, incidentally, still exists. It is Torres de Hércules, the lighthouse at Corunna,
reconstructed in the late eighteenth century about the still massive remains of the pharos.

seventh century and woven into an imaginative pseudo-history based largely on farfetched biblical parallels, I could continue to regard it as but one moderately absurd element in a rather thin fiction. Since then I have had to change my mind. With many others I could wish that *Lebor Gabála* had never been written, or had not been so hugely successful as to become the very center-piece of early and medieval Irish learning; for very early on, it overbore and forever replaced whatever ancient origin legends and pagan cosmogony may have been current among the Irish, so that, apart from what can be gleaned none too certainly from a few tales and from *Lebor Gabála* itself, we have no Irish equivaent of the *Eddas*. Yet obviously this success was no mere accident. When the Irish accepted Christianity they found in the Bible and in Christian literature what their own myths would scarcely have provided them, an authoritative, consecutive history of the world from Creation. The man who composed the original of *Lebor Gabála* united the Irish with this world history on the most honorable terms imaginable and through a narrative many of whose details could be checked out in such impartial authors as Orosius and Isidore of Seville. It would of course be a mistake for us to equate his production with the recensions we now possess, for these are the result of centuries of effort to improve it, to harmonize it with a later alternative version, and to correct, most unsuccessfully, a couple of basic inconsistencies about the temporal relationship of biblical events. They are the result, too, of that genial capacity for wandering away from the point, which the Irish literati possessed to so signal a degree, or for assuming that if one explanation is good, two or three are so much the better. Still, nowadays, even when reading these recensions I hesitate and reflect before presuming to laugh at anything in *Lebor Gabála*. It is enough to smile in admiration at the boldness of the original concept.

Lebor Gabála has clearly discernible purposes, but it is, after all, atypical, since the ideas underlying it were so largely stimulated by non-native sources. When we turn to more purely Irish tales, sagas, and cycles, it is hard to be anywhere near so sure of their purposes, particularly where the story, though written down in the eighth or ninth century, seems to have originated

from that remote realm of myth which is forever obscured by
the interposition of *Lebor Gabála*. Thus in the Ulster Saga,
which all agree is based on or incorporates very old material,
we come on indications that even as the stories were being set
down they were being adapted to and influenced by the artificial
scheme in which the Irish annals and genealogies were linked
through *Lebor Gabála* to Christian world history. In all likeli-
hood the Saga or its mythic prototype had no definite temporal
setting, but was imagined as having taken place in the measure-
lessness of the old gods' time. In the annals, however, which I
think received their intrinsic form about 790, we find that Cú
Chulainn, *heros fortissimus Scottorum,* died in A.D. 2, so that
his life overlapped with that of Christ by one year. The death of
Conchobar mac Nessa, king of Ulster, is at A.D. 33, the date
being confirmed in those stories which tell that he died as the
result of a battle fury excited by a vision of the Crucifixion. The
annals assign the central tale of the Saga, the prose epic *Táin
Bó Cuailgne,* to 19 B.C., the same year as the death of Virgil,
who of course was widely regarded as having prophesied in the
Fourth *Eclogue* the coming of Christianity and who was thus in
a way a Christian figure. Later in the annals the beginning of
Patrick's mission, which is plainly seen as the most important
event in Irish history, is dated not only from the Incarnation but
from the deaths of Cú Chulainn and Conchobar. Nor is it hard
to discover elsewhere in Irish literature implied resemblances
between Christ and Cú Chulainn. Each has an earthly "father"
but is conceived by a divinity who appears in the form of a
bird, each has a marvelous youth, each is supernaturally gifted
and of supreme courage, each has a life-span divisible by three
(thirty-three years for Christ, twenty-seven for Cú Chulainn),
each strives for his people, and each dies erect and wounded by
a spear. Whether the original of Cú Chulainn had all these attributes we have no sure means of telling, but there can be
little doubt that the Christian writers who set down the tales
stressed these or added them deliberately. They also deliberately
made him foster-father of Lugaid Réo Derg, whom they depicted as in a sense the ultimate ancestor of the Uí Néill kings
of Ireland and the initiator of the regular alternation in that
kingship, which they presented as the form of succession proper

to the Sixth Age of the World initiated by the birth of Christ.[3]

To be sure, the purpose of all this, though patent enough, is nowhere directly stated. Yet it is also clear that to the men who were thus inventing the pre-Patrician annals, the Ulster Saga and its heroes had immense prestige which was well worth uniting with their construction, and that once the union had been made the originally disparate elements continued to affect each other. A good example is "The Phantom Chariot of Cú Chulainn," a rather late story in which, centuries after his death, Cú Chulainn appears to Lóegaire mac Néill, who was king of Ireland when Patrick came, urging him to accept the new religion. He has of course been summoned up by Patrick. Most unhistorically, Lóegaire submits after a couple of heavyhanded miracles, and "heaven was decreed for Cú Chulainn." [4]

If we turn to the stories themselves, setting all this Christianizing influence aside for the moment, we find that indeed Cú Chulainn is the very epitome of the Celtic hero. By his own decision and stratagem he takes arms at seven, aware that in doing so he has chosen both the highest fame and an early death. At seventeen he defends Ulster singlehandedly against the host and the champions of the rest of Ireland. At twenty-seven he dies amid wild tragedy, with all his tabus broken, mortally wounded by his own magic weapon the *gae bulga,* yet terrifying and undaunted to the last. He is very beautiful. In some descriptions he is small and dark, boylike in appearance; in others, unbelievably splendid, with seven pupils, seven colors of hair, seven fingers on each hand, seven toes on each foot. But when he is possessed by his battle frenzy he undergoes the *riastra,* in which he swells hugely and becomes frightfully distorted. He is skilled in every conceivable feat of arms and in the arts of poetry and divination; yet, though befittingly capable of heroic boasting, he is sometimes said to be modest to the point of shyness. He can act without thought from sheer pride and valor, or he can reveal his grasp of hidden knowledge, or

3. I discuss this at greater length in "The Táin and the Annals," in a forthcoming number of *Ériu.*

4. Tom Peete Cross and Clark Harris Slover, *Ancient Irish Tales* (New York: Barnes and Noble, 1969), p. 354. In the reissue of this book, which was first published in 1936, Charles Dunn has supplied a bibliography identifying the editions and translations of the tales.

he can give the instructions on right conduct which are the
final proof of wisdom. There are plenty of contradictions in
what we are told about him, but none alter the consistency
with which he is accepted as the supreme hero.

And that at last brings us to the point of this essay. In Irish
literature, apart from the Ulster Saga, there are stories that
are comic throughout, stories that are simply tragic or heroic,
and quite a few that are mixed — generally serious in tone, but
with comic episodes, or generally comic with serious or possibly
serious portions. These mixed stories present more problems
than I care even to mention here, but there seems little reason
to doubt that where comedy or comic satire prevails the basic
intent is to be funny. Also, most of these tales are either isolated or belong to lesser cycles or story-groups. Their protagonists are often historical or semihistorical personages who,
though they may exhibit heroism, are not, like Cú Chulainn,
heroes in the classical sense. As for the Fionn cycle with its
mythical heroes, the comic or parodic stories that belong to
that are as a rule comic and nothing else. Finally, none of these
tales or cycles pretend to anything like the prestige of the Ulster
Saga. That is the hero-cycle par excellence.

But in many ways a very queer hero-cycle it is. It is full of
violence and tragedy, in many of its constituent stories quite
unmixed. In many others, however, though the tenor is tragic
or heroic the narrative may suddenly and quite without warning
lapse into broadest comedy and, shortly after, revert as instantly
to its former level. In the *Táin* this happens repeatedly, most
often in an episode involving Cú Chulainn. But it is best to
begin illustrating with a short example: an old story which is
not quite in the canon of the cycle, *Aided Con Rói maic Dáiri*
(The Tragic Death of Cú Rói mac Dáire).

The Ulster heroes went to besiege the Fir Falgae and to carry
off from them the beautiful Blathnat and three magical cows,
three magical birds, and a magical cauldron.

> Cu Roi mac Daire went with the men of Ulster then to the
> siege, and they did not recognize him, that is, they called him
> the man in the grey mantle. Every time a head was brought out
> of the fort, "Who slew that man?" Conchobar would say. "I and
> the man in the grey mantle," each answered in turn.

When, however, they were dividing the spoil, they did not give
Cu Roi a share, for justice was not granted him. He then ran in
among the cows and gathered them before him, collected the
birds in his girdle, thrust the woman under one of his armpits,
and went from them with the cauldron on his back. And none
among the men of Ulster was able to get speech with him save
Cu Chulainn alone. Cu Roi turned upon the latter, thrust him
into the earth to his armpits, cropped his hair with his sword,
rubbed cow-dung into his head, and then went home.

After that Cu Chulainn was a whole year avoiding the
Ulstermen.[5]

From there on, nothing funny or meant to be funny. For love
Blathnat betrays Cú Rói to Cú Chulainn and arranges the
stratagems by which he is slain; but Cú Rói is avenged by his
poet Ferchetne, who seizes Blathnat in his arms and leaps from
a cliff into the sea where both are drowned. The main theme
of the tale is in fact the praise of Cú Rói for his valor, nobility,
and generosity.

This is from the second version of the story (probably twelfth
century). In the older version (eighth or ninth century) Cú
Chulainn leaps onto the cauldron four times, but is thrown off
by Cú Rói with mounting force so that the last time he sinks
into the ground to his armpits. The tonsorial attentions are absent.

In other tales Cú Chulainn also encounters Cú Rói, most
notably in *Fled Bricrenn* (Bricriu's feast) — a fascinating story,
at once comic and heroic, which ends with a beheading-chal-
lenge like that in *Sir Gawain and the Green Knight* and which
is the source of Yeats's "The Green Helmet." At a feast given
simply to raise dissension among the Ulstermen, Bricriu, the
Thersites figure in the Saga, incites the mutual jealousy of the
three chief heroes, Cú Chulainn, Conall Cernach, and Lóegaire
Buadach, over the question of which of them is pre-eminent and
has the right to the Champion's Portion at the feasts of the
Red Branch. Conchobar advises that they appeal to the judgment of Cú Rói mac Dáire. They agree, but first they go to
other princes and wisemen — none of whom can give a verdict
that satisfies Lóegaire or Conall. At last they arrive at Cú Rói's

5. Ibid., p. 329.

stronghold and are honorably received by Blathnat. Cú Rói, she says, is away; and till he comes back each of them must take his turn guarding the fort for a night. The first night Lóegaire stands watch. In the darkness an immense giant approaches him from the sea "with his hands full of stripped oaks, each of which would form a burden for a wagon-team of six, [and] at whose root not a stroke had been repeated after a single sword-stroke." The giant hurls the oaks at Lóegaire one by one, but Lóegaire avoids them and counters with a spear-cast which also misses.

> [Then] the giant stretched his hand toward Loegaire. Such was its length that it reached across the three ridges that were between them as they were throwing at each other, and thus in his grasp the giant seized him. Though Loegaire was big and imposing, he fitted like a year-old child into the clutch of his opponent, who then ground him between his two palms as a chessman is turned in a groove. In that state, half-dead, the giant tossed him out over the fort, so that he fell into the mire of the ditch of the gate. The fort had no opening there, and the other men and inmates of the hold thought Loegaire had leapt outside over the fort, as a challenge for the other men to do likewise (p. 273).

Lóegaire, deeply shamed, does nothing to dispel the error. Next night it is Conall's turn, and the same business occurs. Cú Chulainn, when he stands guard, has a far busier time, having to kill so many phantoms and monsters that he is already tired and sad when the giant comes. Nevertheless he avoids the giant's grasp, overcomes him, and makes him grant three wishes: the sovereignty of Ireland's heroes for Cú Chulainn, the Champion's Portion without dispute, and precedence over the women of Ulster for his wife. The giant then vanishes.

> Then Cu Chulainn mused to himself as to the leap his fellows had leapt over the fort, for their leap was big and broad and high. Moreover, it seemed to him that it was by leaping that the valiant heroes had gone over it. He tried it twice and failed. "Alas," said Cu Chulainn, "my exertions for the Champion's Portion have exhausted me, and now I lose it through not being

able to take the leap the others took." As he thus mused, he essayed the following feats: he would spring backwards in mid-air a shot's distance from the fort, and then he would rebound from there till his forehead struck the fort. Then he would spring on high until all that was within the fort was visible to him, and again he would sink up to his knees in the earth owing to the pressure of his vehemence and violence. At another time he would not take the dew off the tip of the grass by reason of his buoyancy of mood, vehemence of nature, and heroic valor. What with the fit and fury that raged upon him he stepped over the fort outside and alighted at the door of the hall. His two foot-prints are in the flag on the floor of the hold at the spot where the royal entrance was. Thereafter he entered the house and heaved a sigh (p. 275).

The giant is of course Cú Rói, though this is not known to the champions. Next morning he returns in his proper guise — presumably as a man no bigger than they — and awards Cú Chulainn the Champion's Portion. At the end of the story, in the beheading-test episode, he again appears as an uncouth giant.

But it is not only Cú Rói who is given to sudden changes of size. In the final battle in the *Táin,* Fergus mac Róig, the exiled former king of Ulster, encounters his successor and enemy, Conchobar mac Nessa. Fergus attacks with his sword, Caladbolg (compare Excalibur); Conchobar protects himself with his magical shield, Ochan. Fergus' fury mounts wildly, but when he is appealed to by his fellow exile Cuscraid mac Conchobair, and by his old friend Conall Cernach, not to bring defeat upon the Ulstermen but to vent his rage elsewhere, he turns and chops off the tops of three hills. Nothing is said about his suddenly looming to giant stature, but obviously he does.

Cú Chulainn can also change size, the more dramatically in-deed since he is usually presented as rather small. In the *Táin* he fights a number of single combats at fords, the most famous of which is his three-day duel with Fer Diad, his shield-brother of former days. Cú Chulainn does not want to use the *gae bulga,* the ultimate weapon, against him; but he is hard put to survive, for Fer Diad is not only huge, he is *conganchnes* (horn-skinned), so that by the third day Cú Chulainn is a mass of wounds. To add further to the disparity, Fer Diad wears a leather apron, a stone as big as a millstone outside that for fear of the *gae bulga,* and over both an apron of smelted iron. From earliest morning till midday they cast spears at each other, then they close for the final sword fight.

> Then for the first time Cú Chulainn sprang from the brink of the ford on to the boss of Fer Diad's shield, trying to strike his head from above the rim of the shield. Then Fer Diad gave the shield a blow with his left elbow and cast Cú Chulainn off like a bird on to the brink of the ford. Again Cú Chulainn sprang from the brink of the ford on to the boss of Fer Diad's shield, seeking to strike his head from above the rim of the shield. Fer Diad gave the shield a blow with his left knee and cast Cú Chulainn off like a child on to the brink of the ford. Laeg [Cú Chulainn's charioteer] noticed what was happening. "Alas!" said Laeg, "your opponent has chastised you as a fond mother chastises her child. He has belaboured you as flax (?) is beaten in a pond. He has pierced you as a tool pierces an oak. He has bound you as a twining plant binds trees. He has attacked you as a hawk attacks little birds, so that never again will you have a claim or title to valour or feats of arms, you distorted little sprite," said Laeg.

The berating — one of the charioteer's functions — has its due effect. Cú Chulainn tries again, still more furiously, but Fer Diad "shook his shield and cast off Cú Chulainn into the bed of the ford as if he had never leapt at all . . . Then occurred Cú Chulainn's first distortion [*riastra*]. He swelled and grew big as a bladder does when inflated and became a fearsome, terrible, many-coloured, strange arch, and the valiant hero towered high above Fer Diad, as big as a *fomóir* or a pirate." [6]

The ability to expand suddenly to giant stature may have originally betokened not a hero, but a god, as would also great beauty alternating instantly with horrible distortion or the assumption of the guise of a vast *bodach* or churl. My friend Daniel A. Melia has suggested to me that behind the Ulster Saga lies some great myth-epic like the *Mahabharata,* involving a

6. Cecile O'Rahilly, ed., *Táin Bó Cúalgne from the Book of Leinster* (Dublin: Dublin Institute for Advanced Studies, 1967), pp. 227–228.

war between two septs of a single god-kindred, though in the cycle as we have it all has been euhemerized and the fighting is between Ulster and Connacht. This seems most probable; and I think it is likely too that when the Ulster tales were being written down, in the seventh or the eighth century, in a recently and somewhat spottily Christianized Ireland, the myths were still being told in the old ways among the people and were still being understood and fundamentally accepted in their original meaning.

The literati, on the other hand, would have been thoroughly Christian, proudly conscious of their new learning; however they may have admired the force of the old tales and have recognized their prestige, they would doubtless have been contemptuous of the superstitious veneration accorded the tales by the vulgar. Thus, in those passages where the god-qualities of the protagonists were most evident, they may have deliberately turned the narrative into parody, to mock and deflate, to make reverence impossible. Or there is the possibility that parodic versions already existed, themselves ancient; parody of sacred things is, after all, found everywhere and in all ages and need not be connected with disbelief. If that were so, the serious and comic versions may have been selectively combined, to exploit the old parodies for the new purposes.

I think particularly of *Scéla Mucce Meic Dathó* (The Story of Mac Datho's Pig), in which Conall Cernach is the chief figure. It is a strange and certainly ancient tale, full of the sort of lethal boasting and challenging described by Posidonius in his account of the Celts.[7] The Ulstermen and the Connachtmen are at Mac Datho's house — most likely, as has been suggested, the Celtic otherworld hostel. His famous pig, fattened for seven years on the milk of threescore cows, is slaughtered for their feast, and sixty oxen draw it to the hall. "Nine men were under the hurdle on which was the tail of the pig, and they had their load therein." Contention breaks out over which hero has the right to carve it. One Ulsterman after another advances his claim, only to be savagely squelched by Cet mac Matach of

7. J. J. Tierney, "The Celtic Ethnography of Posidonius," *Proceedings of the Royal Society of Ireland,* 60 C, no. 5 (Dublin, 1960). See esp. pp. 247, 251.

Connacht, who reminds each one of the defeats suffered at his hands. The Ulstermen are in dismay and disgrace, their challenges exhausted, and Cet sits down to carve. With that, Conall Cernach enters and orders Cet away from the pig. Cet yields reluctantly.

> "It is true," said Cet, "thou art even a better warrior than I; but if Anluan mac Matach (my brother) were in the house, he would match thee contest for contest, and it is a shame that he is not in the house tonight."
>
> "But he is," said Conall, taking Anluan's head out of his belt and throwing it at Cet's chest, so that a gush of blood broke over his lips. After that Conall sat down by the pig, and Cet went from it.

But what size is Conall? "Then Conall went to carve the pig and took the end of the tail in his mouth until he had finished dividing it. He sucked up the whole tail, and a load for nine was in it, so that he did not leave a bit of it, and he cast its skin and membrane from him." [8]

There is much here and in the story at large which I would not attempt to assess, yet I would also hesitate to fall back on such venerable non-ideas as "primitiveness" or "Celtic whimsy." I am sure, however, that this passage was not meant to be taken ponderously. The Irish writers of the eighth century were fully as intelligent as we are and, in their own context, quite as witty and sophisticated. And consider the context. For at least a thousand years, and probably more, before the onset of the Viking raids in the ninth century, Ireland had remained uninvaded, a phenomenon for which it would be hard to find a parallel in Europe or Asia. Moreover, when the Irish accepted Christianity and Latin learning they took these on their own terms, for their native culture, not having been pulverized by the Roman steamroller, was still lively and coherent. There can be little doubt that the adoption of Christianity and of writing brought about a huge revolution, with many consequent changes of beliefs and attitudes; but inevitably the revolution was contained and then absorbed by the indigenous culture. And by

8. Cross and Slover, p. 206.

then that culture was no longer barbaric. Eighth-century Ireland was certainly an unusual country, but it was no longer remote and isolated. It was a participating member of Christian Europe. Thus it would be a great mistake to assume that a literate Irishman of the time, writing down an ancient and barbaric tale, would regard it or treat it as his ancestors had.

I doubt such men regarded anything as their ancestors had, even in matters where there was no unbridgeable gap. The old native learning continued to be taught, though mingled with the new. "Poetry," *filidecht,* remained in high esteem, and the *filid* were proudly, even jealously conscious of the antiquity of their tradition. Even the old claims of the poets' magical powers continued to be put forward. But were they advanced with full solemnity? Here is a description from an early metrical tract on how an aggrieved poet should go about cursing a king who had refused to pay him for a proffered eulogy.

> There is fasting on the land of the king for whom the poem has been composed and counsel is taken with thirty warriors (or perhaps "laymen") and thirty bishops and thirty poets about making a satire afterwards. And it is unlawful for them to hinder the satire once the reward has been refused. It only remains for the poet, accompanied by six who have respectively the six degrees of poetry, to go before sunrise to a mound where seven territories meet, and the chief poet faces the land of the king he is about to revile and they all have their backs to a thorn which stands on the summit of the hill, and each man carries in his hand a stone and a spike from the thorn and speaks into both of them a stanza in the measure called *laídh*. The chief poet says his stanza first, and then the other poets chant theirs in unison, and each puts his stone and his spike at the base of the thorn, and if it is they that are at fault the ground of the hill swallows them up; if it is the king, however, that is at fault the ground swallows him and his wife and his child and his horse and his weapons and his clothing and his hound.[9]

If this is not genial self-satire, it is at least very good insurance against having to put one's self on the spot by actually attempting to carry out the threat to curse. Quite apart from

9. Eleanor Knott, *Irish Classical Poetry,* Cultural Relations Committee of Ireland (Dublin, Colm O Lochlainn, 1960), pp. 76–77.

the unlikelihood of finding six colleagues willing to risk being
buried alive by involving themselves in a dispute concerning
royalties, the instructions look difficult to fulfill. Even in Ireland
thorn-crowned hills where seven territories met must have been
scarce, and the chances of getting a unanimous verdict from
thirty laymen, thirty bishops, and thirty poets would always be
rather slight. Doubtless the poets were quite content to have
people believe or even half-believe in their wonderful powers,
but certainly there was one group in Irish society who knew very
well that a poet's curse was not necessarily fatal and that his
best satire would quite probably not raise three highly colored
and disfiguring blemishes on the victim's face. I mean, of course,
the poets themselves; and I think it safest to guess that even if
that passage may incorporate prehistoric injunctions, the man
who wrote it had his tongue in his cheek.

Between us and the men who set down the Ulster Saga lie a
dozen centuries of tumultuous and often chaotic history. The
earliest manuscripts in which the stories have been preserved
were written in the twelfth century, in an Ireland very different
from what it had been four hundred years earlier. Many of the
stories come to us in much later manuscripts and after unknown
vicissitudes. Some have been crudely abridged by less com-
petent scribes, others are fragmentary, and often enough two
versions have been jammed together inexpertly. The *Táin* and
a number of other major tales are first found in the *Lebor na
Huidre* (Book of the Dun Cow), written at Clonmacnois about
the beginning of the twelfth century; as I have argued elsewhere, they may have been copied from books brought from
Louth about 835 which may well have suffered disfigurement
in that long interval. Again, particularly in the case of the *Táin,*
it is hard to see why the writers thought fit to include such an
uneven diversity of material, some of it, like the many little ono-
mastical passages explaining how this or that place in north
Louth got its name, of scant literary merit. As I indicated at
the beginning, one of the hardest things to determine about a
native Irish work may often be its overall purpose. Yet where
humor can be definitely observed and where literary dexterity
is patent we are not at such disadvantage, especially if it be

taken for granted that the writers' attitudes toward what they dealt with were complex.

If parody were first introduced into the Saga for the reasons suggested above — which reasons would become less and less imperative as the memory of the old gods faded — it would in any case soon be enjoyed for its own sake and developed further as a genre. Indeed, I would think it likely that certain episodes in the *Táin* were written simply as comedy. Temptation would not have been lacking. The tale requires that one Connacht or allied hero after another be sent against Cú Chulainn in single combat, and it is axiomatic that none of them has a chance. Most of the duels are treated seriously enough; but as the series is extended a suspicion of burlesque enters. There is for example the case of the surly and unpopular Cúr mac Da Lóth, whose attack is apparently not even noticed by a Cú Chulainn preoccupied with his morning exercises.

> Early on the morrow, then, Cúr mac Da Lóth arose. A cartload of arms was brought by him to attack Cú Chulainn, and he began to try and kill him. Early on that day Cú Chulainn betook himself to his feats. These are all their names: *uballchless, fóenchless, cless cletínech, tétchless, corpchless, cless cait, ích n-errid, cor ndelend, léim dar néim, filliud eirred náir, gai bulga, baí brassi, rothchless, cles for análaib, brúud gine, sían curad, béim co fommus, táthbéim, réim fri fogaist, dírgud cretti fora rind, fornaidm níad.*
>
> Cú Chulainn used to practice each of these feats early every morning, in one hand, as swiftly as a cat makes for cream (?), that he might not forget or disremember them. Mac Da Lóth remained for a third of the day behind the boss of his shield, endeavoring to wound Cú Chulainn. Then said Láeg to Cú Chulainn: "Good now, little Cú, answer the warrior who seeks to kill you." Then Cú Chulainn looked at him and raised up and cast aloft the eight balls, and he made a cast of the ninth ball at Cúr mac Da Lóth so that it landed on the flat of his shield and the flat of his forehead and took a portion of brain the size of the ball out through the back of his head. Thus Cúr mac Da Lóth fell by the hand of Cú Chulainn.[10]

10. O'Rahilly, p. 189.

Nad Crantail, on the other hand, got full attention, though with little better luck. He got Cú Chulainn to agree to an exchange of spearcasts — Nad Crantail naturally having the first shot — with the stipulation that neither target was to dodge.

Nadcrantail throws a cast at him; Cuchulainn leaps on high before it.

"You do ill to avoid my cast," said Nadcrantail.

"Avoid my throw then on high," said Cuchulainn.

Cuchulainn throws the spear at him, but it was on high, so that from above it alighted in his crown, and it went through him to the ground.

"Alas! it is you are the best warrior in Ireland!" said Nadcrantail. "I have twenty-four sons in the camp. I will go and tell them what hidden treasures I have, and I will come that you may behead me, for I shall die if the spear is taken out of my head."

"Good," said Cuchulainn. "You will come back."

Nadcrantail goes to the camp then.[11]

The Irish had no native tradition of drama — the first play in Irish was Douglas Hyde's *Casadh an tSúgáin,* written in 1901 — yet I find it hard to believe there was no acting. In the case of a number of early and late stories which are clearly literary constructions, not set down directly from oral narration, it seems inconceivable that the storyteller, having memorized the text, would not have mimed the action to some extent. At least the spectacle of Cú Chulainn lobbing his spear like a howitzer shell and Nad Crantail waddling stiffly off with a couple of feet of shaft sticking out of the top of his skull ought to have inspired a bit of pantomiming. Then, too, there is the non-duel with Láiríne mac Nóis. I cannot imagine that being narrated by a man sitting with his hands quietly folded in his lap.

By mid-story the field of challengers is getting rather thin. The normal champions have begun to be a little reluctant about going where glory and oblivion wait them; and Medb and Ailill, the queen and king of Connacht, have to keep raising the ante, besides resorting to not a little deceitful persuasion. Still, it is

11. L. Winifred Faraday, trans., *The Cattle-Raid of Cualgne* (London: David Nutt, 1904), p. 58. The text is from *Lebor na Huidre* and the *Yellow Book of Lecan.*

not for the sake of his prowess that they settle on an idiot like Láiríne, but because they calculate that by his inevitable death a much better warrior can be forced to come forward. The man thus indirectly aimed at is his brother, Lugaid mac Nóis, the king of Munster, who is a good friend of Cú Chulainn though he has been compelled to join the hosting. Lugaid recognizes their game for what it is and knows that as usual Medb and Ailill's daughter Findabair will be promised, with the implication that her lucky spouse will inherit the sovereignty of Connacht, and that this, along with the customary deft flattery, will set Láiríne's few wits astray.

> He came to meet Cú Chulainn and a conversation took place between them. Then said Lugaid: "They are urging a brother of mine to come and fight with you, a foolish youth, rough, uncouth, but strong and stubborn, and he is sent to fight you so that when he falls by you, I may go to avenge his death on you, but I shall never do so. And by the friendship that is between us both, do not kill my brother. Yet I swear, that even if you all but kill him, I grant you leave to do so, for it is in despite of me that he goes against you." Then Cú Chulainn went back and Lugaid went to the camp.

Meanwhile Láiríne is getting the full treatment at the royal pavilion.

> Then Láiríne mac Nóis was summoned to the tent of Ailill and Medb and Finnabair was placed beside him. It was she who used to serve him goblets and she who used to kiss him at every drink and she who used to hand him his food. "Not to all and sundry does Medb give the liquor that is served to Fer Báeth or to Láiríne," said Finnabair. "She only brought fifty wagonloads of it to the camp." "Whom do you mean?" asked Ailill. "I mean that man yonder," said she. "Who is he?" asked Ailill. "Often you paid attention to something that was not certain. It were more fitting for you to bestow attention on the couple who are best in wealth and honour and dignity of all those in Ireland, namely, Finnabair and Láiríne mac Nóis" [said Medb]. Then (in his joy) Láiríne flung himself about so that the seams of the flockbeds under him burst and the green before the camp was strewn with their feathers.

Láiríne longed for the full light of day that he might attack
Cú Chulainn. He came in the early morning on the morrow and
brought with him a wagon-load of weapons, and he came on to
the ford to encounter Cú Chulainn. The mighty warriors in the
camp did not think it worth their while to go and watch Láiríne's
fight, but the women and boys and girls scoffed and jeered at his
fight. Cú Chulainn came to the ford to encounter Láiríne, but
he scorned to bring any weapons and came unarmed to meet
him. He struck all Láiríne's weapons out of his hand as one
might deprive a little boy of his playthings. Then Cú Chulainn
ground and squeezed him between his hands, chastised him and
clasped him, crushed him and shook him and forced all his
excrement out of him until a mist arose on all sides in the place
where he was. And after that he cast him from him, from the
bed of the ford across the camp to the entrance of his brother's
tent. However Láiríne never (after) rose without complaint and
he never ate without pain, and from that time forth he was never
without abdominal weakness and constriction of the chest and
cramps and diarrhoea. He was indeed the only man who survived
battle with Cú Chulainn on the Foray of Cúailgne. Yet the after-
effects of those complaints affected him so that he died later.[12]

This, the perforation of Cúr, and the excerpt from the Fer
Diad episode are quoted from the second recension of the *Táin,*
of which the principal manuscript is the *Book of Leinster.* This
recension was written, apparently in the mid-twelfth century, by
a master craftsman who based his work on the *Lebor na Huidre*
text but who polished, rearranged, and omitted or resolved inconsistencies at will. He also invented a new introduction to
explain why the *Táin* took place, the "Pillow Talk of Medb and
Ailill," as witty and elegant a piece of writing as exists in Irish.
Whoever he was, he was living proof of the level of urbanity
that could be reached in a country with no towns except for
the Norse settlements and the great monastic establishments.
So far from being awed by the ancient and recently rediscovered
epic, he was clearly delighted with the possibilities inherent in
a central figure who is by turns engagingly juvenile and an ap-
palling vortex of wrathful destructiveness. Yet, though he im-

12. O'Rahilly, pp. 192–193. At this point a page is missing from the
"Book of Leinster," and the text is supplied from the closely related
Stowe MS. Miss Faraday found the corresponding passage in *Lebor na
Huidre* unpalatable and omitted much of it in her translation.

proved these episodes and heightened their humor, he did not
invent them. They are in the older version and, though less skillfully told, perhaps because somewhat abridged, have nearly all
the same comic elements.

Yet this man was also four centuries further removed from the
society in which the divinity of the Ulster heroes was still both
known and felt; and the consequent difference in his attitude is
discernible throughout his work, as for instance in the way he
treats Cú Chulainn's daily practice of his feats. You will remember that, having named them — and his list is almost identical
with that in *Lebor na Huidre* — he tells us that Cú Chulainn
"used to practice each of these feats early every morning, in
one hand, as swiftly as a cat makes for cream." That, however,
would be more than difficult, for the feats include the salmon
leap, ropewalking, management of the *gae bulga,* the champion's shout, and various weapon-strokes, as well as "climbing
a javelin with stretching of the body on its point, with the binding (?) of a noble warrior." To be sure, the writer was perfectly
aware of this; for the feats were traditional and were named
in a number of stories, where attempts were even made to describe them. Yet obviously he chose to spoof them by exaggerating what might seem impossible to exaggerate, the marvelous dexterity of the hero qua hero, while at the same time enriching the narrative action. In the older version Cú Chulainn
is busy performing the feats in the normal manner when Cúr
arrives.

> Cur was plying his weapons against him in a fence(?) of his
> shield till a third of the day; and not a stroke of the blow
> reached Cuchulainn for the madness of the feats, and he did not
> know that a man was trying to strike him, till Fiacha Mac Fir-
> Febe said to him: "Beware of the man who is attacking you."
>
> Cuchulainn looked at him; he threw the feat-apple that re-
> mained in his hand, so that it went between the rim and the body
> of the shield, and went back through the head of the churl. It
> would be in Imslige Glendanach that Cur fell according to an-
> other version.[13]

13. Faraday, p. 69. Miss Faraday translates some of the feat names.
Miss O'Rahilly leaves them as they stand in the text, feeling it "impossible to translate most of them with any certainty as to the meaning."

It might of course be argued that the second recension writer simply took episodes which struck him as implicitly funny, but were in fact examples of rude heroic exaggeration, and turned them into explicit comedy. He was fully capable of that and perhaps he did so occasionally, but certainly not always. For one thing, he would have known Irish literary forms better than would be possible for anyone today, and would have recognized intentional humor. For another, in the *Lebor na Huidre* version the pommeling of Láiríne and its aftermath, though more briefly told, are essentially as in his account and are at as far a remove from any plausible notion of sober epic.

If I could be transported back to any period in Irish history, I would choose the eighth century. That must have been the high point — when the culture, still freshly invigorated by what Christianity had brought to it, had not yet undergone the terrible battering it took from the Vikings in the next two centuries. The island then must have been, relatively, a land of peace, disturbed only by succession fights and local wars fought by small forces in the most traditional and not very bloody manner. It must, too, have been rather a rich country, full of the products of its own arts, all too few of which were to survive Norse plunder and destruction. By the time the Viking terror had subsided Ireland was on an almost permanent war footing, with constant campaigning by the great provincial dynasts, none of whom proved strong enough to knock out his rivals and establish the single monarchy at which all doubtless aimed. The native church was by then generally in decline, and attempts were being made at a thorough Roman reformation. Yet, though much altered, bent in a new direction, and wracked by warfare, the essential continuity of the culture was still unbroken; the great monasteries remained centers of learning; and quite evidently a considerable renaissance was under way in the eleventh century and in the twelfth, when the earliest of the big codices that have come down to us — *Lebor na Huidre,* the *Book of Leinster* and *Rawlinson B 502* — were written.

The Norman Conquest, beginning in 1170, changed all that. The native society, if still not quite broken, was badly maimed; so that when the first conquest failed in the fourteenth century, partly before the gathering force of Irish recovery, partly because the English had lost interest in a colony that was no longer profitable, the culture had already lost much of its vigor and confidence. The chief art, bardic poetry, was highly elaborated, highly disciplined, often arid. The prose, deeply influenced by romance and crippled by a turgid, overornate style, never approached anything like the old energy and splendor.

Obviously there was a great yearning toward lost wholeness and a romanticization of the past; and whatever remained from pre-Norman Ireland was treated with vast respect, preserved in copy after copy, and generally misunderstood. Since worse defeats and worse destructions came in the sixteenth and seventeenth centuries, those attitudes were naturally further reinforced, especially with regard to whatever helped to bolster national pride. Thus a work like *Lebor Gabála,* which I rather suspect was never taken with total seriousness in pre-Norman Ireland, though its usefulness was certainly appreciated, was accepted practically as gospel by learned Irishmen down to the mid-nineteenth century; and they pointed to it as documentary proof of the seamless continuity of verifiable Irish tradition, a tradition which, interestingly, could be matched only by that of the Jews. They were, to be sure, conventional Christians whose faith in the Bible as world history had not yet been shaken by Darwin, but I think their belief in *Lebor Gabála* was more instinctive than that. Essentially — like the Sligo cobbler who explained to Yeats why, though he put no stock in hell or the Trinity, he believed in the fairies — for them "it stood to reason."

As for the *Táin,* it continued to be copied well into the eighteenth century, though we may suspect for a learned and limited audience. Synopses of it, and translations of single episodes like the duel with Fer Diad, were published in the nineteenth century, but scholarly editions and translations of the whole epic from the oldest texts became available only from 1905 on. Since then there has been constant and fruitful study of it, all motivated by the recognition of its high importance. Yet it may be that reverence has again produced solemnity, which in turn makes it difficult to deal with the *Táin* both as epic and as what it also is, a curious ragbag of the magnificent and the trivial, the tragic and the comic. To overstress the ragbag aspect would of course be the worst mistake of all. Yet there it is, and it needs to be looked at. In doing so, and trying to understand it, I think it helps to assume that the authors of the protoversions were lively, complicated Irishmen, who knew what they were doing (even if we can't quite make out what they were up to), and who were fond of a joke.

MORTON W. BLOOMFIELD

The Gloomy Chaucer

> . . . so he who wishes to see a Vision, a perfect Whole,
> Must see it in its Minute Particulars
> William Blake, *Jerusalem* 91:21–22

One of the few advantages of living past thirty is that with age one's awareness of the ironies of life and history is often sharpened. Not only does one's own point of view change with changing circumstances, but very often public attitudes are completely turned upside down and one can savor — if savor is the right word — the relativity of many opinions. Some ideas persist but some change — and sometimes completely.

In my younger days what concerned many scholars and critics of Chaucer was that he would not be taken seriously by his readers. As Gordon H. Gerould writes, "The common view of him as predominantly a jester, though a jester of genius, has tended to obscure certain elements of his art which are nevertheless very important." [1] In one of the few essays specifically

1. "The Serious Mind of Chaucer," *Chaucerian Essays* (Princeton: Princeton University Press, 1952), p. 82.

on Chaucer's humor,[2] Howard R. Patch is obviously struggling with the same worry. He is concerned in "The Idea of Humor" [3] whether the sublime (the highest level of literature) can be achieved through humor. Chaucer was to Patch obviously a great humorist, but he wondered whether this characteristic eliminated him from the ranks of the greatest writers. Over Gerould and Patch and numerous other writers on Chaucer lies the heavy weight of Matthew Arnold's dictum that he lacked "high seriousness."

A look around at Chaucer scholarship and criticism today reveals a different picture. No one needs to write defending Chaucer's seriousness. He is now widely regarded as a grave and moralistic writer who is fundamentally serious and didactic. His apparent humor is a mere epiphenomenon. Chaucer preaches the vanity of human desires. If we pick up a recent issue of the *Chaucer Review* (4:2 [1970]), devoted largely to the Wife of Bath, we find five essays on that wonderful character. In one of them, David S. Reid tells us it is amazing that "some post-Coleridgean criticism . . . can find redeeming, and more than redeeming, virtues in the Wife" (p. 89). In another, Joseph Mogan tells us that "she reveals the full sensuality of her nature in the lines which end with 'Allas! allas! that evere love was / synne!' (602–614)" (pp. 138–139). Bernard Levy is convinced that medieval man (including Chaucer, of course) would take "a rather harshly critical view of the Wife of Bath," unlike modern man who in his permissive way would excuse her (p. 122). Messrs. Judson B. Allen and Patrick Gallacher end their contribution by admitting that she is not "an overweight Dea Luxura," but " a very particular flawed example of humanity." Furthermore "she convicts herself out of her own mouth," and "those of us who find her too charming would be advised to check the roundness of our ears" (p. 105). Four of the five articles put the Wife of Bath firmly in her place. No enjoyment from her is allowed — if we are entertained it is only evidence of

2. See also D. S. Brewer ("The Criticism of Chaucer in the Twentieth Century" in A. C. Cawley, ed., *Chaucer's Mind and Art: Essays,* [London, 1969, and New York, 1971], p. 8), who says of Chaucer's humor that it is "a subject still worth more examination."

3. *On Rereading Chaucer* (Cambridge, Mass., 1939), pp. 3–24.

our depravity. Our modern Jansenist, Puritan,[4] and Manichean critics will not stand for any appreciation of a character like the Wife — all on grounds of historical truth.

I take these particular examples not because similar examples are hard to find,[5] but because they come together in one issue of a journal dealing with a subject, the Wife of Bath, who has normally been regarded as a great humorous character full of vitality. The treatment of the Wife of Bath's Prologue and Tale forms merely one example of a widespread tendency. As Harry Levin puts it in a discussion of a recent book on Shakespeare, "The treatment of each individual play [read: tale] tends to be a casuistic reckoning of the trespasses that condemn the protagonist. The spectacle is moralized into an evangelical tract." [6] All this leads us to think about the nature of the Chaucerian humor and indeed of humor in general.

It is very easy to reconcile the apparent contradiction I have been discussing and anyone can do it. Chaucer is both serious and humorous depending on the perspective adopted. If we are prepared to say that humor can be serious — and I certainly am — we should have no difficulty at all. The real question raised is the nature of Chaucerian humor. It is possible that the attempt to avoid completely the meaning and seriousness of Chaucer's devotion to Catholicism, which characterized much Chaucerian criticism from say 1880 to 1930, brought on the opposite excess of finding a serious homily in all Chaucerian poetry. Yet one excess does not excuse another. Perhaps a discussion of some of the characteristics of Chaucer's humor will

4. See the disapproving paraphrase of the Wife of Bath's monologue by Richard Brathwait (certainly no Puritan) in his *A Comment upon . . . the "Miller's Tale" and the Wife of Bath* (London, 1665), begun before 1617 and reprinted in part in *Geoffrey Chaucer, A Critical Anthology,* ed. J. A. Burrow (Hammondsworth, Eng., 1969), p. 55.

5. See, e.g., Norman T. Harrington, "Chaucer's Merchant's Tale: Another Swing of the Pendulum," *PMLA,* 86 (1971), 25–31, where we look "in vain [in this tale] for a single act of wisdom, compassion, or good humor" (p. 30). Edmund Reiss's recent articles provide further examples of this attitude. See, e.g., his two-part article "The Symbolic Surface of the *Canterbury Tales:* The Monk's Portrait," *Chaucer Review,* 2 (1967–68), 254–272; 3 (1968–69), 12–28.

6. See his "Evangelizing Shakespeare," *JHI,* 32 (1971), 308. On p. 310, Mr. Levin writes: "Single-minded dogmatism, since it brooks no uncertainties, can feel sure which course is right and which is wrong."

help in understanding this closely balanced duality which is built into the Chaucerian stance.

To attempt to define humor is not only a hopeless task but a ridiculous one in itself. The solemn-faced scholar[7] who attempts to catch under his microscope the "essence" of Chaucerian humor is a natural figure of fun. Yet to attempt to understand some of Chaucer's devices and his point of view, his attitude toward the universe, may be of some help to us in enjoying him — at least in allowing us to enjoy ourselves without feeling that we are morally insensitive clods, or in allowing us to see some of the depths of Chaucer's real seriousness.

One definition of humor is "the perception of this illusion [that the world is a perpetual caricature of itself], the fact allowed to pierce here and there through the convention, whilst the convention continues to be maintained, as if we had not observed its absurdity." George Santayana[8] goes on to distinguish comedy from humor as being "more radical, cruder, in a certain sense less human; because comedy throws the convention over altogether, revels for a moment in the fact." Humor is thus in his view the quiet perception of the incongruities and the irony in human actions. This notion of humor as the perception of incongruity goes back to Kant and Schopenhauer. Louis Hasley in a recent brief article on the subject finds three characteristics of humor in literature: a departure from a norm; detachment (or distance I should say); and playfulness.[9]

On the other hand, Carlyle viewed humor as Jean-Paul Richter did — as warm tender fellow-feeling with all forms of existence, a feeling he himself certainly did not possess to a high degree.[10] Here the emphasis is on kindliness, sincerity, and decency. I can add the quality of self-objectivity, for humor above all does not take on one level itself too seriously. All these qualities, and others too no doubt, argue that humor is a

7. E.g., Wilhelm Ewald, *Der Humor in Chaucer's Canterbury Tales* (*Teildruck*) (Göttingen, 1911).

8. These quotations are from his essay on Dickens in *Soliloquies in England and Late Soliloquies* (New York, 1922), pp. 65–66.

9. "Humor in Literature: A Definition," *CEA Critic,* February 1970, pp. 10–11.

10. See Richard J. Dunn, "Inverse Sublimity: Carlyle's Theory of Humor," *University of Toronto Quarterly,* 40 (1970–71), 41–57.

point of view, a perspective, a way of looking at things. In fact I think that Chaucerian humor, like all humor, is multiperspective and takes all things lightly because fundamentally they are too serious. It is a way of facing the universe with bravery.

The world is of such a nature that one can say it is both rational and irrational and that opposites are often true. It is, for instance, both later and earlier than you think. In the offering of solutions to problems, of panaceas to cures, of final answers to questions, one cannot bother to remember this dialectic of human existence. When one argues for a solution, for a *démarche,* one cannot worry about the other side, about the limitations of one's solutions. The rhetoric of action calls for decisiveness, not for questioning; for a single focus, not for seeing several sides. Chaucer is not an activist. On the other hand, all nonactivists are not Chaucers. Chaucer's view of the universe is deeply colored by his sense of balance, of human weakness. It is also strongly aware of a religious tradition which insists on the imperfection of all human endeavor.

Alfred David's fine analysis of Chaucer's *Envoy to Scogan* presents a sensitive awareness of the mingling of the serious and the comic in this short and delightful lyric.[11] In this poem, Chaucer takes a mock-serious stand which any reader would know could not be serious. Yet the seriousness lies in the theme of mutability that plays around the poem in its bittersweet way.

The essence of the Chaucerian humor comes out, I believe, in Chaucer's portrayal of himself, the persona who may or may not be Chaucer but who certainly bears some relation to the real man. The ubiquitous figure in Chaucer's poetry is the chief character in many of his poems and certainly, I think, makes the strongest impression on us. There is still much to learn about him. He appears and reappears, but has some kind of endearing continuity if not identity throughout. The persona adopts many strategies, and a study of them that keeps in mind Chaucerian irony would be, I firmly believe, profitable.

What I shall be particularly interested in here is one strategy, not especially noticed if at all: the Chaucerian-persona strategy

11. "Chaucer's Good Counsel to Scogan," *Chaucer Review,* 3 (1968–69), 265–274.

of answering a querulous objector. It clearly illustrates some of
the complexities in the portrayal of the persona. It is a gambit
used frequently enough to stimulate the question of what
Chaucer is attempting to do with it. It has its own function, of
course, in each work it appears in, but it will help in understanding Chaucer's humor to see it as a recurrent setting of the
Chaucer figure in many of his poems.

Perhaps the most famous and dramatic use of this device is
to be found in *Troilus and Criseyde* II, 666ff, shortly following
Criseyde's remark after seeing Troilus pass by, "Who yaf me
drynke?" She has fallen in love with him at first sight.

> Now myghte som envious jangle thus:
> "This was a sodeyn love; how myght it be
> That she so lightly loved Troilus,
> Right for the firste syghte, ye, parde?"
> Now whoso seith so, mote he nevere ythe!
> For every thyng, a gynnyng hath it nede
> Er al be wrought, withowten any drede.
>
> For I sey nought that she so sodeynly
> Yaf hym hire love, but that she gan enclyne
> To like hym first, and I have told you whi;
> And after that, his manhod and his pyne
> Made love withinne hire herte for to myne,
> For which, by proces and by good servyse,
> He gat hire love, and in no sodeyn wyse.
>
> And also blisful Venus, wel arrayed,
> Sat in hire seventhe hous of hevene tho,
> Disposed wel, and with aspectes payed,
> To helpe sely Troilus of his woo.
> And, soth to seyne, she nas not al a foo
> To Troilus in his nativitee;
> God woot that wel the sonner spedde he.

Chaucer also assumes an apologetic attitude before lovers in
the prologue to Book II of *Troilus and Criseyde*. Here the objector is assumed rather than portrayed. Chaucer begs to be
excused because he is writing about love although he knows

nothing about it, and asks pardon in advance for his gaucheries in describing elegant love.

A more open variety of the gambit comes again in Book III (491ff) when Chaucer says that some men might expect a complete description of Troilus' love affair with Criseyde, but the persona says that such writing would be too tiresome and lengthy. After the consummation scene in that book, the Chaucer figure says to an unnamed or theoretical objector that he need not ask if Troilus and Criseyde were happy (1681–1687), for they were indeed very happy and no inquiries need be made.

The Knight's Tale at the beginning of Part III (the descriptive and decorative part of the tale, lines 1881ff) affords another example of Chaucer answering an assumed complainer.

> I trowe men wolde deme it necligence
> If I foryete to tellen the dispence
> Of Theseus, that gooth so bisily
> To maken up the lystes roially . . .

And so on.

A more obvious example is to be found in the Franklin's Tale where "an heep of yow" are told that they would no doubt criticize Arveragus for allowing his wife to keep her rash oath to the Squire. This group of querulous objectors is told to wait a little before they leap to criticize, for the tale is not yet finished (1493ff).

The Man of Law's Tale provides several examples of the device. The first occurs at lines 246ff, after Chaucer has been describing the arrangements between Rome and the Sultan of Syria for his marriage to Constance. The persona goes on to say that some men would no doubt expect that he should go into detail about the plans for the Emperor's daughter, but using a familiar excuse, he says it would take too long.

Again when Constance is sent away 'in a ship al steerelees" (439) yet with provisions and clothes, Chaucer's querulous objector raises his ugly head again and asks why was Constance not killed at the feast as were all the other Christians. The persona can only answer by referring to God who wished to display a great miracle through her, the God who saved Daniel,

Jonah, and the Hebrews at the Red Sea. Christ also provided her with food as he did the five thousand folk with five loaves and two fishes (470–504). This is a lengthy reply indeed.

The querulous objector appears again toward the end of the tale (1009ff and 1086ff) when he argues with his Chaucerian interlocutor about details of the story. By implication there is also a querulous objector in the passage beginning lines 932ff when the persona asks how Constance, a weak woman, could defend herself against the amorous steward. Our author again falls back on God and refers to the Goliath and Judith stories.

At one point in the Merchant's Tale (1732ff) Chaucer gives us a very distinguished querulous objector who actually existed — Martianus Capella. Chaucer in a mock attempt to describe the wedding of January and May tells Martianus to hold his peace, because even he who described the wedding of Philology and Mercury would not be able to describe the magnificence of this wedding.

There are no doubt further examples, but I think I have given enough to show the frequency of the persona strategy in Chaucer's poems. It strongly helps to create the tone of some of his works.

Its significance — at least in part — is also clear: it contributes to the picture of the humble Chaucer, the persona, which he frequently promotes. Chaucer wishes to portray himself in his poetry as a meek man who is on the defensive and who seeks to placate his audience. It is perhaps a method of *captatio benevolentiae* of his audience, although to work through a querulous objector to this end is unusual if not rare. I do not think the defence of the author's position against a querulous objector is a rhetorical commonplace. Although there may well be such, I cannot recall other non-Chaucerian examples of this device.

It should furthermore be noted that although the "querulous objector" may have grown out of the humility topos or submission formulas,[12] it is different from them in many ways. It

12. See app. II, "Devotional Formula and Humility," in Ernst Robert Curtius, *European Literature and the Latin Middle Ages,* trans. Willard R. Trask (London, 1953 [Original German 1948]), pp. 407–413.

does not attack one's own character, but rather it implies that there is a hostile audience ready to pick on the persona-poet at any time. Its adoption allows Chaucer to explain his artistic procedures while at the same time building a picture of pseudo-humility. Much of Chaucer's poetry is about the writing of poetry, especially when the persona takes over.

Furthermore, the choice of a querulous objector is what the Russian formalists might call a retardation device. It slows down the action with an extraordinary gratuitousness. Nothing is more gratuitous than the free creation of unnecessary trouble for oneself. Instead of moving to one's goal, one throws up blocks in the way to slow down one's progress deliberately. The prolongation of the extra "business," the retardation of the direct statement and the narrative movement of the story unite to create a temporary dissatisfaction, an elongation of the resolution, which when it comes makes the outcome more desirable and satisfying. The objector thus introduces a playfulness, an elaborateness, a uselessness which ultimately increase our delight and add to our amusement.[13]

M. H. Abrams in a lecture at Harvard a few years ago spoke of Wordsworth's *Prelude* as being its own *ars poetica.* Chaucer's poetry is also its own *ars poetica,* except it is sometimes an ironical *ars poetica* which must be interpreted to be understood. Wordsworth has many virtues, but the "egotistical sublime" is hardly streaked with a sense of humor or self-deprecation. The querulous objector is objecting to Chaucer's treatment of a scene and is making artistic objections. These indirectly stress the artificial reality of the characters. They emphasize the "character" or unreal part of the Chaucerian figures, and at the same time the references to them make one feel that they are real people. These increase our sense of playful gratuitousness.

Placed in a wider context, the "querulous objector" is one method Chaucer uses to build up a whole portrait of himself which gives a particular flavor to his poetry — even more it forms a basic element of his seriohumorous attitude toward life. Chaucer, as the lonely persona of his poetry, an exile in this

13. I owe the basic idea in this paragraph to my good friend and colleague Donald Fanger.

world with only his books, naive and serious, yet comic, a kind of Holy Fool as Donald Howard says,[14] can thereby distance himself from his own being. People ask rude questions of him, but they really don't — the situation is made up by Chaucer. Man is pitted against a hostile world, but such hostility may be overcome by art both human and divine. Art transmutes experience, makes it seem something other than it is. The creator in the form of the persona is defending his own creation and that sometimes on the ground of artistic convenience. We are thus poised in a strange way between reality and unreality.[15]

Placing his own figure defensively before an objector, unknown for the most part, Chaucer is also saying that man is accountable for what he does. There is a greater objector, this situation suggests, before whom we must bow. Yet the querulous objector, because he is the lesser, because he is created by his creator to attack himself, is manageable and can be transcended. Furthermore he is funny. The creator creates that which will question his creation. The Chaucer persona presents other sides and aspects, but they tend to add up to a picture of a warm, naive, and limited man to whom we can feel superior but also one on another level to whose skill we are indebted. We are both above and below our genial guide. This guide is a bookish man who transcends the book — one who is both far from and close to us. His presence distances us from the action within the story. Yet his warmth and simplicity brings us close to him.

The inability to have a truly dialectical sense of the human mind leads either to the view of Chaucer as the clown and jester or to the view of Chaucer as the gloomy preacher of human

14. In "Chaucer the Man," reprinted from *PMLA* 80 (1965) in *Chaucer's Mind and Art: Essays,* ed. A. C. Cawley (New York, 1970), p. 45.

15. See my "Authenticating Realism and the Realism of Chaucer," *Thought,* 39 (1964), 335–358. A number of stylistic devices also contribute to this wavering sense of Chaucer's position. Chaucer's use of tenses may be such a device. The use of a preterite after a sequence of historical presents suddenly denies the presentness of the events; we are suddenly taken out of our vivid relation with experience. See L. D. Benson, "Chaucer's Historical Present: Its Meaning and Uses," *ES,* 42 (1961), 67; and Gero Bauer, "Historisches Presens und Vergegenwartigung des epischen Geschehens, Ein erzähltechnischer Kunstgriff Chaucers," *Anglia,* 85 (1967), 138–160.

vanity. The Manichean mind is at work in either case; Chaucer must either be for God or for the Devil. The Puritan adds to this dichotomy by making God a stern ruler who shows little mercy to sinners. The Jansenist condemns us to God's predestination.

The Wife of Bath presents the same problem as the other sympathetic sinners in Chaucer. Can we condemn her along with Troilus and Criseyde, with the John the Carpenter, the Franklin, Dorigen, and the Chaucer persona himself? There are two types of sinners in Chaucer — the vicious and the human. There are also pagans and Christian sinners. With the pagans we must be generous: they did not have the Christian revelation. With the human sinners we must make allowances. In the last analysis we are all brought before a stern Judge, but we do not know the secrets of His heart. Unlike our Manichean critics we do not know His final decisions. We cannot doubt that the Pardoner and the Summoner will receive their just deserts. But what awaits the Wife of Bath or the Franklin? Can Dorigen and Troilus and Criseyde be saved by the "law of kinde"? After all the last three lived before Christ died for our sins and are victims of invincible ignorance.

All this bespeaks the necessity of regarding matters in their own terms, of suppressing the wider issues for a time, of emptying the mind of condemnation temporarily. After this, we may put one point of view into another — we may admire Troilus and next put him into our postpagan and Christian dimension. He exists in both and indeed in many other dimensions if we will. In this view, a kind of cosmic humor emerges in which the very relativity of our views, the limitations of our own world — when viewed from another set of existential postulates, historic, religious, or social — becomes a cause for laughter as well as tears. Troilus is granted in his own person this translation to another frame and "lough right at the wo / Of hem that wepten for his deth so faste" (V, 1821–1822). We can join in with him when we too can look at ourselves or others thus and be granted the gift of tears and laughter. Chaucer can be comic in many ways, offering us a comic strain which reinforces his humor, but his humor is finally the humor of an absolute autonomy. Chaucer reminds us that whatever we may do we are like him, a bumbling creator who stands before a querulous objector, and need like him to be reminded of it. By reminding us of it we transcend it just as Chaucer does when he both joins and refuses to join his characters. Chaucer passes into a meta-universe in which laughter becomes gloom and gloom laughter.

To those who will be stern and unbending, who have no room for half measures, who know the purposes of our lives and what the Great Judge will say, I suppose nothing can be said to convince them of His mercy and of His mysterious grace. Those who will be sentimental will no doubt find a place for all the Chaucerian figures before the Throne of Glory. Those who recognize their limits, who know and who do not know, who condemn and yet love, those who can appreciate the intolerable and yet understand it, they will leave the decision open. In short the Chaucerian negative capability demands a negative capability from us. True negative capability arises from an objective love. It is this combination that yields the uniqueness of Chaucer's humanism and that creates his humor. Our age is perhaps not one to appreciate humor of this sort. Only black humor will do for some of us. But if we can comprehend this tragic perspectivism, we may grasp something of the Chaucerian humor, which hates human meanness and cruelty and which at the same time pities human weakness and affectation and even at times sin. Even though we may condemn it, we should also acknowledge that this attitude comes from a love for life.

ERICH SEGAL

Marlowe's *Schadenfreude:* Barabas as Comic Hero

A broad-shouldered man clubs a scrawny cripple. The victim staggers in pain, bleeds, begins to weep. Far from being a police report of felonious assault, this is an objective account of the first stimulus to human laughter in the history of Western literature. Though the modern sensibility may recoil at the thought of such brutality as "comedy," Homer is unequivocal in reporting the delight of the Greek leaders when Odysseus beats Thersites: "Though sad and homesick, they laughed with pleasure at him" (*Iliad* 2.270).

Several theorists of the comic could explain this laughter from a psychological standpoint, but it is important to recognize that not a few would decry it from a moral standpoint. We think immediately of Plato, an enemy of laughter in general and Homeric laughter in specific. How wrong of the gods to enjoy "unquenchible laughter" at the sight of the crippled Hephaistos.[1]

---

1. *Republic* 388Eff. To the modern mind, the Homeric term ἄσβεστος γέλως suggests inanimate unfeeling laughter, reminiscent of Bergson's definition of the comic as "something mechanical encrusted upon the living." Henri Bergson, "Laughter," trans. Brereton and Rothwell, in *Comedy,* ed. Wylie Sypher (New York: Doubleday Anchor, 1956), p. 84.

Cruelty should never be a laughing matter, argues Socrates in the *Philebus* (49D) and Aristotle in the *Nichomachean Ethics* (IV.8.3). In the *Poetics* (V.1–2), Aristotle draws the line at what is properly ludicrous: we may laugh at a kind of ugliness which is "neither painful nor harmful." And yet Aristotle's own prescription might well justify the amusement at Thersites' expense, since he was "the ugliest man who came to Ilium" (2.216). Besides, even Socrates allows that we may rejoice at the misfortunes of those we hate.[2] And barely hidden beneath the moralizing in both Plato and Aristotle is the implicit concession that, however ethically reprehensible, people *do* laugh at their friends' misfortunes.[3]

It is almost universally accepted that comedy provides an inward release for various antisocial instincts; even Plato grants this. But one finds less willingless to acknowledge that among the instincts satisfied is man's inherent thirst for cruelty. That man is innately hostile has always been a more difficult notion to accept than the idea that he is innately erotic. Alfred Adler first posited the "agression drive" in 1908 ("every individual really exists in a state of permanent agression"[4]), but Freud fought the concept for twenty years until, in *Civilization and Its Discontents,* he finally conceded its validity: "The bit of truth behind all this — one so eagerly denied — is that men are not gentle, friendly creatures wishing for love, who simply defend themselves if they are attacked, but that a powerful measure of desire for aggression has to be reckoned as part of their instinctual endowment . . . *homo homini lupus.*"[5] Later in the essay, Freud restates this even more emphatically: "The tendency to aggression is an innate, independent, instinctual disposi-

2. *Philebus* 49D. Hating enemies was a standard aspect of the ancient heroic code.

3. Although at one point Aristotle specifically decries *Schadenfreude,* ἐπιχαιρεκακία (*Nichomachean Ethics* II.6.18). Horace objects to *laedere gaudere* in *Sat.* I.4.80ff and *passim.*

4. Alder is retrospectively discussing his first statement on aggression. Cited in *The Individual Psychology of Alfred Adler,* ed. Heinz L. Ansbacher and Rowena R. Ansbacher (New York: Basic Books, 1956), p. 38.

5. Sigmund Freud, *Civilization and Its Discontents,* trans. Joan Rivière (London: Hogarth Press, 1930), p. 85.

tion in man, and . . . it constitutes the most powerful obstacle to culture." [6]

Considering how difficult this was for modern psychologists to accept, one more readily understands the moral indignation of the ancient philosophers at the raising of brutal laughter.[7] Moreover, Aristotle's position was distorted by subsequent misinterpretations. Sir Philip Sidney saw the philosopher as forbidding "laughter in sinful things," [8] and Ben Jonson even argues that Aristotle was against laughter of any kind: "[it is] a kind of turpitude, that depraves some part of man's nature without a disease." [9] We are but one small step from the ultimate agelastic attitude, which Chesterfield urges upon his son — that he never laugh at all in his entire life.[10]

But Sidney notwithstanding, the very essence of laughter is "sinful things," the more hostile the better. Freud observes that the closer we are to the original aggression, the greater the comic delight.[11] Of course none of this is new. The modern view of laughter-as-aggression subtends the Hobbesian "sudden glory" theory which, by the nineteenth century, as W. K. Wimsatt recounts, "became crudified through various physiological, psychological and primitivistic analogies." Mr. Wimsatt questions the worth of inquiries along these lines:

6. *Ibid.*, p. 102. Otto Rank accepts the essence of Freud's view on "this primary evil in man." See "Life Fear and Death Fear," trans. Mabel E. Moxon, in *The Myth of the Birth of the Hero,* ed. Philip Freund (New York: Vintage Books, 1951), p. 275 and *passim.*

7. And yet Socrates was not unaware of "the aggression principle." Throughout the *Philebus* passage already cited, he speaks of man's innate φθόνος toward his fellow man. The Greek term is usually rendered as "envy," but there is legitimate basis for translating φθόνος as "hostility." Compare its usage in *Iliad* 4.55–56; Pindar, *Pythian* 3.71; Euripides, *Ion* 1025.

8. "Defense of Poesie," in *The Complete Works of Sir Philip Sidney,* ed. A. Feuillerat (Cambridge, Eng.: 1923), III, 41.

9. *Timber: Or Discoveries Made Upon Men and Matter,* in vol. VIII of the complete works of Ben Jonson, ed. Herford and Simpson (Oxford: 1947), p. 643.

10. Lord Chesterfield's letter from Bath, 9 March, 1748, is quoted by W. K. Wimsatt, ed. *The Idea of Comedy* (Englewood Cliffs: Prentice-Hall, 1969), p. 150.

11. Freud, *Jokes and Their Relation to the Unconscious,* trans. James Strachey (London: Hogarth Press, 1960), p. 134.

Why do I laugh . . . when an old peddler stumbles and spills
his pencils all over the street? I don't know. Maybe I don't laugh.
But a Fiji Islander would! He will laugh when a prisoner is being
roasted alive in an oven! Confident proclamations about the
nature of anthropoid laughter are invested with importance by
equally confident assumptions that reduction to the lowest common factor is the right way of proceeding. . . . Are such theories
of hidden elements and forgotten origins supposed to increase
my appreciation of jokes or comic situations? [12]

The argument of the present essay dissents somewhat from
Wimsatt's view, believing that there can be value in recalling
"forgotten origins" of ancient stimuli to laughter. The answer to
"why they laughed" may provide many insights to literatures of
the past. There is a ready case in point right from Wimsatt's
essay. His example of the blind peddler recalls a famous incident
in Spanish literature, when Lazarillo de Tormes tricks his blind
master into jumping into a post, causing very painful injury: "da
con la cabeza en el poste, que sonó tan recio como si diera con
una gran calabaza, y cayó luego para atrás medio muerto y
hendida la cabeza." [13]

However it may affect us today, this episode was enormously
popular in sixteenth-century Spain and was imitated by other
writers in prose and song. It may even have been a part of the
folklore well before it found its way into the Lazarillo novel.[14]
Suffice it to say that at the time, this cruel trick earned as much
admiration for Lazarillo as the beating of Thersites did for that
proto-pícaro, Odysseus.

Naturally times change, and likewise objects of laughter. Our
greater "civilization" may come to reject certain brutalities as
too painful to be risible, and the Lazarillo incident may be one

12. Wimsatt, "The Criticism of Comedy," in *Hateful Contraries*
(Lexington: University of Kentucky Press, 1965), p. 91; 94–95.

13. "He hit his head against the post and it sounded loud as a huge
pumpkin. And then he fell down backwards, half dead, his head all
gashed." My trans. from *Lazarillo de Tormes* in *La novela picaresca en
España,* ed. Angel Valbuena y Prat (Madrid: Aguilar, 1962), p. 91.
Unless otherwise indicated, all translations in this essay are my own.

14. Moreover, the first extant French farce in the vernacular is the
late thirteenth-century *Le garçon et l'aveugle.*

of them. Emotion is ever and always the foe of laughter. And yet every age produces new cruelties and new possibilities for comic *Schadenfreude*. In the preface to *Joseph Andrews,* Fielding discusses the limits, in fact, the *ne plus ultra* of the Ridiculous: "What could exceed the Absurdity of an Author who should write *'The Comedy of Nero,* with the *merry Incident* of ripping up his Mother's Belly'; or what would give a greater shock to humanity . . ." But in 1742 de Sade was still in swaddling clothes, the childish brutalities of Jarry's King Ubu were more than a century away, and the Absurdity of "The Comedy of Nero" would be exceeded in 1959 by *Oh Dad, Poor Dad, Mamma's Hung You in the Closet and I'm Feelin' So Sad.* Martin Esslin recently observed that the spirit of von Masoch has become increasingly congenial to modern comedy.[15] And who could have imagined a comedy that would invite us to relish the annihilation of the human race? But then who could have imagined that the absurd optimism of Dr. Pangloss would be surpassed by the insouciant glee of Dr. Strangelove?

But since our concern is cruelty in comedy past, it will be useful to examine several stories which are told in a "framed" context and include the reaction of a fictive audience. The Eighth Day of Boccaccio's *Decameron* contains many tales of brutality, much of it perpetrated by two rogues, Bruno and Buffalmacco, "uomino sollazzevoli molto, ma per altro avveduti e sagaci." [16] In the third story, they dupe Calandrino, hit him with stones till he whines in pain, and then abandon him, "con le maggior risa del mondo." The victim then vents his frustration by brutally beating his wife. Boccaccio's fictive listeners welcome this story with great delight. Their reaction is even more enthusiastic for the ninth tale, in which Bruno and Buffalmacco victimize one Maestro Simone, a dimwitted doctor, finally hurling him down a latrine. This malodorous mayhem evokes enormous laughter: "Quanto la novella . . . facesse le donne ridere, non è da domandare: niuna ve n'era a cui per

15. Esslin, "Violence in Modern Drama," in *Reflections: Essays on the Modern Theater* (Garden City: Doubleday, 1969), p. 167.

16. "Fun-loving men who were also perceptive and shrewd." Giovanni Boccaccio, *Il Decameron,* ed. Charles S. Singleton (Bari: Laterza & Figli, 1955), II, 111.

soperchio riso non fossero dodici volte le lagrime venute in su gli occhi." [17]

And yet there are limits. The seventh tale of this same Day, the cruel revenge wrought by the scholar Rinieri on a woman who scorned him, evokes icy silence. Unlike Panurge's revenge upon the haughty Parisienne, this tale engages our pity. As Bergson explains, "to produce the whole of its effect . . . the comic demands something like a momentary anesthesia of the heart. Its appeal is to the intelligence, pure and simple" (pp. 63–64).

The *Canterbury Tales* afford another opportunity to study the success or failure of comic *Schadenfreude* on an audience. For example, Oswald the Reeve tells a lusty tale which involves aggressive sexuality: two scholars "swyve" the wife and daughter of a miller as revenge for his having shortchanged them. At the end there is much physical violence:

> And on the nose he smoot hym with his fest
> Doun ran the blody streem upon his brest.
>
> (4275–4276)

As a final coup, the miller's wife accidentally smashes him with a staff "on the pyled skulle":

> That doun he gooth and cride, "Harrow I dye!"
> Thise clerks beete hym weel and lete hym lye.
>
> (4307–4308)

And yet, although the Reeve can tell such a story, he is the only pilgrim who did *not* laugh at the Miller's tale just preceding his. In fact, Chaucer describes him as being angry and upset. Surely it is not due to the grossness of the Miller's tale (which involves some hostile flatulence), or even its explicit brutality:

> The hoote kultour brende so his toute
> And for the smert he wende for to dye.
>
> (3812–3813)

17. "No need to ask how much the story . . . made the women laugh. Every single one of them laughed so hugely that tears came to their eyes at least twelve times." *Ibid.*, p. 173.

Actually, the scatology and cruelty help to explain the near universal laughter with which the pilgrims greet the tale.[18] Oswald the Reeve is discomfited not because the young student was branded, but because the old carpenter was cuckolded. As he himself explains his ill humor:

> But ik am oold, me list not pley for age
> Gras tyme is doon, my fodder is now forage . . .
> We olde men, I drede, so fare we . . .
>
> (3867–3868, 3874)

Schadenfreude is delight at someone else's misfortune. For Oswald the Reeve, the cuckold in the Miller's tale was too close to himself. He sympathized; he feared ("We olde men, I drede . . ."). Clearly, this is *Schade* without *Freude*. Successful comedy must subliminally reassure us that the victims could not possibly be ourselves. How curious, though, that Chaucer's Reeve could tell of cuckoldry and yet not listen to it. One thinks of how Molière could transmute the pain of his personal life into the joy of such plays as *Ecole des femmes*.

This brief detour has demonstrated that what might today be considered excessive cruelty was greatly enjoyed in times past. The entire discussion began with Homer, and to Homer it now returns. We can only speculate on what sort of effect the Thersites episode had upon the bard's audience. And yet it is not unreasonable to think that Homer's listeners would laugh much the way the Greek leaders did. They too might even regard Odysseus' manhandling of Thersites as "the very best thing Odysseus had done since he got to Troy" (*Iliad* 2.274).[19] Homer's audience knew well that Odysseus would go on to better things, but it is significant to note that his actions here attract so much attention and comment among his fellow

18. The Reeve's Prologue, 3855–3858. All quotations from Chaucer are from the 2nd ed. of F. N. Robinson (Boston: Houghton Mifflin, 1957).
19. Certainly Sir Thomas Elyot appreciated "the witty Ulisses" at this moment. Compare *The Governour,* ed. A. T. Eliot (London, 1834), p. 13.

warriors. This episode is especially important as presaging the Odysseus we will come to know, the comic hero who will "live up to his name."

For the essence of Odysseus is in his name, as George Dimock has emphatically demonstrated.[20] The newborn son of Laertes was named by his grandfather, Autolycus ("Lone Wolf"), who said: "I have odysseused many in my time, up and down the wide world, men and women both; therefore let his name by Odysseus." [21] As Dimock argues: "In the Odyssey *odyssasthai* means essentially 'to cause pain (*odynē*) and to be willing to do so.' " [22] Thus from birth, by name and by nature, the first comic hero in Western literature is an inflictor of pain. In a certain sense, the Thersites episode in the *Iliad* anticipates the entire epic devoted to the satisfaction of comic *Schadenfreude* through the agency of a wily aggressor. And, as Dimock also notes, there is not always rational provocation for Odysseus' behavior. Not all his wild actions can be attributed to a *force majeure* like the Wrath of Poseidon. More often than not, Odysseus is merely following his own instinct "to plant evils," κακὰ φυτεύειν: "So let us think no more of 'wrath' which implies provocation and mental perturbation, but rather of a hand and mind against every man, by nature, or as a matter of policy" (p. 55).

Odysseus is a rogue by nature and heredity. We should never seek psychological explanations *for* his behavior. Rather, we should acknowledge the psychological appeal *of* his behavior. Cedric Whitman sees Odysseus as the antecedent of the crafty Aristophanic protagonist, "the self militant, and devil take the means." [23] Whitman uses *poneria,* the modern Greek word for wiliness, to describe not only the amoral Aristophanic hero, but

20. George E. Dimock, Jr. "The Name of Odysseus," *Hudson Review,* 9 (Spring, 1956), 52–77, reprinted in several anthologies including *Essays on the Odyssey,* ed. Charles H. Taylor, Jr. (Bloomington: Indiana University Press, 1963), pp. 54–72; my page references are to the latter.

21. Dimock's translation of *Odyssey* 19.407–409, p. 55 of his essay.

22. *Ibid.,* p. 55. Compare the joyous laughter explicit in the name of Isaac (*Yitzhák*), Genesis 21:6.

23. Cedric H. Whitman, *Aristophanes and the Comic Hero* (Cambridge, Mass.: Harvard University Press, 1964), p. 52.

the essential characteristic of a popular Greek folk hero whose appeal through the ages has never diminished.[24]

Throughout the comic tradition, the hero's attitude may be called by different terms, but its essence is childish aggression, a behavior pattern noted even by Socrates.[25] Suzanne Langer cites Punch as "the most forthright of these infantilists," [26] but in great comedy we are never very far from "givers of pain" in the Odyssean sense.

Take the Aristophanic hero, an insouciant breaker of laws, jaws, and his own wind. Hostility incarnate. This aspect of his character has not always pleased the scholars. Gilbert Norwood, for instance, objected to *The Knights* for being too much "an anthology of verbs meaning 'to kick in the stomach.' " [27] But Aristophanes' art merely lyricizes the cruelty of his characters. Philocleon in *The Wasps,* one of the playwright's "rejuvenated" heroes, gets drunk at the final *komos,* grossly insults the guests (adding flatulence to verbal hostility), steals his son's flute-girl, and heads homeward, punching people in the street (1292ff). It should be noted that the word *hubris* or its compounds is used four times in the account of Philocleon's antisocial behavior.[28]

In *The Clouds,* there is the famous finale in which a young man beats up his father and threatens to do likewise to his mother (1321ff); the psychology of this *Schadenfreude* is obvious. Grosser — and less comprehensible to the modern sensibility — is the joy described by the chorus of *The Birds* as being one of the added pleasures of possessing wings: airborne excretion (790ff). Psychologists have established the relation between hostility and defecation.[29] In the *Ecclesiazusae* the

24. *Ibid.,* p. 30. In an appendix (pp. 281ff), Whitman discusses Karaghiozes, the roguish hero of the modern Greek shadow plays who shares many of the "Odyssean" features we are discussing.

25. In *Philebus* 49A, Socrates refers to "childish hostility," τὸν παιδικὸν . . . φθονόν.

26. Suzanne Langer, "The Comic Rhythm," in *Feeling and Form* (New York: Charles Scribner's Sons, 1953), pp. 342–343.

27. Gilbert Norwood, *Greek Comedy* (New York: Hill and Wang, 1963), p. 208.

28. *Wasps* 1303, 1319, 1414, 1441. All references to Aristophanes are to Victor Coulon's five-volume ed., Belles-Lettres ser. (Paris: 1958–1963).

fantasy of beating one's parents makes this duality explicit. Blepyros objects to the formation of a communistic state envisioned by his wife, Praxagora. Among the many reforms she proposes is that children be raised by the state. This, argues Blepyros, would invite mass murder. Youngsters would regard all old people as their parents, strangle them . . . and excrete upon them (637ff).

As mentioned above, the word *hubris* is common in the works of Aristophanes, often in the literal sense of violent physical assault. Per contra, in the tragic authors, *hubris* is almost always something mental.[30] Aristotle, advocate of restrained laughter, defines wit as educated *hubris*,[31] doubtless implying that the activities of the comic hero should not transcend the verbal assault. But Aristophanes is not the only comic author who sees physical *hubris* as a comic virtue. One thinks immediately of Restoration comedy, cruel and cynical, whose prime weapon was called "wit," a word less refined in the usage of that time than in ours. "Wit" can be almost any antisocial act, as described, for example, in Wycherly's *Plain Dealer* (V.ii):

> *Novel*: I wonder . . . that young fellows should be so dull, as to say there's no humor in making a noise, and breaking windows! I tell you there's wit and humor too in both . . .
>
> *Oldfox*: Pure rogue! There's your modern wit for you! Wit and humor in breaking of windows; there's mischief, if you will, but no wit or humor.
>
> *Novel*: Prithee, prithee, peace old fool! I tell you, where there's mischief, there's wit.

29. A. H. Maslow and Beta Mittelman, *Principles of Abnormal Psychology* (New York: Harper, 1951), pp. 331ff; Norman Cameron, *Personality Development and Psychopathology* (Boston: Houghton Mifflin, 1963), p. 65. Henry A. Murray cites a case history involving fantasies of airborne excretion in "American Icarus," *Clinical Studies of Personality,* ed. Burton and Harris (New York: Harper, 1955), II, 635.

30. Examples of ὕβρις as physical assault in comedy: *Clouds* 1299; *Wasps* 1418; *Birds* 1047; *Lysistrata* 658; *Ecclesiazusae* 664. Examples of ὕβρις as a mental attitude in tragedy: Aeschylus, *Eumenides* 533; Sophocles, *Oedipus Rex* 873, *Electra* 881; Euripides, *Hippolytus* 474.

31. *Rhetoric* II.12.16. Aristotle's phrase is πεπαιδευμένη ὕβρις.

In this case, and indeed as a rubric of comedy, one might define wit as what has oft been thought but ne'er so well repressed. There is often wit in *hubris*. There is always *hubris* in wit.[32]

Aristophanes is also replete with verbal aggression. Every *agon* begins with an exchange of insults, and not every *agon* rises above this level. But Greek New Comedy, infused with Menandrian *philanthropia,* substituted *ethos* for *gelos.* Laughter was not its aim. In fact, the famous Menandrian-Terentian maxim about nothing human being alien explains why there could be no laughter in this sort of comedy. Feeling is fatal; *qui pense rit, qui sent pleure. Philanthropia* is admirable, but uncomic. [33] Even Terence, notoriously lacking *vis comica* (which might here be rendered "comic violence"), is best remembered for a character who delights in physical assaults:

> *Phormio*: quot me censes homines iam deverberasse usque ad
> necem,
> hospites, tum civis? quo mage novi, tanto saepius.[34]

Why does Phormio beat people to death, especially since he claims to be living only for the pleasure of life (338ff)? The question is its own answer. He is a descendent of the Autolycan-Odyssean rogue, an inflictor of pain for pleasure.

Of course the Plautine slave is an Odyssean hero, as both he and the playwright are wont to remind us:

> *Chrysalus*: ego sum Vlixes quoiius consilio haec gerunt.
> (*Bacchides* 940)

32. Compare Martin Grotjahn, *Beyond Laughter* (New York: Mc-Graw-Hill, 1957), p. 10: "Increasing demands for repression through the ages have changed aggression from assault into wit."

33. This formula fits Menander's *Dyskolos* precisely. What little laughter is evoked centers about the title character, old Knemon, ἀπάνθρωπός τις ἄνθρωπος σφόδρα (6), "a human exceedingly inhumane."

34. "How many men do you think I've already beaten to death — citizens as well as foreigners? And the more I do it the more I want to do it!" *Phormio,* 327–328. The Latin is Kauer & Lindsay's Oxford text (1926). John Sargeaunt, trans. of the Loeb Library ed. (Harvard University Press, 1912), omits line 328 without explanation.

Simo: superauit dolum Troianum atque Vlixem Pseudolus.[35]

(*Pseudolus* 1244)

He delights in mischief for its own sake,[36] and his aggressive attitude is that expressed by Epidicus: *apolactizo inimicos omnis* (678), "I kick the hell out of all who oppose me." There is no need to go into great detail, for clearly one factor unites Aristophanic *poneria,* Plautine *malitia,* and Rabelasian *panourgia*.[37] And the machinations of the *commedia dell'arte* Brighella and the massacres of Père Ubu are part of the same phenomenon. For the baton with which Scapin beats Géronte is no different from the club with which Odysseus beats Thersites. The effect in each case is comic *Schadenfreude.*

The argument thus far has been but a prologue to a discussion of Marlowe's *Jew of Malta.* T. S. Eliot pointed out the essential truths: the play is not tragedy but farce. Marlowe, like Ben Jonson writes what Eliot calls "savage comic humour." [38] But Jonson's brutality has been discussed far more often than Marlowe's cruelty, though it is everpresent in his plays. As in Tamburlaine's torture of Bajezeth and sack of Babylon; in Faustus' willingness to "offer luke warme blood of new borne babes." [39] And in Barabas' entire raison d'être.

35. *Chrysalus* (a slave): "I'm Ulysses, whose brains are running this whole enterprise!" *Simo:* "Pseudolus has surpassed Ulysses and the Trojan Trick!" All Plautus references are to the two-volume Oxford text of W. M. Lindsay, (1903).

36. For the Plautine slave's concern only with the guile of the game, see my *Roman Laughter: The Comedy of Plautus* (Cambridge, Mass.: Harvard University Press, 1968), pp. 61ff.

37. The Greek word *panourgia* means sheer villainy. In *Rabelais: A Study in Comic Courage* (Englewood Cliffs: Prentice-Hall, 1970), Thomas M. Greene discusses Panurge's "unpredictable creative malice" (p. 28). Greene also observes that "the pranks of Panurge can be seen as gratifications of that spontaneous cruelty, visible in products of folk fancy, which cultured people deny themselves, but enjoy" (p. 29).

38. Eliot's essays, "Notes on the Blank Verse of Christopher Marlowe" and "Ben Jonson," are published in *The Sacred Wood* (London: Methuen, 1920), pp. 86–94, 104–122. The words quoted here are from the essay on Marlowe, p. 92. For further comparisons between Marlowe and Jonson, see Harry Levin, *The Overreacher: A Study of Christopher Marlowe* (Cambridge, Mass.: Harvard University Press, 1952), pp. 148ff.

39. *Doctor Faustus* 446. All quotations from Marlowe are from the C. F. Tucker Brooke ed. (Oxford: 1910).

Bernard Spivak has recently demonstrated Barabas' relation to the Vice of morality plays, "a single intriguer, a voluble and cunning schemer, an artist in duplicity, a deft manipulator of human emotions." [40] But Barabas existed long before medieval drama, before Christianity, and even before morality as Socrates "invented" it. Before he was called Vice, he was called Odysseus.

To best understand the *Jew of Malta,* we must seek not ancestors, but analogues. Dimock's description of Homer's wanderer is quite as apt for Marlowe's Jew: "a hand and a mind against every man, by nature, or as a matter of policy." Harry Levin has pointed out that "policy" is a key word for Barabas, and Mario Praz has pointed out that "policy" enters the English language in 1406 — associated with Ulysses.[41]

By now the Romanticized views of Marlowe's hero have lost currency, although at least one critic in the last decade has referred to Barabas as "a sensitive and helpless victim" for whom the Elizabethan audience might have felt "genuine sympathy." [42] But rationalism dies even harder than Romanticism. There are still critics who try to argue cause and effect for Barabas' behavior. But one does not have to explain Harpagon's greed or Volpone's acquisitiveness; that's the "humour of it." And Barabas is also a humourous character. No doubt the earnest attempts to "understand" the Jew of Malta were influenced by the dimensions Shakespeare later added to his Jew of Venice. But Barabas is not Shylock; if you prick him, he will not bleed.

Barabas' humor is the *poneria* of the Aristophanic hero, and he too is essentially "the self militant." All of Marlowe's heroes are what Levin calls "monomaniac exponents of the first person" (p. 157), but none as much as Barabas, for he contains multitudes, a cast of thousands in a malevolence of one. He is not only every *thing* orthodox Elizabethans were against, he is every *one.* A Jew was a gargoyle much the same as a Turk. In fact, an Elizabethan writing in 1590 remarks: "Turcismus enim Judaismo

40. Spivak, *Shakespeare and the Allegory of Evil* (New York: Columbia University Press, 1958), p. 141.

41. Levin, *Overreacher,* p. 61. Praz, "Machiavelli and the Elizabethans," *The Flaming Heart* (New York: Doubleday, 1958), p. 104.

42. David M. Bevington, *From Mankind to Marlowe* (Cambridge, Mass.: Harvard University Press, 1962), pp. 222, 224.

cognatus admodum et affinis est." [43] And both Turk and Jew were associated with the Devil.[44] The Devil-Jew-Vice was a familiar stage figure, but surely never was there an ambiance of villainy to match that of Marlowe's Malta. The prologue sets the tone. It is Machiavelli's first appearance on the English stage.[45]

> Albeit all the world thinke *Macheuill* is dead,
> Yet was his soule but flowne beyond the *Alpes,*
> And now the *Guize* is dead, is come from France . . . (1–3)

Here is yet another Elizabethan bugbear: atheism and villainy incarnate. Interestingly, Machiavelli too was frequently considered an incarnation of the Devil. Moreover, his soul (unlike Faustus') enjoys Pythagorean metempsychosis, and after having visited that infamous Protestant-killer the Duke of Guise, he now flies across the Channel to present "the Tragedy of a Iew" (30). To Machiavelli, of course, Barabas' ultimate fall *is* a tragedy, "because he fauours me" (35). To add to his innate sins, the Jew is also a Machiavellian, and it should be noted that when he boasts of his successul co-religionists throughout the Mediterranean world, he specifically points out that there are "many in *France*" (165).

But of course the Maltese are more or less Italians. No need to emphasize what that nation evoked in the Elizabethan imagination. In *Pierce Penilesse* Thomas Nashe calls Italy "the Academie of man-slaughter, the sporting place of murther, the Apothecary-shop of poyson." And worst of all, these men are Catholics. Here again we confront the diabolical, for the Pope is in league with the Devil, as Satan himself admits in the morality play, *The Conflict of Conscience* (1581): ". . . the Pope, who is my darling dear, / My eldest Boy, in whom I do

43. From an anonymous tract quoted by Leon Kellner in "Die Quelle von Marlowe's 'Jew of Malta'," *Englische Studien,* 10 (1887), 110.

44. Barabas is "bottel-nosed" like the morality devil (Spivak, pp. 134ff). An equation between Turks and devils is made by Urbanus Regius in *An Homely or Sermon of Good and Euill Angels* (1583).

45. That the Marlovian caricature has not a single real characteristic of the Florentine philosopher is demonstrated by Irving Ribner, "Marlowe and Machiavelli," *CL,* 6 (Fall 1954), 348–356.

delight." [46] Indeed, Marlowe's Malta is a kind of Devil's Island.

The name Marlowe chooses for his protagonist makes it perfectly clear: he is the antithesis of Christ. And as Anouilh says of one of his mythological heroines, "Elle s'appelle Antigone et il va falloir qu'elle joue son rôle jusqu'au bout." Quite simply then, Barabas plays "hate thy neighbor." And his primary humour is not miserliness. He does not even share Volpone's enthusiasm for lucre. Even for silver the fox of Venice would not say, "Fye, what a trouble 'tis to count this trash" (42). To Barabas, fantastic wealth is only useful "to ransome great Kings from captiuity" (67); money is equated only with policy. Since the real essence of Barabas is motion, the instant he has told us the sole value of "infinite riches in a little roome" (72), he asks the first question of the play: "But now how stands the wind?" (73). Barabas will always be moving — and shifting with the wind. The importance in what follows is not so much that his ships immediately arrive laden with goods, but rather the interesting revelation that he is always taking risks. When he asks about his argosy at Alexandria, a merchant replies:

> . . . we heard some of our sea-men say,
> They wondred how you durst with so much wealth
> Trust such a crazed Vessell, and so farre.   (115–117)

But Barabas realized his ship was damaged: "Tush . . . I know her and her strength" (118). And four lines later, the "crazed Vessell" arrives safely in Malta port. Barabas will risk sinking more than once in this play.

When his co-religionists tell him that the Turk has arrived in Malta, Barabas implies his concern for them all. But he immediately tells the audience in an aside:

> Nay, let 'em combat, conquer, and kill all,
> So they spare me, my daughter, and my wealth.
>   (191–192)

46. Nathaniel Woodes, *The Conflict of Conscience* I.i.83–84, ed. Edgar T. Schell and J. D. Shuchter, in *English Morality Plays and Moral Interludes* (New York: Holt, Rinehart and Winston, 1969).

We cannot take too much stock in his affection for his daughter, since he has already told us he loves her "As *Agamemnon* did his *Iphigen*" (176).[47] And by the same token that he is richer than Job (414ff) Barabas surely owns more than a thousand ships. His first love is not even Volpone's for gold, "far transcending . . . children, parents, friends" (I.i.16–17). Rather, Barabas salutes his co-religionists, "Assure your selues I'le looke vnto [*aside*] my selfe" (212).

Barabas' true policy is selfmanship — which he indulges immediately after the departure of "these silly men" (218). He is not concerned with the Jews' problem or even Malta's:

> How ere the world goe, I'le make sure for one,
> And seeke in time to intercept the worst,
> Warily garding that which I ha got
> *Ego mihimet sum semper proximus.*
> Why let 'em enter, let 'em take the Towne.   (225–229)

And he is always against the universe, even in moments of prosperity. This is not the only time Barabas wishes the rest of humanity dead. In act five he exclaims, "For so I liue, perish may all the world" (2292). Marlowe's Faustus is tempted with a Deadly Sin who says much the same.[48] This unchained infantilistic aggression is also evident in Jarry's unchained infantilistic hero:

> *Père Ubu:* Vous vous fichez de moi! Dans la trappe, les financiers. *On entourne les financiers.*
>
> *Mère Ubu:* Mais enfin, Père Ubu, quel roi tu fais, tu masacres tout le monde!
>
> *Père Ubu:* Eh merdre! [49]

47. And Barabas must once again have Agamemnon in mind when he comments on Lodowick's desire for his daughter's hand: ". . . e're he shall haue her / I'le sacrifice her on a pile of wood" (812–813).

48. "I am *Enuy* . . . O that there would come a famine through all the worlde, that all might die, and I liue alone." *Doctor Faustus* 744ff.

49. *"Père Ubu:* You're all impertinent! Down the trap door with the financiers! (*They are shoved in.*) *Mère Ubu:* Enough is enough, Père Ubu. What kind of king are you? You're slaughtering everybody! *Père Ubu:* Oh shlit!" Alfred Jarry, *Ubu Roi* III.2. Later in the same scene Ubu rephrases his sentiment: "avec ce système, j'aurai vite fait fortune, alors je tuerai tout le monde et je m'en irai."

Those who would have us feel for the plight of Barabas inevitably point to his "persecution" in the scene of the confiscation of his wealth. But there is no reason why Barabas should refuse to pay something in order to keep much more than half his property (remember what he has hidden away). He could, in fact, keep all his wealth merely by the application of a little holy water. After all, to a Machiavellian, religion is "but a childish Toy" (14); and he will immediately persuade his own daughter to feign conversion, arguing that

> A counterfet profession is better
> Then vnseene hypocrisie.   (531–532)

When Abigail tells him his house (with hidden horde) has already been occupied, it becomes a challenge to outfox the little foxes, or as Barabas himself says in more Odyssean Language:

> No, I will liue; nor loath I this my life:
> And since you leaue me in the Ocean thus
> To sinke or swim, and put me to my shifts,
> I'le rouse my senses, and awake my selfe,   (501–504)

With the full awakening of his militant self, his splendid creative malice will now be fully displayed. He will epitomize his last advice to his daughter, "be cunning *Abigall*" (539).

Marlowe's "balcony scene" (640ff) ends with Barabas and his gold reunited and his ecstatic effusion: "hermoso placer de los dineros" (705). Why in Spanish? It could be a tag in any one of the many languages he knows, but Marlowe is ironically anticipating the arrival (in the next line) of one more Elizabethan devil, the Spaniard del Bosco, "Vizadmirall vnto the Catholike King" (712). In granting del Bosco permission to sell his slaves, the Maltese governor is breaking faith with his ex-allies, whom he now calls "these barbarous mis-beleeuing *Turkes*" (751). This note of international treachery sets the stage for the most memorable confrontation in the play: between the Jew Barabas and the Turk Ithamore.

Barabas enters brimming over with sweet hostility, for he is not really bitter or vengeful. He is already as rich as he ever was

(772) and now can devote himself entirely to mischief. To Lodowick, his hostility is but thinly veiled:

> . . . 'tis a custome held with vs,
> That when we speake with *Gentiles* like to you,
> We turne into the Ayre to purge our selues   (805–807)

He speaks of the "burning zeal" with which he regards the nuns who live in his former home, adding in an aside, "Hoping ere long to set the house a fire" (851); but then he must excuse himself to buy a slave. We need seek no emotional reason for Barabas' wanting a new servant. It is not, as some critics would have it, that he feels lonely, for Barabas does not *feel* anything. He has always been alone; there has never been a Leah to whom he gave a ring. He lives in a continuum of active aggression. And Ithamore will merely be a weapon.

At their first meeting, Barabas and the lean Turk each sing an aria of evil, an amoebean song of cruelty. This is a set piece with much precedent in comic literature. In Aristophanes' *Knights,* for example, there is perpetual rivalry between the Sausage Seller and the Paphlagonian, a "super-panurgist and super-diabolist." [50] They constantly exchange threats of violence and scatalogical attack. The Chorus enjoys the prospects of the Paphlagonian being bested (or worsted):

> But we are delighted to say that a man has
> come on the scene, far more corrupt than you, and it's
> clear he'll harass you and surpass you in villainy,
> boldness, and dirty tricks.   (328–332)

The *agon* here is nothing less than a bragging contest of crimes past and better crimes to come. At the end, the Paphlagonian must concede defeat, with a uniquely Aristophanic play on words: Οἴμοι κακοδαίμων, ὑπεραναιδευθήσομαι, "Aieeh, bad luck — I'm absolutely ab-rogue-ated!" (1206).

But the "aria of evil" which can best be compared with Barabas' occurs in Boccaccio. While, strictly speaking, it is prose

---

50. Παφλαγόνα / πανουργότατον καὶ διαβολώτατόν τινα (*Knights* 44–45).

narrative, we everywhere sense the speaker's delight in presenting the achievements of Ser Ciapelletto:

> Testimonianze false con sommo diletto diceva, richesto e non
> richesto . . . Aveva oltre modo piacere, e forte vi studiava, in
> commettere tra amici e parenti e qualunque altra persona mali
> ed inimicizie e scandali, de' quali quanto maggiori mali vedeva
> seguire, tanto più d'allegrezza prendea. Invitato ad uno omicidio
> o a qualunque altra rea cosa, senza negarlo mai, volonterosa-
> mente v'andava, e più volte e fedire e ad uccidere uomini con le
> proprie mani si ritrovò volentieri . . . Perchè mi distendo io in
> tante parole? Egli era il piggiore uomo, forse, che mai nascesse.[51]

Ciapelletto is like Molière's Dom Juan, according to Sganarelle
"le plus grand scélérat que la terre ait jamais porté." [52] But
Barabas is more than a match for the grandest rogues of comedy,
and his outrageous brag bears quoting at length:

> As for my selfe, I walke abroad a nights
> And kill sicke people groaning under walls:
> Sometimes I goe about and poyson wells . . .
> Being young, I studied Physicke, and began
> To practise first vpon the *Italian;*
> There I enric[h]'d the Priests with burials,
> And alwayes kept the Sexton's armes in vre
> With digging graues and ringing dead mens knels:
> And after that was I an Engineere,
> And in the warres 'twixt *France* and *Germanie,*
> Vnder pretence of helping *Charles* the fifth,
> Slew friend and enemy with my stratagems.

51. (I quote only a small portion.) "He gave false witness with supreme delight — and whether asked to or not . . . He took inordinate
pleasure in stirring up enmities, scandals, and other misfortunes among
friends, relatives, and anyone else. And the greater the misfortune, the
greater his amusement. If invited to a homicide — or some other das-
tardly event, he not only always accepted and went with great enthusiasm,
but very often his enthusiasm found him striking the blows and killing
men with his own hands . . . But why am I going on at such length?
He was perhaps the very worst man who was ever born." Boccaccio,
Il Decameron, I, 29.

52. Molière, *Dom Juan* I.i. Sganarelle continues, describing his master
as "un enragé, un chien, un diable, un Turc, un hérétique, qui ne croit ni
Ciel ni Enfer, ni loup-garou" (a madman, a dog, a devil, a Turk, a
heretic who doesn't believe in Heaven or Hell or the Big Bad Wolf!).

> Then after that was I an Vsurer,
> And with exorting, cozening, forfeiting,
> And tricks belonging vnto Brokery,
> I fill'd the Iailes with Bankrouts in a yeare,
> And with young Orphans planted Hospitals,
> And euery Moone made some or other mad,
> And now and then one hang himselfe for griefe.
>
> (939–941, 946–961)

There are, of course, aspects of Barabas' "career" which derive from medieval stereotypes of the Jew. In any case, we are not meant to take any of his words at face value or believe that he has actually traveled to all the places he mentions. Marlowe's style is always one of exaggeration, especially in this play.[53] We note in Barabas' brag, which begins significantly, "As for my *selfe*,"[54] that his interest is always in malice, not money. As a doctor his delight was enriching the priests (with burials). As a usurer, his joy was in the pain he caused (suicides, insanity, and so on). Most interesting is his behavior while "helping" Charles the fifth, for here he slew friend as well as enemy.[55] This delight in totally indiscriminate cruelty is exactly like Ser Ciapelletto's in stirring pain and trouble among relatives and friends. Both Boccaccio's and Marlowe's descriptions are intended to arouse the laugh of *Schadenfreude* through a comic hero who unabashedly relishes the inflicting of pain, "o qualunque rea cosa."

Whereas Barabas' exploits may be imaginary, before the play is out, he will have committed almost all the atrocities of which he boasts. And Ithamore, who begins as one of Barabas' dupes, will end as one of his victims. For the Jew merely baits his slave with the Volpone-trick. Whereas he may flatter him as

53. For example, Barabas' hyperbolic allusions when discussing the poison for the nuns (1399ff). The characters in the subplot are also given to exaggeration; see Bellamira's boast that clients once came to her from as far as Padua and Venice (1155ff). Barabas' "aria of evil" can also be compared with the boasts of Lightbone in *Edward the Second* ("I learned in Naples how to poison flowers," and others, 2363ff).

54. In significant contrast to his daughter's first words in the play, "Not for my selfe . . ." (462).

55. Some have sought a historical model for Barabas among the Jews who were skilled at designing war machines; see Kellner, pp. 89ff. But the best model is Dr. Faustus, who also "helps" Charles V (917ff).

"my second self" (1317), and chant litanies of "I here adopt
thee for mine onely heire" (1345), Barabas wastes no time in
telling the audience that he is but guiling Ithamore:

> Thus euery villaine ambles after wealth
> Although he ne're be richer then in hope . . .
>
> (3154–3155)

How little veiled is the hostility in Barabas' expression of gratitude to his collaborator in the poisoning of the nuns: "Ile pay
thee with a vengeance, Ithamore" (1418). In fact, Barabas buys
Ithamore to enlarge his own scope of hate.

Barabas' purchase is followed by a crescendo of comic
cruelty. First, the Jew schemes to set Lodowick against Mathias
in a heartless perversion of what Sir Toby stirs up between
Viola and Sir Andrew Aguecheek. But in Shakespeare the trick
adds to the midsummer madness; here it adds to Maltese murder.
And there is so much gusto on the part of the murderer that we
feel no sympathy at the death of the two young men.

It is even difficult to grieve for Abigail. For as she gasps her
last breath, we cannot help but think of an offstage chorus of
her fellow nuns, all dying at the same time. The many other
murderous pranks of Barabas which have analogues on the
comic stage cannot be listed here. Sometimes Ithamore will lend
a helping hand — to strangle a friar, for example (Boccaccio's
Ser Ciapelletto was likewise generous when it came to killing
people). But he is a mere zany to his master, who has no real
need of him. In fact, after Ithamore's defection, the speed and
scope of villainy actually increase. Here, as throughout the play,
Barabas' single aim is to outdo himself in evil:

> Now I haue such a plot for both their liues,
> As neuer Iew nor Christian knew the like . . .
>
> (1626–1627)

That is why he persists in scheming even after he becomes
governor, which could be ambition's *ne plus ultra*. He must
continue in malice; it is his humour. This is that Odyssean quality
in Barabas (and we cannot ignore how he led the Turk through

the city walls in Ulysseslike fashion). Just as when Mosca believes that he and Volpone have achieved "our master-peece: We cannot thinke, to goe beyond this" — and Volpone immediately comes up with yet another scheme to "torture 'em rarely" (V.i.30–31, 128). So too Barabas' instinct urges him to undo others till he himself is undone.

Thus, immediately following the brutal sack of Malta, Barabas switches sides. We need seek no explanations in reason or *Realpolitik*. The motive is far more basic: are there not Turks to kill? Barabas is a man who could laugh at the annihilation of the world. He cares no more for Turk than for Christian (2213); he cares for himself. And at the end, he is quite the same person he was at the outset, ever risking, shifting, testing the wind, and delighting in his villainy:

> . . . why, is not this
> A kingly kinde of trade to purchase Townes
> By treachery, and sell 'em by deceit?
> Now tell me, worldings, vnderneath the sunne,
> If greater falshood euer has ben done.   (2329–2330)

His opening monologue had already explained his views on "the policy" of riches.

His last trick is both his best in quantity of victims and his worst — since he is one of them. Shakespeare's Jew ends at the baptismal font, but Marlowe's ends in hotter water. Barabas' cauldron is also an ancient comic prop (it rejuvenated Demos in *The Knights*). Surely the last glimpse of Barabas, boiling mentally and physically, and cursing the "damn'd Christians, dogges, and Turkish Infidels" (2370) was intended to raise a "heartless laugh." [56] It must have, for audiences packed Henslowe's playhouses to see Marlowe's wildly successful play. Today we may find such laughter as foreign as that of Wimsatt's Fiji Islander delightedly watching a prisoner roast. But that was in another country. Yet so was Barabas, and as Baudelaire wrote in his essay on laughter: "Pour trouver du comique féroce et très

56. Eugene Waith, "Marlowe and the Jades of Asia," *SEL*, 6 (Spring 1965), 239.

féroce, il faut passer la Manche et visiter les royaumes brumeux du spleen." [57]

Schadenfreude is a childish pleasure, say the psychologists, and Marlowe often displays a rather adolescent delight in cruelty. It is perhaps difficult to accept this as a laughing matter, but the beast in man does not always evoke pity and terror — as in the case of Lear's pelican daughters or that Spartan dog Iago. There is also Jonson's fox of Venice, and Marlowe's snake of Malta, both of whom make laughter of what Freud had to concede was a basic human trait: *homo homini lupus*. Did Freud know he was quoting Plautus?[58]

57. "To find a ferocious, in fact very ferocious sense of the comic, one has to cross the Channel and visit the foggy kingdoms of spleen." "De l'essence du rire," in *Curiosités ésthétiques* (Paris: Garnier, 1962), p. 256.

58. *Asinaria* 495.

JOHN M. BULLITT

Swift's "Rules of Raillery"

"Agreeable B——tch." With this *discordia concors* of approval
and abuse Swift affectionately concluded his *Journal to Stella.*[1]
The final word was strong language in the eighteenth century,
as we may infer from the novels of one of Swift's most gifted
admirers, Henry Fielding. The "chaste" Laetitia Snap, Jonathan
Wild's "adwhorable creeture" whose timely compliance had
prevented her from being, in a literal sense, raped by Fireblood,
was righteously incensed when her husband, Wild, abused her
with the term; in *Joseph Andrews,* the warmhearted and more
agreeable Betty, the chambermaid, bore with patience Mrs. Tow-
wouse's epithets of slut, trollop, and whore, but she was stung
to the quick with the name of that "terrible word so odious to
female ears." And yet we can be sure that Stella, who, with
Rebecca Dingley, was accustomed to Swift's epithets of "saucy
rogue," "saucy jades," "naughty girls," and "slut," responded

1. The quotations from Swift are from the following editions: *Jonathan Swift: Journal to Stella,* ed. Harold Williams, 2 vols. (Oxford,
1948); *The Poems of Jonathan Swift,* ed. Harold Williams, 3 vols. (Oxford, 1937); *The Correspondence of Jonathan Swift,* ed. F. Elrington
Ball, 6 vols. (1910–1914); *The Prose Works of Jonathan Swift,* ed.
Herbert Davis et al., 14 vols. (Oxford, 1939–1968).

to the most terrible word of all with tranquil satisfaction. Swift's playfulness had not transgressed the rules of raillery.

Swift knew the dangers of being witty. "Since I must laugh, or cannot live / Good natur'd Stella will forgive," he wrote in "Stella's Distress," but forgiveness of his sin of wit had not always been granted him,

> Since there are persons who complain
> There is too much satire in my vein,
> That I am often found exceeding
> The rules of raillery and breeding.
>
> ("A Dialogue Between an Eminent Lawyer and
> Dr. Swift," ll.1–4)

The complaints of Swift's victims were no more strident than his own when, after a decade of nursing his wounded sensitivities, he let his anger at Thomas Sheridan break out at the end of his pen in *The History of the Second Solomon*. Sheridan, the "Second Solomon," apparently had written a poem called "The Funeral," shortly after becoming acquainted with Swift in early 1718. The content of the poem survives only in Swift's pained description of it in *The History*, probably written in 1729: "In three months time, Solomon, without the least provocation, writ a long poem, describing that person's [Swift's] muse to be dead, and making a funeral solemnity with asses, owls, &c. and gave the copy among all his acquaintance." Swift's initial response to Sheridan's raillery is recorded in a letter to Patrick Delany on 10 November 1718, written in confidence "else I may be thought a man who will not take a jest." Swift's complaint was "that I have long thought several of his papers, and particularly that of the Funeral, to be out of all the rules of raillery I ever understood."

In eighteenth-century usage, "raillery" was as Protean a word as wit, humor, ridicule, or satire itself;[2] and Corbyn Morris' *An Essay Towards Fixing the True Standards of Wit, Humor, Raillery, Satire and Ridicule* (1744) can be taken as typical of the many attempts to establish clear distinctions and to fix rules of

2. See Norman Knox's discussion of the definitions of raillery in his chapter on "Raillery and Banter" in *The Word Irony and its Context, 1500–1755* (Durham, N.C., 1961).

usage. Morris' definition of raillery, which, in its emphasis on good humor, seems to be close to the OED's definition as "good humored ridicule," expressed a prevailing view: "Raillery is a genteel poignant Attack of a Person upon any slight Foibles, Oddities, or Embarrassments of his, in which he is tender, or may be supposed to be tender, and unwilling to come to a free Explanation." But Morris distinguished raillery from ridicule by the seriousness of the subject matter and the intended response: raillery is used on slight subjects and its purpose is to give pleasure by causing only "a little embarrassment of a person," whereas ridicule aims at more serious faults and its aim is "to degrade the person attacked and to render him contemptible." Clearly, Swift felt that Sheridan's "The Funeral" had exceeded the limits of good humor and had descended, however unwittingly, into degrading abuse; the poem had violated the cardinal rule of raillery, that it communicate good humor and not offend its object.

That Swift sometimes thought of raillery as a form of ridicule is apparent from his lines in "An Epistle to a Lady" in which, paraphrasing Horace, he says that

> Ridicule has greater Pow'r
> To reform the World than Sour,   (ll.199–200)

and a few lines later he explains:

> I may storm and rage in vain;
> It but stupifies your Brain.
> But, with Raillery to nettle,
> Set your Thoughts upon their Mettle.   (ll.209–212)

But Swift's more habitual usage was to exclude from raillery all painful subjects: "The complaint you make of a disorder in one of your eyes," he wrote Mrs. Pendarves (22 February 1734/5), "will admit no raillery." And the raillery between friends should never "nettle." In "Cadenus and Vanessa" a group of "glitt'ring Dames" are loudly obnoxious visitors, and after the usual vapidity about clothes and scandal "They raill'd next *Vanessa's* Dress; / That Gown was made for Old Queen *Bess*." For this and the censure that followed, masking as raillery, Vanessa was "Fill'd with disdain, with Rage inflam'd, / Both of her self and Sex asham'd." Those "fair Detractors" not only had broken the rules of raillery, they had broken "one of the best Rules in Conversation," which, Swift notes in his *Hints Towards an Essay on Conversation,* is "never to say a Thing of which any of the Company can reasonably wish we had rather left unsaid; nor can there any Thing be well more contrary to the Ends for which People meet together, than to part unsatisfied with each other, or themselves."

The proper word for detraction which aims at degrading the person attacked was not raillery but "railing"; stupid and malicious people, lacking good manners and ignorant of the rules of civilized conversation, confound the cheerful and harmless wit of raillery with the malice and rudeness of "railing." Such confusion is part of "The Furniture of a Woman's Mind":

> For Conversation well endu'd;
> She calls it witty to be rude;
> And, placing Raillery in Railing,
> Will tell aloud your greatest Failing.   (ll.17–20)

In "To Betty the Grizette," Swift mocks the female "Hybernian Asses" who go to playhouses

> Where, in Eighteen-Penny Gall'ry
> *Irish* Nymphs learn *Irish* Raillery:
> But, thy Merit is thy Failing,
> And, thy Raillery is Railing.   (ll.25–28)

In the *Hints Towards an Essay on Conversation* Swift deplores that "rude Familiarity" which passes "for innocent Freedom, or Humor" but which, "among the *Romans,* was the Raillery of Slaves, of which we have many instances in *Plautus.* It seemeth to have been introduced among us by *Cromwell,* who by preferring the Scum of the People, made it a Court Entertainment." This "Irish raillery," this "raillery of slaves," is a product of false refinement and a veneer of gentility concealing gross Billingsgate:

> So, the pert Dunces of Mankind
> Whene're they would be thought refin'd,
> Because the Diff'rence lyes abstruse
> 'Twixt Raillery and gross Abuse,
> To show their Parts, will scold and rail,
> Like Porters o'er a Pot of Ale.
>
> ("To Mr. Delany," ll.45–50)

Again in his *Hints,* Swift devotes a paragraph to raillery, which he calls "the finest Part of Conversation," and he begins by describing its misuse: "It now passeth for Raillery to run a Man down in Discourse, to put him out of Countenance, and make him ridiculous, sometimes to expose the Defects of his Person, or Understanding; on all which Occasions he is obliged not to be angry, to avoid the Imputation of not being able to take a Jest." The last phrase echoes closely his own anxieties as he complained to Delany about Sheridan's use of raillery, and the whole paragraph is so close in meaning to the poem "To Mr. Delany," which Swift enclosed with his letter to Delany, that we may suppose it to have been written at the same time. Swift proceeds: "The *French,* from whom we borrow the Word, have a quite different Idea of the Thing, and so had we in the politer Age of our Fathers. Raillery was to say something that at first appeared a Reproach, or Reflection; but, by some Turn of Wit unexpected and surprising, ended always in a Compliment, and to the Advantage of the Person it was addressed to."

For this definition Swift may have had in mind his much admired La Rochefoucauld, "who is my favorite," he wrote Pope, "because I found my whole character in him." La Rochefoucauld, in the sixteenth of his *Réflexions Diverses,* "De la Différence des Esprits," wrote: "il y a une manière de railler, délicate et flatteuse, qui touche seulement les défauts que les personnes dont on parle veulent bien avouer, qui sait déguiser les louanges qu'on leur donne sous des apparences de blâme, et qui découvre ce qu'elles ont d'aimable, en feignant de le vouloir cacher." If La Rochefoucauld provided Swift with a hint toward defining raillery, it was Voiture whom Swift acknowledged to be the inventor of "the Rule" of raillery. The works of Vincent de Voiture were in Swift's library, and in two letters to Pope he

praised the French letter-writer as "an author I am fond of"
(26 February 1729/30) who had given him "entertainment"
(21 October 1735). Pope recorded his own admiration in his
"Epistle to Miss Blount with the Works of Voiture," and although there is no foundation to Curll's charge that Pope had
"very politely pillaged his [Voiture's] Letters," the influence of
Voiture upon some of Pope's early letters is unmistakable. A
number of editions of Voiture's letters in translations by Dryden,
Dennis, and others began appearing in 1696; and John Ozell
translated *The Works of the Celebrated Monsieur Voiture* in
1715, prefaced by Pope's poetical tribute and a life of Voiture
"Written by his Nephew." [3]

"To Mr. Delany" is a poetic essay ("Which might as well
have been in Prose") on the art of conversation and good manners, which Swift defined in his *Hints on Good Manners* as "the
art of making every reasonable person in the company easy,
and to be easy ourselves."

> What Use in Life, to make Men frett?
> Part in worse humor than they met?
> Thus all Society is lost,
> Men laugh at one another's Cost;
> And half the Company is teazd
> That came together to be pleased.   (ll.71–76)

Swift's prescription for good conversation is that it combine
"Humor, Raillery, and Witt" without making anyone uneasy:

> Our conversation to refine
> True Humor must with Wit combine:
> From both, we learn to Railly well;
> Wherein French Writers most excell:
> Voiture in various Lights displays
> That Irony which turns to Praise,
> His Genius first found out the Rule
> For an obliging Ridicule:
> He flatters with peculiar Air

---

3. This two-volume edition is not listed in the CBEL. A copy, from
which I quote later in this paper, is in the Houghton Library, Harvard
University.

> The Brave, the Witty, and the Fair;
> And Fools would fancy he intends
> A Satyr where he most commends.   (ll.29–40)

Although Voiture's letters hardly deserve Samuel Johnson's harsh epithet of "despicable remains," they rarely exhibit the strength of intellect or diversity of style that inform Swift's practice in the same vein of humor. Characteristically, the letters begin in a tone and with the vocabulary of complaint, which then gracefully turns into the language of compliment. As his nephew wrote in the "Life" prefaced to Ozell's 1715 edition: "Tho' he was a great Lover of Rallery, yet he never writ any thing Satirical; and in all his writings, there is nothing but what is to the Advantage of those he speaks of."

Writing to one of "the Fair," Mlle. de Paulet, Voiture adopts a caustic, injured tone as he complains that she sent him "a great Packet" but with only a "little Letter in it" with which she tried "to cover a Piece of Injustice with a great deal of Civility." Voiture is careful to call attention to his ironic simulation of anger lest he be misunderstood and his flattery received as satire: "But to speak seriously (for I know, Madam, you would not for the World that I should mean what I say) instead of complaining of this, I have Reason to return you a thousand Thanks for the Honour you cause me to receive from so many deserving Persons" (Letter XXX). Some such clear signals of intent were obviously absent in Sheridan's poem, but if one's ridicule is to be "obliging," Swift, like Voiture, knew the jest must be explicit:

> But those who aim at Ridicule
> Shou'd fix upon some certain Rule,
> Which fairly hints they are in jest,
> Else he must enter his Protest.
>   ("Cadenus and Vanessa," ll.664–67)

There is, of course, no "certain Rule" beyond that of showing that no truth underlies the jest:

> No Raillery gives just offense
> Where Truth has not the least Pretense.
>   ("Stella's Distress," ll.61–2)

Voiture's graceful skill in the irony of inverting blame and praise is illustrated in his letter to one of "the Brave," the Duke of Anguien, after his victory at the battle of Rocroy in 1643. The Duke was said to be a modest man who despised flattery, and Voiture's letter of compliment labels the Duke as unreasonable, unrespected, revengefully bold, violent, obstinate, heated, and intolerable.

> My Lord, At a Time that I am so far remov'd from your Highness, that you cannot possibly lay your commands upon me, I am fully resolv'd to speak freely my Mind to you, which I have so long been oblig'd to disguise, lest it should bring me into the same Inconveniency with those who before me have taken the like Liberties with you. But let me tell you, my Lord, you have done too much to pass without being taken Notice of, and you are unreasonable, if you think to behave yourself as you do, without being loudly told of it. If you did but know how strangely all Paris talks of you, I am very confident you would be asham'd of it; and you could not without Confusion hear, with how little respect and how little Fear of Displeasing you, all the World presumes to discourse of what you have done. I must confess, my Lord, I wonder what you could mean: You have shewn yourself Bold with a Vengeance, and Violent to the last Degree, in putting such an affront upon two or three old Captains, whom you ought to have respected, if it had been only for their Antiquity . . . I heard, indeed, you are obstinate as a Devil, and that it was not to much Purpose to dispute about anything with you: But yet I never thought, that your Heat would have transported you so far. If you go on at the rate you have begun, you will shortly grow intolerable, I assure you, to all Europe, and neither the Emperor nor the King of Spain, will either of them be able to endure you . . . But now . . . I felicitate your Highness for the Victory . . .   (Letter XX)

The irony is sufficiently transparent to avoid misunderstanding, and the concluding panegyric is a flattering reinforcement of his good-humored intention.

We may pause, finally, on one pattern in Voiture's habitual use of raillery which is conspicuous and formulaic: an act or sentiment of kindness by his correspondent is attributed to malice and his own response is a threatened revenge. Voiture's formula of malice-revenge is clear, for example, in a letter to another one of "the Fair," Mlle. Rambouillet, written in answer to her having teased him for teaching French to a young English girl: "Madam . . . I had much ado to understand what you say of *la Corneille,* and *the Son of the King of England,* but if I have guessed rightly at the meaning, 'tis the greatest Piece of Malice that ever was forg'd. You never said any Thing to me, that provok'd me so much; and 'tis an Affront I shall never forget, 'til I have had my Revenge for it . . . All these Injuries, Madam, put me into a terrible Fury; but the sweet Sauce you sent me, appeas'd it" (Letter LVII). The charge of malice, provocation, and injuries and the promise of revenge became a staple in Swift's manipulation of "that Irony which turns to Praise."

Swift's voluminous correspondence has been widely used by scholars as a source of biographical information, but it has been too much neglected as a form of literature. And yet, as Oliver W. Ferguson has suggested, "for Swift, writing a letter was a literary activity," [4] and his letters written in raillery are among his most accomplished literary acts. Lord Orrery, Swift's early biographer, quoted Swift as saying: "When I sit down to write a letter, I never lean upon my elbow, till I have finished it." As Ferguson shows, this claim to unstudied spontaneity conceals a world of art; and Swift himself said in response to the artful raillery of Lord Bathurst that "your Lordship is the first person alive that ever made me lean upon my elbow while I was writing to him" (October 1730). One may doubt the sincerity of the remark, but it suggests that Swift took the art of raillery seriously.

The exchange between Bathurst and Swift shows Bathurst to have been a worthy practitioner of the art. Expressing his pleasure in reading Swift's letters to him, Bathurst demands more of them:

> But if you grow obstinate, and will not answer me, I will plague and pester you, and do all I can to vex you. I will take your

4. See his " 'Nature and Friendship': The Personal Letters of Jonathan Swift," in *The Familiar Letter in the Eighteenth Century,* ed. Howard Anderson, Philip B. Daghlian, and Irvin Ehrenpreis (Lawrence: University of Kansas Press, 1968), pp. 14–33.

works to pieces, and show you that they are all borrowed or
stolen. Have you not stolen the sweetness of your numbers from
Dryden and Waller? Have not you borrowed thoughts from Virgil
and Horace? At least, I am sure I have seen something like them
in those books. And in your prose writings, which they make
such a noise about, they are only some little improvements upon
the humour you have stolen from Miguel de Cervantes and
Rabelais. Well, but the style — a great matter indeed, for an
Englishman to value himself upon, that he can write English;
why, I write English too, but it is in another style.

(9 September 1730)

Bathurst continues in the same vein about Swift's political tracts
and concludes that "I have twenty other points to maul you
upon, if you provoke me; but if you are civil and good-natured,
and will send me a long, a very long letter, in answer to this, I
will let you alone a good while."

Swift delighted in this kind of obliging wit, and his answer to
Bathurst, complaining ironically of the "unspeakable injury"
done to him, Bathurst's "highest degree of malice," and his
"injustice," forces him to the compliment: "I pretend to have
been an improver of irony on the subject of satire and praise,
but I will surrender up my title to your Lordship." His surrender was certainly a gesture of rhetoric. Swift had several
correspondents who could also "rally very well," as he wrote
of Esther Van Homrigh (3 September 1712), but few, if any
(including Bathurst), improved more elegantly than Swift upon
the irony of raillery.

Swift was acutely sensitive to the response of his audience,
and he knew that raillery is a form of irony so susceptible to
misinterpretation that its success depends almost as much upon
the wit of the reader as that of the practitioner. The reason
that the witty Archbishop King was so often "misunderstood"
and his "innocent" meanings "misapplied" was because of the
"gross understandings" of the people in Ireland who "do very
ill understand raillery," Swift wrote (10 April 1711). "I can
rally much safer here [London] with a great Minister of State
or a duchess, than I durst do there with an attorney or his wife.
And I can venture to rally with your Grace, although I could
not do it with many of your clergy. I myself have been a wit-

ness, when want of common sense has made people offended with your Grace, where they ought to have been the most pleased. I say things every day at the best tables, which I should be turned out of company for if I were in Ireland."

In conversation, as in letters, it behooves the ironist to choose his company well and avoid the error of those "men of wit and good understanding," Swift wrote in his *Hints on Good Manners,* who conceive a "better opinion of those with whom they converse than they ought to do. Thus I have often known the most innocent raillery, and even of that kind which was meant for praise, to be mistaken for abuse and reflection." Swift knew his audience when he adopted the language of proud insolence to Henry St. John (7 January 1710/11), who had invited him to dine with an "early notice, to prevent you from any other appointment":

Sir,
    Though I should not value such usage from a Secretary of State, and a great Minister; yet when I consider the person it comes from, I can endure it no longer. I would have you know, Sir, that if the Queen gave you a dukedom and the garter to-morrow, with the Treasury just at the end of them, I would regard you no more than if you were not worth a groat. I could almost resolve, in spite, not to find fault with my victuals, or be quarrelsome tomorrow at your table; but if I do not take the first opportunity to let all the world know some qualities in you that you take most care to hide, may my right hand forget its cunning. After which threatening, believe me, if you please, to be with the greatest respect, Sir,
    Your most obedient and most humble servant,

                                                              J. Swift

The ironic double meaning behind Swift's threat to expose "some qualities in you that you take most care to hide" is a piece of witty flattery that St. John would admire and Voiture never achieved.

Voiture's formula (the complaint of malice, provocation, and injustice met by resentment and revenge) provided Swift a rhetorical model which he much improved. In Swift's favorite "variations on the device" of raillery (letters of thanks and letters of reproach to a friend for writing at all [5]), he often opens with a charge of malice. He complains to Thomas Tickell (19 July 1725) that his "whole behavior . . . hath tended maliciously to hinder me from writing or speaking anything that could deserve to be read or heard. I can no sooner hint my desire of a favour of a friend, but you immediately grant it, on purpose to load me, so as to put it out of my power to express my gratitude."

Writing to Gay (8 January 1722/3), Swift asks: "What can be the design of your letter but malice, to wake me out of a scurvy sleep, which however is better than none?" And again, writing to Robert Cope (26 May 1720), who had invited Swift to visit him, he begins: "If all the world would not be ready to knock me down for disputing the good-nature and generosity of you and Mrs. Cope, I should swear you invited me out of malice; some spiteful people have told you I am grown sickly and splenetic, and, having been formerly so your-self, you want to triumph over me with your health and good humor, and she is your accomplice." Swift opens his letter (October 1726) to Pope's friend Mrs. Howard with vengeance: "Madam, Being perpetually teased with the remembrance of you, by the sight of your ring on my finger, my patience at last is at an end, and in order to be revenged, I have sent you a piece of Irish plaid . . ." How far Swift could develop Voiture's simple formula into witty arabesques of flattery is seen in his charming letter to the Duchess of Ormond upon receiving pictures of her and her husband:

Any other person, of less refinement and prudence than myself, would be at a loss how to thank your Grace, upon the surprise of coming home last night, and finding two pictures where only one was demanded. But I understand your Grace's malice, and so here affirm you to be the greatest prude upon earth. You will not so much as let your picture be alone in a room with a man, no not with a clergyman, and a clergyman of five-and-forty: and therefore resolved my Lord Duke should accompany it, and keep me in awe, that I might not presume to look too often upon it. For my own part, I begin already to repent that I

5. *Ibid.,* p. 26.

ever begged your Grace's picture; and could almost find in my heart to send it you back: for, although it be the most beautiful sight I ever beheld, except the original, yet the veneration and respect it fills me with, will always make me think I am in your Grace's presence; will hinder me from saying and writing twenty idle things that used to divert me; will set me labouring upon majestic, sublime ideas, at which I have no manner of talent; and will make those who come to visit me, think I am grown, on the sudden, wonderful stately and reserved. But, in life we must take the evil with the good; and it is one comfort, that I know how to be revenged. For the sight of your Grace's resemblance will perpetually remind me of paying my duty to your person; which will give your Grace the torment, and me the felicity, of a more frequent attendance.

When Samuel Johnson defined "raillery" in his *Dictionary* as "slight satire; satirical merriment" he did not have in view Swift's conception of "the finest part of conversation," in which the corrective truths of satire have no place. But if Swift's good-mannered raillery never aimed at discomforting its object, it did allow him room to include what could be called "parallel satire" in which the ironically blamed good qualities of the recipient are contrasted with the generality of mankind. The device is seen briefly in Swift's affectionate abuse of the Duchess of Queensbury (3 October 1732) when he complains that

you can neither spell, nor talk, nor write, nor think like a courtier; that you pretend to be respected for qualities which have been out of fashion ever since you were almost in your cradle; that your contempt for a fine petticoat is an infallible mark of disaffection; which is further confirmed by your ill taste for wit, in preferring two old-fashioned poets [i.e., Gay and Swift] before Duck or Cibber. Besides, you spell in such a manner as no Court lady can read, and write in such an old-fashioned style as none of them can understand.

Two witty, spirited, and more extended examples of this variation of raillery appear in letters written to ladies who had sent presents to the aging Swift. Swift's friend William Richardson had a niece, Katharine Richardson, whom Swift had never met; she had sent Swift "half a dozen of shirts." In his letter to

her (28 January 1737/8) Swift accuses her uncle, who, with
no "provocation" other than that of dining with Swift, had
gratified the "revenge in his breast" by sending him wines and
salmons "that surfeited my self and all my visitors; whereby it
is plain that his malice reached to my friends as well as myself." Similarly, his niece, "maliciously bribing a useless man,"
was "cruel" enough to send the shirts, "although I never once
gave you the least cause of displeasure." Upon inquiry among
her neighbors, Swift continues, he finds Katharine is reputed to
be a "Lady adorned with all perfections . . . and even good
housewifery, which last is seldom the talent of ladies in this
kingdom." He concludes:

> Our common run of ladies here dare not read before a man, and
> much less dare to write, for fear, as their expression is, of being
> exposed, so that when I see any of your sex, if they be worth
> mending, I beat them all, call them names, until they leave off
> their follies, and ask pardon; and therefore, because Princes are
> said to have long hands, I wish I were a Prince with hands long
> enough to beat you at this distance, for all your faults, particu-
> larly your ill treatment of me. However, I will conclude with
> charity. May you never give me cause to change, in any single
> article, the opinion and idea I have of your person and qualities,
> may you ever long continue the delight of your uncle and your
> neighbors round, who deserve your good will, and of all who
> have merit enough to distinguish you. I am with great respect
> and the highest esteem, Madam,
>   Your most obedient and most obliged humble servant,
>   Jon. Swift.

The other letter (4 June 1734), written in cheerful raillery
but barbed with parallel satire, is to Archbishop Hoadly's
daughter, who had pleased Swift with gifts of pork and butter
— "great offenses, contrived on purpose to corrupt my integrity." But Swift promises revenge:

> However, I have two ways to be revenged: first, I will let all
> the ladies of my acquaintance know, that you, the sole daughter
> and child of his Grace of Dublin, are so mean as to descend to
> understand housewifery, which every girl of this town, who can
> afford sixpence a month for a chair, would scorn to be thought

to have the least knowledge in, and this will give you as ill a reputation, as if you had been caught in the fact of reading a history, or handling a needle, or working in a field at Tallaght. My other revenge shall be this; when my Lord's gentleman delivered his message, after I put him some questions, he drew out a paper containing your directions, and in your hand: I said it properly belonged to me, and, when I had read it, put it in my pocket, and am ready to swear, when lawfully called, that it is written in a fair hand, rightly spelt, and good plain sense. You now may see I have you at mercy; for, upon the least offence given, I will show the paper to every female scrawler I meet, who will soon spread about the town, that your writing and spelling are ungenteel and unfashionable, more like a parson than a lady . . . I lay it upon you, Madam, to bring housewifery in fashion among our ladies, that by your example they may no longer pride themselves on their natural or affected ignorance. I am, with the truest respect and esteem, Madam,

> Your most obedient and obliged, etc.

Parallel satire based on raillery had wider applications for Swift than the *jeux d'esprit* of epistolary compliment, and it may be found in such satiric contexts as the dedication to Lord Somers in *A Tale of a Tub* and at greater length as the rhetorical device central to *A Vindication of His Excellency, the Lord Carteret* who

could never wipe off the stain, nor wash out the tincture of his University acquirements and dispositions . . . I cannot omit another weak Side in His Excellency. For it is known, and can be proved upon him, that *Greek* and *Latin* Books might be found every Day in his Dressing Room, if it were carefully searched; and there is Reason to suspect, that some of the said Books have been privately conveyed to him by *Tory* Hands. I am likewise assured, that he hath been taken in the very Fact of reading the said Books; even in the Midst of a Session, to the great Neglect of public Affairs.

I own, there may be some Grounds for this Charge; because I have it from good Hands, that when His Excellency is at Dinner, with one or two Scholars at his Elbows, he grows a most unsupportable, and unintelligible Companion to all the fine Gentlemen round the Table.

It is always disappointing when intelligent men take what in the eighteenth century were called "short views," but how else can one respond except with uneasy disappointment to F. R. Leavis' remark, made in his celebrated essay "The Irony of Swift," [6] that "in his use of negative materials . . . the aim always is destructive." The materials of raillery are, indeed, negative, but the positive affirmations in Swift's humor shine through the epithet of "agreeable b——tch" just as they do through Swift's lament over the fault of Arbuthnot, who "has every quality and virtue that can make a man amiable or useful; but, alas, he has a sort of slouch in his walk."

6. Most recently reprinted in *Swift: A Collection of Critical Essays,* ed. Ernest Tuveson (Englewood Cliffs, N.J.: Twentieth Century Views, 1964), p. 21.

JEAN-JACQUES MAYOUX

De Quincey: Humor and the Drugs

When Thomas De Quincey first burst upon the reading world
— at any rate, upon the readers of the *London Magazine* —
in 1821 with the *Confessions of an English Opium-Eater,* it
was obvious, and remains so in spite of a later preface classify-
ing the work as "impassioned prose," that he was determined to
be funny. Why? Perhaps it was not only natural bent but self-
preservation, for the Society for the Suppression of Vice was
then on the upgrade, and if opium was held to be no worse than
brandy as an intoxicant, surely it was as bad and demanded at
least some sort of deprecating attitude, like the hypocritical
distance in Lamb's *Confessions of a Drunkard.*

From our point of view, the first question set by the *Confessions* should be this: for whom does De Quincey play buffoon, for his reading public or for himself? The playing buffoon
being the setting up of oneself for an object, the obvious answer
is, for the public. Marmeladov, or Karamazov the father, do not
behave otherwise. But Marmeladov is drunk, and his buffoonery
is compulsory, irresistible.

Our genial drunk, in fun of course, often works out his ag-
gressions, as associations provide, in the course of his ramblings.
So does De Quincey, who starts by settling his scores with

S. T. Coleridge in a rich comic-farcical scene, with Coleridge
having paid attendants to dog his steps and hold him back from
the laudanum-selling druggist's shop, then, as they try to fulfill
their commission, easily revoking his own authority:

> *Porter.* . . . really you must not; consider, sir, your wife and —
> *Transcendental Philosopher.* Wife! What wife? I have no wife.
> *Porter.* Didn't you say no longer ago than yesterday —
> *Transcendental Philosopher.* Pooh, pooh! yesterday is a long time
>   ago . . .[1]

Here, of course, the "what wife? I have no wife," pretending to
recall *Othello,* is very much and very maliciously a hit ad
hominem.

Coleridge as a treacherous fellow opium-eater appears in the
Confessions on page 3. This is on page 10. The spread of a side
subject should be, provisionally, noted and left.

Of a very different sort and nearer to our quest of De
Quincey in his humor is the next comic scene, set in the course
of his running away from the school in Manchester. It shows
his enormous and heavy trunk escaping the grasp of the groom
and "trundling down from step to step with accelerated pace
and multiplied uproar" (p. 94). This, to me, is curiously mind-
ful of the djinn in *Vathek* rolling himself up into a ball which
somehow compels each and all to rush kicking after him as he
bounds on and on. A kind of "comic wilfulness" (De Quincey's
phrase) of bewitched animation is here almost equally compelling ("it trundled or rather leapt right across with the noise
of twenty devils"). Something noticeably irrational as well as
fanciful is an index to much of De Quincey's comedy. Naturally
enough, since the "paradise of opium-eaters" is around him,
the druggist who sold him his first laudanum is playfully given
divine status, in a "beatific vision of the immortal druggist sent
down to earth on a special mission to myself" (pp. 194–195).
This, since he has disappeared from Oxford Street, leads to the

    1. Vol. I (*Confessions of an English Opium-Eater*), p. 10, in the
collected ed., 16 vols. (Edinburgh: A. & C. Black, 1878). All references
will be to this edition. Apart from titles and indications, italics unless
otherwise stated are mine.

proposition, "I believe him to have evanesced." The jocular treatment, I suggest, covers a mode of vision.

De Quincey did not set up as a comic writer, but as a humorist. It is superfluous to remind learned and practised readers of a distinction that has been clear, even if not clearly stated, for many generations; or, again, of that between wit and humor, but we must recall it briefly, with an eye to the personal sequel.

Let me take, as it comes unsought to my mind, a plain, average instance of wit: a lady visits Voltaire at Ferney for the second time and goes into ecstasies over the trees: how tall they have grown since her first visit. "Madam," Voltaire answers, "they have nothing else to do!" Or again, to a remark made by a wit that all the Condés are fools, somebody retorts that M. de... is no fool. "No," the wit replies, "but how clearly you perceive that he is the son of a fool." The sayings, once uttered, retain, if they have deserved it, an impersonal glory; once we have thanked him for obliging, we can dismiss even Voltaire. Humor, on the other hand, requires not one but two living people; the second a listener or reader, the first one a "humor," in Jonsonian terminology, in his own person, or an inventor of humors. Humor is born, and held between them like some kind of current, and needs a continued presence. Think of Charles Lamb meeting in the Strand a countryman carrying a hare, and asking him, "Prithee my good fellow, is this thy own hare, or a wig?" The pun in itself is as it may be. But to become a source of humor it has needed two mental processes, including that of the utterly puzzled and nonplussed countryman.

Or we may take the tale — again as it comes to me not out of a file — of the soldier carrying a wounded comrade from the battlefield. As he proceeds, a cannonball strikes off the head of his charge, whom he deposits before an infuriated surgeon who asks what he means by bringing him a headless body to look after. "Devil take me," the soldier says, "he told me it was his leg." If the story, instead of being sheer horror, is in fact good "black" humor, it is because of the fantastic absurdity of the situation and of the reply. Is not absurdity connected with humor, from the first, from Ben Jonson himself and Master Stephen's "Have you a stoole there to be melancholy upon?"

Congreve has progressed to formulation when he remarks that humor is "a singular manner of doing or saying anything peculiar and natural to one man only." [2] The absurdity is, as a rule, a relation between a warped or disturbed subjectivity and the supposed sane, staid, solid, objective world of common sense. The English have invented humor in their dislike of conferring validity on the products of the intellect, making, as they have gone along, the shrewd discovery that every head, including their own, was thus warped; the game being then an understanding and appreciation of mutual absurdity. The arch-humorist is Sterne, because he generalizes the absurd. This is the vast and glorious difference between Shandyism and Pantagruelism, and the formula of it is that "a man cannot dress, but his ideas get cloath'd at the same time" (*Tristram Shandy,* vol. IX, chap. xiii). The clothing is of his own flesh. Sterne is the first to spread the humorous vision over the whole intellectual field: all thinking, in a manner, has become humorous.

Now the absurdity in the humorous exchange is always conscious at some point or level, but not always the same. The writer may create a "humor" — an unconsciously absurd character like Parson Adams or Matthew Bramble — or a humorist or, more frequently, perhaps, an intermediary nature, a faddist with a twinkle like Walter Shandy. In the Romantic heyday of humor, the writer will tend to do without humorous characters, and to be humorous in his own name. It is a subtler game, already played by Sterne — subtler because the humorous communication will only be built up and materialize at a distance, in the reader's mind: because what we may term the pause of feigned innocence between the utterance and the perception of humor will be infinitely lengthened.

This, then, is what we may term the revolution in humorous writing, the second form of humorous consciousness, the final contrast, say, between Burton and Lamb. De Quincey defines it clearly and modestly: dealing with Lamb, he remarks (what

2. *Concerning Humour in Comedy* (1695).

of course seems to us in retrospect a glimpse of the obvious),
"the character of the writer cooperates in an undercurrent to
the effect of the thing written . . . you must have some insight into the particular bias of the writer's mind . . . There
is," he goes on, "in modern literature a whole class, though not
a large one, standing within the same category; some marked
originality of character in the writer becomes a coefficient with
what he says to a common result . . . the objective in the
thought becomes confluent with the subjective in the thinker." [3]

Subjectivity being, then, an essential of humorous writing, an
obvious point is implicit or, as explicit, is missing here, which
brings us back to our remarks about buffoonery: the humorist
is playing a part. If he dispenses with the humorous character,
he becomes himself a humor by becoming conscious of peculiarity, of oddity even, cultivating it and flaunting it. But here
is the necessary subtlety of the humorist: he must feign innocence; now, in his own name, he must handle and misuse words,
logic, values, in pretended naivety, as humorous characters had
done before in various degrees of real innocence.

The "serious" writer withdraws and conceals his idiosyncra-
sies, as much as he can, behind the objectivities of the subject.
The humorist thrusts himself to the fore, drawing attention to
himself by various antics, a sort of verbal clowning; hence,
every definition of humor includes the incongruous as an element. Of the incongruous, De Quincey makes heavy use; he
obviously enjoys the various forms of burlesque writing, including anachronism. The fun of the *Confessions* hangs on suc-
cessive and interlaced motives. One of them is the letter to
Monsieur Monsieur de Quincy, scribbled in the illegible hand
which is supposed to be the mark of French penmanship.[4] One
can follow the workings of a mind indulging in free association
and then transcribing into common terms points emerging from
a sort of fanciful private monologue. Illegibility brings enigma,
enigma brings Sphinx, here is the Sphinx facing a letter brought
by the post office. Now, if the Sphinx "conducted her intercourse with Oedipus by way of letter and propounded her

3. VIII ("Charles Lamb"), 110–111.
4. I (*Confessions*), 79–80.

wicked questions through the post office of Thebes," she needed only to use French penmanship to be beyond deciphering.

Or here is the girl he has met by Deeside, as the "bore" rushed the waters of the river upstream with the appearance of a threatened Flood. She will become Pyrrha to his Deucalion. But, as with the Sphinx, to clench the absurdity she must be involved in some anachronistic activity. The letter is still there and its disposal will be woven into the game. The girl will be dispatched — Pyrrah, I mean, will be dispatched, "O ye powers of moral anachronism," to the Chester Post Office. No episode has been the object of more baroque-humorous decoration. The parodying function of language takes endless turnings. De Quincey as actor in the story gets mixed up with De Quincey the fanciful story-teller who, in legal jargon, propounds about the supposed indiscretion of speaking to an unknown girl a new but retrospectively valid social ruling: in times of natural catastrophes or similar emergencies it shall be lawful to speak to a person without having been introduced (I, 107).

Like all clowning, De Quincey's verbal clowning may be said to imply disguise, and with the heroi-comic disguise there is in alternation the burlesque proper. The "cop" or artificial mound where De Quincey and the girl take refuge from the rushing waters is supposed to be made by "ancient Danish hands possibly not yet paid for their work." The Danes have been granted an odd form of immortality, to find themselves turned into modern laborers with wage problems (I, 103). The usual distance of simple statements is replaced by various crude colorings for more vividness. "Science," particularly arithmetic, but also geometry, alternates in the function with the law and other techniques. The simple statement that at school "we had no playground" brings before us, by the flimsiest liaison, Bacon's reflections on tables, square (having "two polar extremities . . . a perihelion and an aphelion, together with equatorial sides") or triangular ("if the triangle should be right-angled, then the Lucifer seated at the right angle might argue that he *subtended* all the tenants of the hypotenuse") (I, 39).

And so, to the accompaniment of groans from the reader who is not preeminently interested in mental revelation, the text rambles on through John O'Groats' house, Charlemagne, and the Round Table, to two little girls sharing an orange: "You divide and I choose." The logical or, indeed, any common ground with the absence of playground is so weak that we have the feeling of being carried along in some kind of rambling daydream.

Humor is an aspect of the human problem of communication. It is, in fact, one of the subtlest forms of communication ever devised. Sterne, who shows the almost total lack of mental communication between Walter and Toby Shandy, never doubts that he himself communicates successfully — through humor — with the reader. At the start of the humorous exchange and perception there is the awareness of difference, of oddity, of, finally, the individuality of language. The listener hears a man speaking, not a thing spoken of, and he will perceive the man precisely through the particular distortion of the thing. The voice of the opium-eater replaces the mere objective fact of opium-eating with the mocking, easily granted admission "if you eat a good deal of it, you must do what is disagreeable to any man of regular habits, viz., die" (I, 196). A genial triangular structure, bringing together, under the aegis of opium, *disagreeable, die,* and *regular habits,* trips up any attempt at hasty valuations and embarrasses not only the man of "regular habits," but also the man of orthodox judgments.

Since *Confessions of an English Opium-Eater* was self-seen as "impassioned prose," I suppose that as a humorist's credentials De Quincey would present first and foremost the scherzo "On Murder Considered as One of the Fine Arts." [5] This is a model; no better could be found for an analysis of the conscious and peculiar processes of humor. It could be said that all of it is derived from the title. Once you have set yourself to deal with the artistic aspects of murder, you must redispose all notions around this new perspective; and if you have previously admitted that each individual is entitled to his own perspective and oddity of vision, you must concede a willing suspense of ethical creed and social judgments and let yourself be temporarily carried along, not unresisting, but enjoying the strength

5. IV (*The English Mail Coach and Other Writings*), 1–110. But what starts on p. 58 is the postscript, which offers some of De Quincey's most tense and vivid prose but no humor.

of the pull. The misuse of language is here a constant delight.
Who says "art" must seek genius? He will find it. "All the
Cains were men of genius." An art has "amateurs," "connois-
seurs"; we can look for them in literature. "Milton was an amateur . . ." "As to Shakspeare, there never was a better . . ."
General history must undergo severe revaluations: "Greece,
even in the age of Pericles, produced no murder, or at least
none is recorded, of the slightest merit." On the other hand, in
the years 1588–1635, "what a glorious pleiad of murders . . .
3 Majesties, 3 Serene Highnesses, and 1 Excellency."

But what matters is the history of the art, and the schools
distinguishable in it. "The Jewish school was always respectable." We know how artistic development can be arrested by a
blighting influence. Thus, of Catiline, Clodius, and their friends:
"It is to be regretted that the priggism of Cicero robbed his
country of the only chance she had of distinction in this line."

Philosophers, we learn — or, at least, I learn — are singularly appreciated as murderees. Hence De Quincey finds it very
much against Locke that "though he carried his throat about
with him in this world for seventy-two years, no man ever
condescended to cut it."

An art must have its scholars, as well as its luminaries whom
they study and commemorate. A recent luminary has been
Williams; thus it is the Williams Lecture that has been given us
to expound these great principles and to show us the progress
made from the Dark Ages to "this age when masterpieces of
excellence have been executed by professional men" (IV, 3).

They must correspond, of course, to the public and reflect its
demands: "Design, gentlemen, grouping, light and shade, poetry,
sentiment are now deemed indispensable." Williams is hailed
by our lecturer (nicknamed Toad-in-the-hole) as inaugurating
"a second age of Leo the Tenth." The contemporary poison-
ings, of course, are mediocre art for the masses, and there is
severe criticism in our murder club of Mr. Thurtell's feats.
"Mere plagiarism — base plagiarism from hints that I threw
out! Besides, his style is as harsh as Albert Dürer, and as coarse
as Fuseli . . . There was, however, an unfinished design of
Thurtell's for the murder of a man with a pair of dum-bells,

which I admired greatly; it was a mere outline that he never filled in, but . . ."

De Quincey's achievement through many of these pages is in his so skillful imitation of the individual enthusiasm of a living voice in its modulations; so convincingly and so fantastically identifying with it, so cleverly echoing, in this new and far more extreme creation, the various Hellfire Clubs of the more spacious eighteenth century. The inversion of values that goes with the inversion of facts to form one of the bases of the humorous paradox (remember Falstaff) is carried on, one is tempted to say, rather discreetly, and in general, almost abstract terms, rendered efficient by literary skill and superb tempo; as if, after all, our author were slightly afraid of his subject and took some time to warm up to the gruesomeness of it. It is at about page 30 that this new degree is reached, with the remark that "people will not submit to have their throats cut quietly . . . and whilst the portrait painter often has to complain of too much torpor in his subject, the artist in our line is generally embarrassed by too much animation." This difficulty is all to the good, however. Murder, as an efficient stimulation to extraordinary displays of liveliness even in torpid subjects, is specially meritorious. The English boxer who had to fight twenty-seven rounds against a wheezy Munich baker before he could bring out "his tools" and finish the job is a shining instance. Facility must be avoided, and as an artist the murderer should observe certain rules: "the subject chosen should be in good health . . . no tailor ought to be chosen who is above twenty-five, for after that age he is sure to be dyspeptic." The subject "ought also to have a family of young children wholly dependent on his exertions, by way of deepening the pathos."

A deplorable, a disastrous passage (IV, 45) tries with flat-footed ingenuity to practise inversion within inversion on the theme that "many a man has dated his ruin from some murder or other that perhaps he thought little of at the time." A course that starts in murder will be found going from bad to worse, to end in procrastination. This, the reader will admit, is merely cute, and shows that any trick of inversion is not enough; it must go with genuine perversion.

The learned lecturer with his sponsor, in the end — and this may be, in part at least, due to the requirements of the Victorian atmosphere — shelters behind Swift's "extravaganza" (his term), *A Modest Proposal.* Can we assess the truth, or trace the limits, of the parallel?

There has always been something very perilous in the *advocatus diaboli* position. It seems to take no account of our mixed natures, unless it is so well aware of them that it invites us to work the devil out of our systems by first bringing him out, uncomfortably, into the open. A blend of attraction and repulsion is in us, even for what ethically we must call the worst. Cannibalism is not for nothing a recurrent theme in humor.[6] If De Quincey had been able to look forward instead of back, he would have found something much closer to his own achievement if not to his professed purpose: Mark Twain's *Cannibalism in the Cars.* The procedure is the same: solemn misappropriation of language; men eaten to the accompaniment of congressional speeches and motions, as the murders of those others had been appreciated in relation to aesthetic values: "Mr. Halliday of Virginia: 'I move to further amend the report by substituting Mr. Harvey Davis of Oregon for Mr. Messick. It may be urged by gentlemen that the hardships and privations of a frontier life have rendered Mr. Davis tough; but, gentlemen, is this a time to be fastidious concerning trifles? . . . No, gentlemen, bulk is what we desire, substance, weight, bulk — these are the supreme requisites now — not talent, not genius, not education.' "

The American ethos being as watchful as the British, Mark Twain, who might have found it unwise to take shelter behind De Quincey as De Quincey had behind Swift, prefers a typical American turn: "I had only been listening to the harmless vagaries of a madman instead of the genuine experiences of a bloodthirsty cannibal."

De Quincey is less blatantly dishonest. But how far can we

6. That there is so much cruelty and death-dealing in psychedelic literature, and some in the life of the addict, means, of course — and this should be ceaselessly recalled — not a creation but, again, failing control, a release of the aggressive instincts present in us all. It has been so since the time of the haschischins or original assassins.

equate his unholy fun to Dean Swift's savage irony? Swift, whatever obscure sadistic instincts may be remotely involved in the
Modest Proposal, has a precise and *useful* aim in view: by
shock tactics to rouse attention, to create disgust, revulsion, and
pity, a sense of forgotten human solidarity, a self-accusation,
an active impulse. If we try to assume that De Quincey is prac-
tising similar irony, it leads us, I am afraid, nowhere. Create an
aversion to murder? We are supposed to have it. Increase it?
Not a bit. The aversion is disarmed until we get to the utterly
heterogeneous postscript. This is the difference: that in fact
there has been what I have termed a willing suspension of
ethical reaction. Bergson's distinction between humor and irony
might be adduced to show that this is irony, but as such it would
prove to be formal and logical, not imaginative. The true distinction between the two, to my mind, lies in the gratuitous
nature of humor, whereas irony — to be worth its bitter salt —
must be directed toward an aim. It is clear to me that De
Quincey remains very much this side of straight irony. Could
we again try to follow the spontaneous, barely just conscious,
working of his mind? The idea of treating murder as one of the
fine arts was probably not primary. What was primary is perhaps revealed by the postscript, to be connected with "On the
Knocking at the Gate in *Macbeth*" (XIII, 192–198) and many
other pieces. The fascination of murder, seen in sadomasochistic
participation, is that of the point of time that brings together
murderer and murderee and the preceding tension which perhaps reveals the most secret nature of human, of personal, time
moving up (De Quincey points the way to Faulkner) to this final
point of awful, ecstatic concentration and confrontation. Then
comes the release, of whatever kind. May it not be suggested
that to the temporal structure of tension and release corresponds
the mental pattern that we find reversed — in print — in *On
Murder*? The postscript is tense to the bursting point; the "extravaganza" is pure release. The connection, in any case, is so
certain that in "On the Knocking at the Gate" we have the very
theme of *On Murder* brought up: of the Williams murders, "I
must observe that *in one respect* they have had an ill effect, by
making the connoisseur in murder very fastidious in his taste
. . . All other murders look pale by the deep crimson of his;

and as an amateur once said to me in a querulous tone, 'There has been absolutely nothing *doing* since his time.' " [7]

The fun of the Murder Club, very distant in my judgment from the ironical vision, is tied to temporary release from social values, to the enjoyment of total freedom, which is an essential of humor.

A tendency to the jovial sinister, to be amused by the macabre, is spread over the works, frequently going along with what the reader can hardly help noticing and what is perhaps the mark of a peculiar mental condition, an insistent presence, a thrusting forward of the object. At the end of the *Autobiographic Sketches,* De Quincey tells the story of the private museum of Mr. White, the surgeon, who preserved there the embalmed body of a grateful and whimsical patient who, against a large bequest, had stipulated this attention to her remains. The sarcophagus used for the purpose was a large grandfather clock. Hence, De Quincey remarks, "had Mr. White . . . furnished us with the key of the museum . . . restricting us only (like a cruel Bluebeard) from looking into any ante-room, great is my fear that the perfidious question would have arisen amongst us — what o'clock it was." [8]

Nor by "object thus thrust forward" do I mean the reader to understand this particular good lady making shift for a timeless clockface but, rather, the deathly essence which radiates from her. Grisly associations must come in her train. They fill a passage of Poe-like merriment:

> The mummy, therefor, was not seen; but the skeleton *was* . . . It is not every day that one makes the acquaintance of a skeleton; and with regard to such a thing — thing, shall one say, or person? — there is a favorable presumption from beforehand; which is this: As he is of no use, neither profitable nor ornamental, to any person whatever, absolutely *de trop* in good society, what but distinguished merit of some kind or other could induce any man to interfere with that gravitating tendency that by an eternal *nisus* is pulling him below ground? Lodgings are dear in England. True it is that, according to the vile usage on

7. De Quincey's italics.
8. XIV (*Autobiographic Sketches*), 432ff.

the Continent, one room serves a skeleton for bedroom and sitting-room; neither is his expense heavy as regards wax-lights, fire, or "bif-steck." [9]

It is a passage that would do wonderfully as the text for a course in creative humor, it is so blatantly full of all the tricks of the game, all relying on incongruity, conjuring visions of an indiscreet skeleton entering a drawing room, a modest skeleton sitting down in a narrow corner to his modicum of "bif-steck," alternating with the at-last-pure skeleton obeying the laws of all matter without protest. For a very similar bout of "black" humor we may go, in the *Confessions,* to "The Pains of Opium," where we find De Quincey's treatment of the Victorian legend of spontaneous combustion — starting typically, according to my proposition that his humor is release from tension, with the obsessive fear, "Might I not myself take leave of the literary world in that fashion? . . . Upon one variety of this explosion," he goes on, "a man blew up in the dark . . . leaving nothing behind him but some bones, of no use to anybody, and which were supposed to be his only because nobody else ever applied for them." De Quincey thinks some external means of ignition should be required: "If so . . . what should hinder the 'devouring element' . . . from spreading through the throat to the cavity of the chest: in which case, not being insured, the man would naturally become a total loss" (I, 238–239).

How different this is from Dickens' straight, realistic-fantastic treatment of the end of Mr. Krook, supported in his Preface[10] by an array of earnestly invoked credentials. De Quincey's play is intellectual, it handles notions and relations in the spirit of paradox: "nobody else" applying for the bones — as his own — suggests the complementary idea of the rightful owner bringing his claim. Back we are in the reanimated skeleton's company, but with the added logical piquancy of the reflexive. Alternately, the total passivity of manmade things brings the application — read misapplication — of the ideas of lack of insurance and total loss.

9. XIV, 435; De Quincey's italics.
10. *Bleak House.*

In the constant desultory playfulness, there seems to be perceptible an impulse to let the words run free, or, rather, stand free, with a sort of presence that they do not normally possess. They soon begin to play like the imps they are. If the author notes in his *Confessions* "I should not have absolutely disdained the humble station of 'devil,' " he goes on, in time and in his musing manner, to remark, "to the perfection of the diabolic character, I fear that patience is one of the indispensable graces" (p. 174). The shift is again, through language, from reality to oddity as if the temptation just could not be avoided.

We may by this time suggest that the attraction of oddity could be termed the sense of the inappropriate, to be satisfied through misuse of language. We have heard a farcical Coleridge talking down his attendants in defense of his shopping for opium. But we also hear him, in pompous herald's jargon, proclaim: "Know all men by these present that I, Samuel Taylor Coleridge . . . am a Licensed opium-eater, whereas this other man . . ." There is perhaps something of a childish regression in the amusement that our author takes everywhere in speaking a pseudo-scientific language which we have already sampled. To express the point that as a child he was made to memorize every one of the sermons of his clerical tutor that he heard, but that, fortunately, going only to one of the two Sunday services, he heard only half the lot, he puts it as $\frac{330}{2}$. He can at no time resist these sidetracking solicitations of his fancy and these trains of words. We have not forgotten the letter addressed to Monsieur Monsieur de Quincy. Let us try to see how his mind works around that, noting that he pretends, preposterously, to be recalling from the past what of course he is fabricating in the present: "I *was* astonished to find myself translated by a touch of the pen not only into a Monsieur, but even into a self-multiplied Monsieur; or speaking algebraically, into the square of Monsieur; having a chance at some future day of being perhaps cubed into Monsieur[3]." A half page later he remarks, "In a moment I saw too plainly that I was not Monsieur[2]. I might be Monsieur but not Monsieur to the second power" (pp. 78ff).

Earlier there was the story of the apothecary and his medicine for the liver trouble which, by then, had become for the boy a neurotic obsession. "He confined himself to one horrid mixture, that must have suggested itself to him when prescribing for a tiger." The idea "medicine for a tiger" tickles him. The word "tiger" takes over and directs the story: "I should think that in the same spirit of reasonable equation, three such tiger-drenches must be equal to one apoplectic fit, or even to the tiger himself." After a comic scene of a tea party with the now drowsy and pompously inarticulate tiger-doctor, his very trade has taken possession of the writer's imagination, so that nearly three pages later, having got on to negotiations with the guardian, we have this curious blending: "If I, acting on the apothecary's precedent of *repetatur haustus,* had endeavored to administer another bolus or draught of expostulation, he would have followed my course as to the tiger-drench." And so on, to the last appearance of "my three tormentors (guardian, Archididascalus and the professor of tigrology)" (pp. 65–70).

That De Quincey is a very conscious (at exasperated moments one would say conscientious) humorist is obvious. What seems to me much less certain is that he knows the way his humor is going, or that he guides it. In Alethea Hayter's brilliant study, *Opium and the Romantic Imagination,* there is, to my knowledge, nothing that concerns humor. Yet, thinking also of another intoxicated brain of genius, that of Poe with his "angel of the odd," I have come to wonder whether the influence of the intoxicant should not be traced in this field.

Sterne is the great and constant digressor, as we know. This is part of his teasing temper; every digression becomes part of a fanciful pattern, which he draws for his own and our amusement at the end of volume VI of *Tristram Shandy.* Through meandering, Sterne is trying to achieve freedom from time, until he discovers that time carries him on inflexibly, digressing or not. A free writer he is otherwise determined to be and to remain: precisely one of those subjective, capricious ones whom De Quincey gathers around Lamb. He is painstakingly so: he hardly ever digresses without nudging us — "Mind, I am digressing." How different De Quincey's lengthy digressions and endless digressive notes, how sincere his apologies: he just could not help it, whatever started him — a subject, a theme, a mere

word. As soon as he has stepped aside, not only has all sense
of proportion been lost, but the main subject is as if it did not
exist any more. There is an interlude, which may be short or
long, what he would call a trance, in the conscious personal
time, during which an irrepressible fascination takes over.

Obviously a mental control has ceased to work, and what
Baudelaire will call the thyrsus — the Bacchic wand thrusting
right and left any amount of florid ornament — will come before our eyes.

A Beckettian radio drama, *Words and Music,*[11] presents three
characters: Croak, Words, and Music. They have no other
existence than as three elements of a personality whose inter-
mittent center of control is Croak, also known as "Milord." It
seems to me that as one reads on through De Quincey's pages,
one is aware of Milord's frequent absences. It is as if De Quincey were that sort of, not split, but disintegrated personality of
the Beckettian vision. The writer qua writer seems to have no
power of judgment left, no sense of construction and, least of
all, as suggested here, no sense of proportion. The imagination
(or is it, as Coleridge would say, the fancy?) on the other hand
seems perpetually ready to answer any new call, and to start
in a new direction. A word will do, not always with a clear justification, as if the pen had stopped almost accidentally and the
fascination had taken over. Words are amusing. They have, if
one decides or agrees to let them go, a life of their own, which
it is a pleasure to watch developing, until one is simply carried
along and away with them. It is De Quincey's form of the
angel of the odd.

The Thing — a word, in this connection, being a thing — is
temporarily magnified. It also tends to come alive and, frequently, to be humanized. Among the many memories of his
childhood, De Quincey counts one connected with Lord Monboddo's theories of the origin of language and of mankind itself. For, according to his bullying brother, the citizens of
Thomas' fictional kingdom were still afflicted with the original
tails of Monboddo's vision. Now De Quincey cannot resist the
irrelevant, which is that their tutor's interest in Monboddo went
quite another way to some grammatical points, such as the

11. London: Faber & Faber, 1968.

function of the *aoristus primus*. The fascination works. "It (or shall we say *he*?) was known to the whole Christian world by this distinction of Primus; clearly, therefore, there must be some low, vulgar tense in the background . . . had it been possible to meet an Aoristus Primus in the flesh, I should have bowed to him submissively" (XIV, 81).

This animation may become either a trick or a habit: I fancy a habit, a sort of distortion of the vision. For in volume XIII we have the same sort of anthropomorphic procedure on the subject of *Orthographic Mutineers*. "Take *abalienate,* and *ablaqueation.* They are most respectable words — but so exceedingly retired in their habits that I never once had the honor of meeting either of them in any book, pamphlet, journal . . . though haunting such a society myself all my life."

Remember the Bore, seen as a disease of rivers. The theme reappears here connected with "proposed revolutions in spelling." They can be seen as "a sort of cutaneous affection, like nettle-rash, or ringworm." Or as the infliction of bodily injury. Of reformer Mitford, De Quincey hopes that his grave is not "haunted by the injured words whom he had tomahawked."

"Inasmuch as the final *e* in the singular is mute, *that is . . .* has been allowed to retire upon a superannuation allowance, it is abominable to call it back upon active service — if the nation and Parliament mean to keep faith, they are bound to hire a stout young *e* to run in the traces with the old original *e,* taking the whole work off his aged shoulders" (XIII, 101).

A spirit of active metamorphosis, it seems, is active in the object itself; a spirit that underlies the animation we have detected. The Bore, as it races on, from water becomes animal. It "did not gallop but went at a long trot . . . that most frightful of paces in a tiger, in a buffalo, or in a rebellion of waters. Even a ghost would appal me more if coming up at a long diabolical trot, than at a canter or gallop" (I, 106).

In the freedom of such humor, the total effect is secured more by parallelism than by subordination. The invention of the long trot as a gait for a ghost is somehow reprojected on the advancing waters, in, of course, a comic key.

Once life has been granted, it must under pain of failure be sustained by some peculiarity. The Bore is all the more a form of life if it becomes *a sickness*: "it was an affection to which only some few rivers here and there were liable . . . I had never heard of such a nervous affection in rivers . . . I found that . . . the neighboring river Severn . . . suffered at spring-tides the same kind of hysterics."

What needs not to be animated can all the more easily be humanized or feminized; thus of the Welsh cows whose excessive proximity might prove inconvenient to his outdoor sleep: "I do not suppose any fixed hostility to English faces in Welsh cows; but everywhere I observe in the feminine mind something of beautiful caprice, a floral exuberance of that charming wilfulness which characterizes our dear human sisters I fear through all worlds"; where again, as in most of the humorous-imaginative clusters I have considered, there has been a gliding so that the possible action of the cows is now identified with alleged womanly qualities and disappears behind them, leaving little more than a cow's gentle smile in a woman's face.

I am stressing this point of metamorphosis and animation, perhaps tediously, because while the structure of the incongruous is static, this is dynamic, and the tension between the terms is what is resolved in humor. An extreme instance of terms far separate and preposterously brought together marks a paper where nothing is quite serious after the title, "System of the Heavens as revealed by Lord Rosse's telescopes." [12] De Quincey associates this with a paper "from the German of Kant" on the age of the earth, published by some person — "I believe it was myself" — and less well known than it should be (III, 167). In this mood, the subject takes his fancy and he just lets it play. As in the scherzo on murder *considered as one of the fine arts,* the datum here does give much. The earth is feminine. How then shall we set about finding her age? Ask her? "A man deserves to be cudgelled who could put such improper questions to a lady planet." What, then, about "a certificate of our dear little mother's birth and baptism"? Once again the thing is done and the humorist can let the humor work itself out: "I am satisfied that she is very much admired throughout the solar system: and in clear seasons, when she is seen to advantage, with her bonny wee pet of a Moon tripping round her like a lamb, I

12. III, (*Immanuel Kant and Other Writings*) 167ff.

should be glad to see the planet that could fancy herself entitled to sneeze at our earth" (III, 168). But again, rambling
variations are the very substance of Quinceyan humor. So we
must be back at it: "Is she that kind of person that you would
introduce to a waltzing partner, some fiery young gentleman
like Mars; or would you rather suggest to her the sort of partner-
ship which takes place at a whist table?"

She could be seen as a playful twelve- or thirteen-year-old,
perhaps a romp "but not a hoyden, observe; no horse-play."
Earthquakes, volcanoes, and so on, will cease "as soon as our
Earth reaches the age of maidenly bashfulness. Poor thing! It's
quite natural, you know, in a healthy growing girl" (III, 169).

Others see her as decayed: "they absolutely *hear* the tellurian
lungs wheezing." The humor here, we perceive, is very near
burlesque, a sort of travesty cosmology, the planets com-
mented upon in the language of our daily streets dealing with
the affairs of the family just around the corner. Humor appears
as a game of free language transpositions. Thus it goes on.
These stars and planets, one of De Quincey's fanciful authorities feels, are dismally regular:

> What he wished for was something like Lloyd's list:
> *Comets* — due 3; arrived 1.
> *Mercury* — when last seen, appeared to be distressed; but made
> no signal.
> *Pallas and Vesta* — not heard of for some time; supposed to have
> foundered.   (III, 192)

We have here a double plane, the earthly one, of indiscreet
familiarity, competing with a fantastically animated universe.
It is tempting to mix the two. Astrology will be, to bring them
into relation, a satisfactory middle-term. His horoscope, given
by a grimy Welsh astrologer, informs him that "he shall have
seven-and-twenty children . . . also . . . he shall desert
them." The astrologer having yielded his quota of farcical fun,
the author turns his indignation against the stars: "that's not
only a lie in the stars, but a libel; and if an action lay against
a constellation, I should recover damages." [13]

13. VII ("Sortilege and Astrology"), 261, 283; 277, 231.

Words, words, words. Precisely: words are all the fun. It is
not the supposed relation between two men and the stars that
finally counts, but the relation in the language of a nineteenth-
century lawsuit between constellation and recovering damages;
it is again incongruity brightened by the genius of the odd.

We are left with a certain use, misuse, liberation of language.
A potency, also; and, after all, this may be the link between
the "impassioned" and the humorous in a work like the *Confessions*. Can a word bite? The paper on *Modern Greece* (III,
453–497) — a dog-ridden country — brings back his old obsessive fear of hydrophobia. Writing about it, what if he should
catch it? "Think, excellent reader, if we should suddenly prove
hydrophobous in the middle of this paper, how would you distinguish the hydrophobous from the nonhydrophobous parts?"

A strange world indeed, not unlike that of sleep from which
sudden unexpected forms rise and act as obsession (even dis-
guised as accident) commands. Modern Greece will produce
dogs; dogs will recall the fear of rabies, this will lodge where it
may, since the writer is alone with his paper and pen: in the
very words. If he caught it, obviously the writing would catch it
back.

I have presented my instances massively so as to bring out
the habitual working of De Quincey's imagination. I have
stressed the singularly free (if uncontrolled means free) rambling. Can it not be connected with the unwise passivity of the
ordering mind in a more or less drugged state, while the imagination is released and activated? Baudelaire, who lifted so much
of the *Paradis artificiels* out of De Quincey but who was in his
person a distinguished haschischin, has some interesting remarks to make on the neglected point of the comic effect of the
drug. That opium may not work in the same manner is an obvious caveat; it should only make us the more attentive to coin-
cidence and discrepancy. Clearly there are similarities between
the two artificial paradises. Baudelaire, describing the first effects
of his drug, writes: "D'abord une certaine hilarité saugrenue et
irrésistible s'empare de vous. *Les mots les plus vulgaires,* les
idées les plus simples prennent une physionomie bizarre et nou-
velle . . . Des ressemblances et des rapprochements incongrus,

impossibles à prévoir . . . des ébauches de comique, jaillissent continuellement de votre cerveau." [14]

Wherein, the stress is on the odd, on the powerlessness of controls, on the freeing and metamorphoses of language, on the continuous gushing of queer fancies. Language is indeed central: "Il arrive quelquefois que des gens tout à fait impropres aux jeux de mots improvisent des enfilades interminables de calembourgs [sic], des rapprochements d'idées tout à fait improbables." [15]

Then, after pages of reiterations on this point, comes a second phase: "Les objets extérieurs prennent des apparences monstrueuses. Ils se révèlent à vous sous des formes inconnues jusque là. Puis ils se déforment et transforment, et enfin ils entrent dans votre être, ou bien vous entrez en eux." [16]

This seems to be a step further in the loss of grip and disintegration of the united self, in its invasion.

"La grammaire, l'aride grammaire elle-même, devient quelque chose comme une sorcellerie évocatoire; les mots *ressuscitent revêtus de chair et d'os*."

Have we not seen something like it? — ". . . barren grammar itself" behaving like conjuring witchcraft, words coming alive, "clad in flesh and bones"?

14. "In a first stage, a queer, irresistible hilariousness gets hold of you. *The most commonplace words,* the simplest ideas put on a new, an odd face . . . Innappropriate associations and assimilations, that you cannot foresee . . . incipient comicalities, unceasingly burst out of your brain."
I have brought together two sets of passages, each a variant of the other, surprisingly retained side by side by the author: the first in "Du vin et du haschisch," the second in "Le poème du haschisch."
15. "It sometimes happens that people quite incapable of verbal play extemporize endless chains of puns, quite improbable connections of ideas."
16. "External objects appear in monstrous shape. They are revealed to you in hitherto unknown forms. Then they become distorted and transformed, and finally they enter your very being, unless you enter theirs" (my translations).

DONALD FANGER

Dickens and Gogol: Energies of the Word

"Dickens bears a good deal of resemblance to Gogol," the Russian critic Shevyrev observed in 1841, "and, if it were possible to suppose an influence of our literature on the English, we might conclude with pride that England was beginning to imitate Russia." [1] It was, of course, impossible to suppose any such influence: even half a century later, when Constance Garnett's translations were making Englishmen look at each other with a wild surmise, and the English taste for Russian exoticism was at the full, Gogol was to have no share in it. In his own lifetime (he died in 1852), only one of his stories, "The Portrait," appeared in English; and if Dickens read it, the fact went unrecorded. [2] As for Gogol's knowledge of Dickens, we have only the report of a Moscow professor of literature that on one afternoon in 1841, in a Roman cafe, he found Gogol

1. S. P. Shevyrev, "Vzgliad russkogo na sovremennoe sostoianie Evropy," *Moskvitianin* (1841), 237–238 (Chast' 1, otd. III, "Nauki"). All translations from the Russian are my own.

2. The sole indication that he knew any of Gogol's work comes in a letter of 1867, where he commends to Bulwer-Lytton Gogol's least characteristic work — "a story . . . called *Tarass Boulla* [sic] [in Louis Viardot's translation of] the *Nouvelles Russes* of Nicolas Gogol." *Letters of Charles Dickens,* ed. Walter Dexter, III (Bloomsbury: Nonesuch Press, 1938), 562.

engrossed in the reading of an unspecified novel of Dickens (it could have been *Pickwick,* or *Nicholas Nickleby,* or *Oliver Twist*) in an unspecified language. Beyond this — to use a favorite Gogolian expression — everything becomes shrouded in fog.

It is clear, then, at least that neither writer knew any of the other's most representative work; and if there is nonetheless an element of truth in Prosper Mérimée's calling Gogol "the Russian Dickens," or in Maurice Baring's assertion that "Gogol begins where Dickens leaves off," it must be sought outside the area of influence. Members of the same generation (Gogol was born in 1809, Dickens in 1812), both men achieved an unrivaled popularity in the decade of the 1830s — and gave popularity a new dimension by finding it with a new and enlarged public that included classes not previously given to reading fiction. (The emblematic group of paupers who met in a London locksmith's shop to hear the shilling numbers of *Pickwick* read have their counterparts in the Petersburg typographers who collapsed with laughter while setting Gogol's first collection of stories.)[3]

Each made his reputation as a humorist, via an improvised, exuberant first fiction whose comedy, grounded in a mythified past, had (as Walter Allen remarks of *Pickwick*) "no designs [on the reader] and no ulterior motive."[4] Both, moreover, would continue to the end to write under the general license of the comic, though both were quick to circumscribe the gratuitousness of "pure" comedy — to select targets rather than simply occasions for laughter, and to seek them with increasing deliberateness in the spectacle of contemporary life. Both saw the platform available to the popular humorist as representing

3. See Edgar Johnson, *Charles Dickens: His Tragedy and Triumph,* I (New York, 1952), 155; and *Letters of Nikolai Gogol,* ed. Carl R. Proffer (Ann Arbor: University of Michigan Press, 1967), p. 38.

4. "How amazed we were," Pushkin wrote of Gogol's first volume of stories, "at a Russian book that made us laugh — we, who had not laughed since the time of Fonvizin!" (that is, since the eighteenth century). Compare Belinsky, who four years later praised Gogol as the master of "a purely Russian humor." *N. V. Gogol' v russkoi kritike i vospominaniiakh sovremennikov* (Moscow-Leningrad, 1951), pp. 37, 58.

On Dickens: Walter Allen, "The Comedy of Dickens," in Michael Slater ed., *Dickens 1970* (London: Chapman and Hall, 1970), p. 22.

a serious social responsibility; and while it would be hard to say that the quality of comedy itself becomes attenuated in either writer, it does, in both, become progressively more problematic by being made to border on material of another tonality, which suggests alternative ways of viewing even the comic passages themselves. Already in Dickens' second novel, the "merry old gentleman" is at the same time a sinister old gentleman, and though Mr. Bumble is memorable because he is comic, he is significant because of the way he stands for an inhuman system. Implicit polyvalence of this sort appears early in Gogol's work, too; the absurd story of the two Ivans ends with the narrator's cry, "It's dreary in this world, ladies and gentlemen!" — and in chapter 3 of *Dead Souls* he stresses how "the gay can in an instant turn into the sad, if only you stand too long contemplating it, and then God knows what may wander into your head."

Grounds for gaiety, Gogol is saying, are at the same time grounds for its opposite; indeed, he (and Pushkin before him) spoke of "laughter through tears" as the formula most appropriate to his best comedy; and Russian criticism was later to confirm this duality as underlying the very metaphoric structure of his style, with its tendency to employ "metaphors upward" or "metaphors downward," that is, comparisons which demean the object in question, producing comedy, and comparisons which exalt it, producing pathos, lyricism, and grandiloquence. The larger point at issue is put by Taine in his discussion of Dickens: "This sensibility can hardly have more than two issues — laughter and tears." [5] Add a third — the shudder that comes from the horrific and macabre — and the statement seems fair enough for either writer; nor will it be easy to think of another major nineteenth-century figure of whom the same might be said.

These are some of the warrants for pursuing a juxtaposition that has hardly escaped mention by any critic of either writer who was at all familiar with the work of the other. But the heart of the matter remains, as V. S. Aksakova noted in 1845, "in the *means of expression,* in *the turn of the phrase,* in *narra-*

5. H. A. Taine, *History of English Literature,* trans. N. Van Laun, II (New York and Chicago, n.d.), 443.

tive devices: in those apparently insignificant details . . . [which show] so great a likeness that it sometimes seems as if [Dickens' writing] were a translation from Gogol." Indeed, Dickens in Russian "demands utterly Gogolian expressions." By the same token, if one were to translate Gogol, "of course only the language of Dickens would do." [6]

A peculiar address in the management of words is the ground of the affinity — and a key as well to the larger strategy of comic fiction which both men employed. Contemporary mistrust of "style" in both countries for a long time impeded recognition of the fact that each was a virtuoso stylist — and, we can see now, in terms both of originality and range, the most considerable prose stylist of the century in his country.[7] Writing in an age when the cognitive aspects of prose literature were becoming paramount, they addressed readers accustomed to regard fiction as a picture *of* something — "real life" — and disposed to discuss the one in terms of the other. Such a view regards words merely as a means tending ideally to a kind of transparency; when on occasion the "vision" they engender is too eccentric to be ignored, that vision itself becomes an ontological datum, measured for correction against the reader's notion of life, all curiosity about the manner of its genesis eschewed.

Yet Dickens and Gogol deal in transparencies only as a kind of realistic relief. Where they force recognitions on us, it is seldom without a shock of surprise (the "sudden glory" of Hobbesian laughter when comic effects are in question), and if their oddities take on a semblance of naturalness, it is from the dynamics of style — an elusive matter, to which I shall return. The point here may be put most simply by saying that Dickens and Gogol regard words more in the manner of poets than of prose writers, and invite a corresponding adaptation from their critics. Resisting the tendency of fiction to masquerade as history or biography, each creates a style that can fairly be called opaque — not in the sense of being obscure, but in the

6. Letter to M. G. Kartashevskaia, 8 March 1845, in *Literaturnoe nasledstvo*, 58 (Moscow, 1952), 670–672. My italics.

7. Leskov might well vie with Gogol for this title, as Meredith might with Dickens, but it is at least arguable that neither Leskov nor Meredith produced such sustained or influential achievements.

sense that it constantly directs attention to the words themselves, to the brilliance of the artifice (and so, ultimately, to the artificer himself). It was the critic Rozanov who first found the characters — indeed, the whole created world — of Gogol to arise from some "waxy mass of words," or, in an alternative image, to consist in a "mosaic of words." The same can be said of Dickens.

Dickens wrote very little about his art, but a characteristic phrase in a letter to Forster does suggest something of the all but autonomous value and vitality he found in language: urging his friend to prune his verbal excesses, he encourages him to "knock out a word's brains here and there." Gogol is more theoretical and more general. "One is astonished at the preciousness of our language," he writes in *Selected Passages*. *"Every one of its sounds is a gift;* everything is coarse-grained and tangible, like a very pearl, *and indeed the name for a thing may on occasion be even more valuable than the thing itself."* [8]

Proper names in both writers are a reminder of this, exploiting as they do some of the deeper associations of their respective tongues: Akaky Akakievich Bashmachkin, Anton Prokofievich Pupopuz, Ivan Ivanovich Pererepenko, Ivan Nikiforovich Dovgochkhun, Evtikhii Evtikhievich, Elevferii Elevferievich, Dobchinsky and Bobchinsky, Lyapkin-Tyapkin — the Gogolian list is long. In Dickens it is even longer — and more familiar, and better studied.[9] No one could ask, with reference to his work, what's in a name, who was not prepared to stay for a lengthy answer.

8. *Letters of Charles Dickens,* I, 808; quoted by Park Honan in his very interesting article, "Metrical Prose in Dickens," *Victorian Newsletter,* 28 (Fall 1965), 2. Gogol, *Polnoe sobranie sochinenii,* 8 (Leningrad, 1952), 279. My italics.

9. On names in Gogol, see Vladimir Nabokov, *Nikolai Gogol* (Norfolk, Conn., 1944), pp. 42–43, 83–86; Simon Karlinsky, "Portrait of Gogol as a Word Glutton," *California Slavic Studies,* 5 (Berkeley, Los Angeles, London), 177–181; and Andrei Belyi, *Masterstvo Gogolia* (Moscow-Leningrad, 1934), pp. 215, 233. On names in Dickens, see G. L. Brook, *The Language of Dickens* (London, 1970), pp. 208–222; C. A. Bodelsen, "The Physiognomy of the Name," *Review of English Literature,* 2 (July 1960), 39–48; Elizabeth Hope Gordon, *The Naming of Characters in the Works of Charles Dickens* (Lincoln, Nebraska, 1917); and John Forster, *The Life of Charles Dickens,* bk. IX, chap. 7 (any ed.).

By the same token, there does not seem to be much at this point in time that needs saying about the typical bearers of Dickensian names. No longer subject to reproach for flatness, their general mode of being is accepted as having its own legitimacy. Each one speaks, as Walter Allen puts it, in a kind of soliloquy, in a "language of personal obsession" that expresses his "permanent fantasy of [himself]." [10] And their comic life comes from the energy and resourcefulness each one shows in clinging to his peculiar selfhood against temptations to flexibility which lesser personages might find overwhelming. They do not simply bear the brilliance of their creator: they flaunt it as their own. Sairey Gamp and Pecksniff are merely the best known of this legion of inspired artists in comic monologue — the high point of a scale on which Randolph Quirk has noted examples (from Dickens' working plans) of characters who appear to have been imagined "entirely and solely as a particular kind of linguistic behavior." [11]

Once more, the same is true of Gogol: in his most characteristic works behavior and relationship — like selfhood — are primarily verbal matters. His most memorable vulgarians (*poshlyaki*), as George Ivask has pointed out, are, paradoxically, "great wordsmiths," "even esthetes," their moral nonentity at once established and redeemed by the artistry Gogol lends them.[12] Repeatedly and inexhaustibly, the characters of the short stories, of *Dead Souls,* and of *The Inspector General* justify their subhumanity in a plotless world by the lively economy of their garrulousness and the furious energy of their stasis. It is not psychological curiosity they reward with each appearance, but esthetic curiosity; we await something like the counterpart of rhyme in a comic poem. This applies as much to the minimal utterances of Akaky Akakievich in "The Overcoat" as to the verbal floods of Nozdrev or Khlestakov (or Flora Finching).

Stylists and rhetoricians, the characters of both writers are themselves the creation of style and rhetoric. The familiar tendency of both to confound character and milieu (not Krook's

10. Allen, p. 15.

11. Randolph Quirk, *Charles Dickens and Appropriate Language* (Durham, Eng., 1959), p. 23.

12. Iurii Ivask, "Literaturnye zametki," *Mosty,* 12 (1966), 174ff.

room but Krook himself explodes in flame, while in *Dead Souls* the bearlike landowner's stocky furniture proclaims, "I, too, am Sobakevich!") is one way of implicating the disparate ingredients of the depicted world in the service of a single-keyed vision, the dramatized monologue of the personalized narrator, all of whose notations — of clothing, gesture, surroundings, landscape, weather — are made to serve a single given theme.[13] Thus when, as in the case of Mr. Turveydrop in *Bleak House,* the theme is artificiality, all other aspects drop away, and the very syntax with its repetitions enacts this theme:

> He was a fat old gentleman with a false complexion, false teeth, false whiskers, and a wig. He had a fur collar, and he had a padded breast to his coat . . . He was pinched in, and swelled out, and got up, and strapped down, as much as he could possibly bear . . . He had, under his arm, a hat of great size and weight, shelving downward from the crown to the brim; and in his hand a pair of white gloves, with which he flapped it, as he stood poised on one leg, in a high-shouldered, round-elbowed state of elegance not to be surpassed. He had a cane, he had an eye-glass, he had a snuff-box, he had rings, he had wristbands, he had everything but any touch of nature; he was not like youth, he was not like age, he was not like anything in the world but a model of Deportment.   (Chapter 14)

Compare the way Manilov is introduced in chapter 2 of *Dead Souls*:

> God alone might be able to say what kind of character Manilov's was. There is a kind of people known as so-so, neither-this-nor-that, neither fish nor fowl, as the proverb has it. It is among them, perhaps, that Manilov should be numbered . . . During the first minute of conversation with him you couldn't help saying, "What a pleasant and kind man!" The next minute after that you wouldn't say anything at all; while the minute after that you'd say, "The devil knows what all this is about!" — and you'd get as far away as possible . . . No amount of patience could get you any lively or even emphatic word out of him, of the kind you can hear from almost anybody if you touch on a

13. See, e.g., C. B. Cox, "A Dickens Landscape," *Critical Quarterly,* 2, no. 1 (1960), 58–60.

subject close to his heart. Everyone has some passion of his own: the passion of one man may have turned to wolfhounds; another fancies himself a great lover of music and amazingly sensitive to all its profundities; a third is a master at valiant dining, a fourth at playing a role ever so slightly higher than the one assigned to him; a fifth, with a more limited desire, sleeps and dreams of how he might be seen strolling with an aide-de-camp for the benefit of his friends, acquaintances, and even those who don't know him at all; a sixth is already gifted with a hand preternaturally impelled to bet on some ace or deuce of diamonds, while the hand of a seventh just itches to set things right somewhere . . . in short, everyone has something all his own, but Manilov didn't have a thing.

The point of view here (as in the characterization of Mr. Turveydrop) is hardly one that a Tolstoy or a George Eliot could permit himself. There is no room for genuine curiosity about either character: they are phenomena, not problems. (Gogol applies the same technique to his introduction of Manilov's wife, albeit with greater economy: "His wife — however, they were perfectly content with each other.") Here and elsewhere, a complicity operates between narrator and reader to enjoy the spectacle of these unfree characters. It is an enjoyment which works at their expense: a pleasure in superiority, reinforced by the pleasure of appreciating the narrator's verbal adroitness.

From the repetition inherent in such unitary emphasis, from the prominence necessarily given to *words* by such repetition, it is not surprising to find words themselves engendering things. Nabokov makes much (perhaps even too much) of this in his brilliantly onesided study of Gogol, calling attention to the way a whole auxiliary population is called into momentary being by the sheer momentum of the Gogolian language. The most spectacular instance is the expanding simile in *Dead Souls* whereby Sobakevich's head, seen in a window, engenders a comparison with a pumpkin which, in its turn, engenders a whole evanescent scene of youthful rustic flirtation, complete with two kinds of music and a chorus of "white-bosomed and white-necked country lasses."

A comparable eclipse, during which the scene undergoes a

quasi-surrealistic transformation, occurs in *Our Mutual Friend*. It begins as simple metaphor: among the Podsnaps' friends are some "who were not entitled to be asked to dinner, but had a claim to be invited to come and take a haunch of mutton vapour-bath at half past nine." These guests, that is, are to come after dinner; it is their lot to share the ghost of the dinner, the aroma of the meat that lingers in the air after the dishes have been removed. Two pages later, the metaphor begins to expand. "The bathers" arrive: "Bald bathers folded their arms and talked to Mr. Podsnap on the hearthrug; sleek-whiskered bathers, with hats in their hands, lunged at Mrs. Podsnap and retreated; prowling bathers went around looking into ornamental boxes and bowls as if they had suspicions of larceny on the part of the Podsnaps, and expected to find something they had lost at the bottom; bathers of the gentler sex sat silently comparing ivory shoulders" (Book I, Chapter 11). This is not, we may note, the simple fanciful-picturesque transformation that both writers employ at the beginning of their careers. Despite Nabokov's assurance that "fancy is only fertile when it is futile," there is a point to all such passages when they occur, as these examples do, in the later works. With Dickens the point is satirical: the subject of this section of *Our Mutual Friend* is the unreality of social life. With Gogol the point is rather more remote, but related; it has to do with the insignificance, the meaninglessness, of the lives being displayed. The auxiliary population of *Dead Souls* — including Sobakevich's famous list of deceased serfs — is at least as memorable and alive as the cast of primary characters: and this fact is a commentary and a judgment.

Even such apparent digressions actually work in the service of the dominant and unifying *themes* of these two writers, each of whom might with justice claim the title that Baudelaire awarded to Gautier: *magicien-ès-lettres*. Thematic unity, word-enforced in the sense of recurrent verbal motifs and refrains, is common in a strikingly strict way to Gogol, for all his digressive vagaries, and to Dickens, despite the red herring of conventional and often melodramatic plot. This is clearer — as almost everything is clearer — in the Dickensian novel, with its stylistic set pieces which are, as it were, nodal points, resuming theme and sustaining atmosphere. Halfway through *Our Mutual Friend* we find this set piece — not precisely narration, rather, a pause in the narration, a drawing-back to recall, from a new angle, the theater in which the narrative action takes place:

> A grey dusty withered evening in London city has not a hopeful aspect. The closed warehouses and offices have an air of death about them, and the national dread of colour has an air of mourning. The towers and steeples of the many house-encompassed churches, dark and dingy as the sky that seems descending on them, are no relief to the general gloom; a sun-dial on a church-wall has the look, in its useless black shade, of having failed in its business enterprise and stopped payment for ever; melancholy waifs and strays of housekeepers and porters sweep melancholy waifs and strays of papers and pins into the kennels, and other more melancholy waifs and strays explore them, searching and stooping and poking for anything to sell. The set of humanity outward from the City is as a set of prisoners departing from gaol, and dismal Newgate seems quite as fit a stronghold for the mighty Lord Mayor as his own state-dwelling.
>
> (Book II, Chapter 15)

Here is all of the physical City in little, along with its wretched citizens. The paired nouns in "warehouses and offices," "towers and steeples," "keepers and porters," find an echo in "an air of death," "an air of mourning," "set of humanity" and "set of prisoners," and in the thrice-repeated "melancholy waifs and strays." Not only words are repeated, but sounds: in the alliteration of "dark and dingy," of "papers and pins," of "searching and sweeping" — and in the assonance of "waifs and strays." All this supports the emphasis on "death," "dread," "gloom," "melancholy," "dismal." The places of business are *closed,* the churches are *house-encompassed,* the sky is *descending*: the city is a prison. The people are like the trash in the streets; and the trash is more than a simple metaphor for money, the god of this civilization and the nemesis of authentic life. It could be further demonstrated how this passage manages, by verbal association, to recall most of the other important settings in this large book, and many of the main motifs (for example, the scavengers in the street recall not only the Hexams and Riderhoods, but the respectable scavengers, the Vereerings, Fledgeby, the Lammles).

Theme and motif, as organizing agents of this fictional world, have been well enough treated in the criticism of recent decades. Less observed (even by writers on style, who have tended to stop short with lexicon) is the more basic function of syntax in the broadest sense — the characteristic patterns of relationship into which words themselves are set. In Gogol's case a start was made in the work of Eikhenbaum and Biely, Eikhenbaum stressing the Gogolian narration as *performance* (compare Robert Garis, *The Dickens Theater*) and Biely the role of *zvukopis'*, that orchestration of sounds which constitutes something like the molecular structure of Gogol's prose and produces the materials out of which he builds his peculiar world. Examples from Gogol would be out of place here, but Biely's cardinal observation deserves to be quoted for the light it can shed on Dickens. Gogol, Biely writes,

is a master at reflecting the sounds of a word in a verbal group; the basic sound, on which the vocal accent falls, becomes, as a result of the law of reflection, phosphorescent . . . Gogol's verbal fabric is a merging of assonances, alliterations, a gradation of intersecting sound groups . . . In [his] orchestration of sound, there is a transition from musical gesticulation to artistic representation. There is no getting around it; otherwise, you won't understand a good deal (in the colors, as in the plot) — just as you will not understand the operatic nature of the poses: without music, they are *conventional*: with it — *real*.[14]

Biely's use of "conventional" is paradoxical here; in his context, it means artistically unmotivated — the point being that the music of this prose, by giving a cue to its shaping conventions, offers a key to its proper understanding. That seems to me a just claim, and one capable of extension: recognition of the syntactic and euphonic peculiarities of this prose can clarify our understanding of comic narrative itself (as opposed to humorous instances) in both writers — and ultimately help define the nature of the world each creates. Three Dickensian passages

14. Belyi, *Masterstvo Gogolia,* p. 228.

— one humorous, one pathetic, and one ostensibly neutral —
may serve as illustrations.

> In a rather ill-favoured and ill-savoured neighborhood, though
> one of its rising grounds bears the name of Mount Pleasant, the
> Elfin Smallweed, christened Bartholemew, and known on the
> domestic hearth as Bart, passes that limited portion of his time
> on which the office and its contingencies have no claim. He
> dwells in a little narrow street, always solitary, shady, and sad,
> closely bricked up on all sides like a tomb, but where there yet
> lingers the stump of an old forest tree, whose flavour is about
> as fresh and natural as the Smallweed smack of youth.
>
> (*Bleak House,* Chapter 21)

> As Oliver gave this proof of the free and proper action of his
> lungs, the patchwork coverlet which was carelessly flung over
> the iron bedstead, rustled; the pale face of a young woman was
> raised feebly from the pillow; and a faint voice imperfectly articu-
> lated the words, "Let me see the child, and die."
>
> (*Oliver Twist,* Chapter 1)

> The cold, wet, shelterless midnight streets of London; the foul
> and frowzy dens, where vice is closely packed and lacks the room
> to turn; the haunts of hunger and disease, the shabby rags that
> scarcely hold together; where are the attractions of these things?
>
> (Preface to the third edition of *Oliver Twist*)

One can only wonder what a practitioner of speed reading
would make of writing like this, intended as it so obviously is
for the ear. Stumbling through the rhymes, the assonances and
the clumps of alliteration in the Smallweed passage leaves us
so far from the realm of nature and youth (delusively mentioned at the end) that the one-liner immediately following
comes almost as an anticlimax: "There has been only one child
in the Smallweed family for several generations."

As for the passage from *Oliver Twist* (Chapter 1), the force
of its pathos comes in considerable part from the rhythmic ordering of alliterations on f and p (with a symmetrical sprinkling
of r's), joined just before the climactic statement in "imper-
fectly." Even the third example shows the same tendency, all
the more strikingly because it does not come from fiction at all.

The *things* Dickens cites clearly have no attraction in themselves — but what he denies to them in reality, he supplies in the obtrusive verbal music — through his characteristic assonances, alliterations, and strong tonic emphases.[15]

It is regrettable that no one has undertaken to diagram the chief varieties of the Dickensian sentence, as Biely did with daunting rigor for its Gogolian counterpart. What that would show, I think, is the thoroughgoing and unprecedented *dynamism* of the Dickensian prose — which works on the reader through an astonishing range of concentric signals to produce a series of orchestrated effects. There is (often) guiding metaphor; there is rhythmic movement toward a skillfully deferred climax; there are vigorous and unexpected words. Ingenious punctuation guides the verbal traffic; and — at the most fundamental level — phonemes signal paronomastically to each other over the walls of their lexical prisons. It is ultimately the presence of this teeming subliminal energy that gives all of Dickens' writing its characteristic cohesiveness and lets us know, however disparate the works we examine, that they belong to a particular "world," single, self-contained — and comic.[16]

15. John Holloway ("Dickens' Word-World," *Encounter,* June 1970, p. 66) cites the phrases Dickens inserted to enliven a piece written by Henry Morley for *Household Words:* "a wet Sunday . . . rustics lounge under penthouse roofs, festooning their smock-frocks with their pocketed hands, and yawning heavily . . . dripping umbrellas make a dismal dance all down the street . . . splashed and draggled stragglers fagging along . . . the flat little church bell seems vexed . . . and tinkles discontentedly, while the very beadle at the door seems quenched and querulous." Reference to the Dickens-Morley text (*Charles Dickens' Uncollected Writings from Household Words, 1850–1859,* ed. Harry Stone, I [Bloomington and London: Indiana University Press, 1968], 286) makes clear the extent to which the somewhat more discursive published text has been gutted to produce this phrasal skeleton, which I have further abridged. Still, Holloway's conclusion holds: this kind of artist, "for whom words themselves form a great independent empire with its own inexhaustible resources," is constantly drawn to infringe the "reality principle" that underlies conventional perception, and to "substitute for it the much larger freedom of inter-play and interchange which belongs to *the world of words*" (my italics).

16. The metaphor of a novelist's created "world" is, of course, well worn; all the same, it tends to be applied to Dickens' work with noteworthy frequency, and by particularly cliché-resistant critics, among them V. S. Pritchett ("The Comic World of Dickens," see note 20 below), Dorothy Van Ghent ("The Dickens World: A View from Todg-

Aside from the obvious argument that comedy is so much more in Dickens (and Gogol) than comic relief, its generic primacy is evident in what I have called syntax: the special ways in which words are made to behave. Showing at least the same "grain, entanglement, and local interplay as things themselves have," [17] their behavior keeps us open to surprise, gives us "familiar experiences in a new perspective," "jerks the mind out of its dim, associative jogtrot along the beaten tracks of habit," and so "adds a new dimension to sensation and thought," bringing about "a deepened and intensified state of awareness."

These phrases are Arthur Koestler's characterization of bisociation — the device he finds basic to humor and comedy alike (as well as to creative cerebration in general).[18] It is implicated in the creation of "worlds" by the demands of sustained narrative, bridging and containing comic scenes, and I have tried to suggest how strong syntax[19] can do this. The strategic direction of that strong syntax in both Gogol and Dickens, as has been often remarked, comes (in contrast to most eighteenth-century comedy, which is based on adult experience) from the point of view of the outsider — more specifically, of the child — who is moved to laughter, indignation, fear, or tears: but always moved, by what the men of his time are content merely to register, or ignore.[20] Here are the terms of bisociation — but a criticism interested in the nature of humorous narrative might

ers's" *Sewanee Review,* 58 [1950]), J. Hillis Miller (*Charles Dickens: The World of his Novels*), Humphry House (*The Dickens World*), and Angus Wilson (*The World of Charles Dickens*).

17. Holloway, p. 66.

18. Arthur Koestler, *Insight and Outlook* (New York: Macmillan, 1949), p. 95.

19. See Alice Meynell's stimulating discussion of Dickens' style, with its recognition that in his humorous writing "the idea is inseparable from the phrase," its fresh and sympathetic treatment of caricature, and its argument that "strong grammar is like strong drawing." The article in question appeared in two substantially different variants: "Charles Dickens as a Man of Letters" in her *Hearts of Controversy* (London, 1917), and "Charles Dickens as Man of Letters" in George H. Ford and Lauriat Lane, Jr., eds., *The Dickens Critics* (Ithaca: Cornell University Press, 1961).

20. Compare Pritchett: "In Dickens the ground [of comedy] is the high visual sense and sharp ear of the experienced child who is insecure." "The Comic World of Dickens," in Ford and Lane, *The Dickens Critics,* p. 313.

well wish to emphasize that if no adult writer had chosen to
see the world thus before Gogol and Dickens, no child had
ever commanded such a vocabulary or such a syntax, or put
such an arsenal of sophisticated expression in the service of
simple norms.

ROBERT KIELY

Victorian Harlequin: The Function of Humor in Thackeray's Critical and Miscellaneous Prose

In *Roundabout Papers,* Thackeray tells an anecdote which, as usual, is partly at his own expense. He was visiting a church in Antwerp when the beadle told him that his walking about was disturbing the service. Thackeray pointed to others who seemed to be moving around less quietly than he: " 'They come to pray,' says the beadle. 'You don't come to pray, you ————' 'When I come to pay,' says I, 'I am welcome,' and with this withering sarcasm, I walk out of church in a huff. I don't envy the feelings of that beadle after receiving point blank such a stroke of wit." [1]

It is the kind of story that Boswell probably would have let pass unrecorded, for, despite his love of the eighteenth century, Thackeray was not a great creator of bons mots. The sharp retort and the well-shaped epigram were not his style. He was not a wit and, as his tone of exaggerated satisfaction makes plain, he knew it.

1. *The Works of William Makepeace Thackeray,* Oxford Edition, ed. George Saintsbury, 20 vols. (London: Oxford University Press, 1908), XX, 444. Quotations from this edition will be indicated henceforth in the text by volume and page number.

Thackeray's gift was for something less taut, less pointed and quick than what is usually called wit. His best effects are cumulative, indirect, and elusive. By his own definition, he was a humorist — a term which may seem comfortably imprecise, but one which may also be used to imply brainless geniality or a tendency to conceal one's own vices while ridiculing those of others. Thackeray himself was restless in any single role, but throughout his career he was fond of comparing himself, as well as his subjects, to clowns and jesters. One of his favorite words was "quack," and his most typical metaphorical guises were those of Harlequin and Punchinello. The usual explanation for this — indeed, one that Thackeray sometimes offers — is that all men are, in one way or another, actors and frauds; that each of us shows sides of himself in public which are different from the man within.

A famous passage at the beginning of the lectures on *The English Humourists* tells the story of a man in deep depression who asks his physician for a cure and is advised to visit the theater where Harlequin is playing. The advice turns out to be useless because the patient is himself the actor who plays Harlequin. At first, the anecdote seems to suggest that the humorist is one who puts up a good front, conceals with tricks and laughter the sorrow that he really feels. But it is always dangerous to quote from the beginning of a paragraph by Thackeray without following the rest. For as he expands his definition, humor becomes something much more than surface gaiety: "If Humour only meant laughter, you would scarcely feel more interest about humourous writers than about the private life of poor Harlequin just mentioned, who possesses in common with these the power to make you laugh" (XIV, 469).

Harlequin, whose public and private selves are as different as night and day, is not the model humorist after all, but only a convenient contrast to the genuine article: "The humourous writer professes to awaken and direct your love, your pity, your kindness — your scorn for untruth, pretension, imposture — your tenderness for the weak, the poor, the oppressed, the unhappy" (XIV, 469). It is such a familiar Victorian catalogue that one is tempted to pass quickly over it in search of something more "original." But that would be a mistake, for the core of Thackeray's idea of humor is here. Obviously, but also very importantly, humor, for Thackeray, is not a cover-up, a simplification of reality, but an evocation of complex, even contradictory, responses. The seriousness and sadness of the true humorist show through his best jokes, not in spite of them, but in subtle combination with them.

It is also clear from the catalogue that the humorist appeals to the heart more than to the mind — to love, pity, tenderness, even to "scorn" rather than to reasoned disapproval. He is one who "feels the truth" and therefore "takes upon himself to be the week-day preacher." The idea that the capacity to feel things deeply gives a man special moral insight is, in part, a Romantic legacy familiar in much Victorian literature. The wit shows himself to be superior to other men through his ability to make quick and sharp distinctions. The humorist, on the other hand, is just like everybody else, only more so. His art depends less on his power to surprise or impress his reader than on his ability to create an affective bond with him. The humorist, defined as a passionate and, especially, compassionate moralist, becomes the descendant not so much of Swift and Pope as of Wordsworth and Keats. As George Eliot put it in 1856, "Humour, in its higher forms, and in proportion as it associates itself with the sympathetic emotions, continually passes into poetry; nearly all great modern humourists may be called prose poets." [2]

Thackeray's distaste for Romantic extravagance and his sympathy for the eighteenth century make it difficult to consider his work in terms even remotely connected with the Romantic imagination. Yet there is something to be gained from examining his humor not as a faltering attempt at balance and intellectual clarity but as a continuing process, a feeling into things and situations, making judgments and withdrawing them, forever enlarging possibilities and resisting conclusions. Like many Romantics, he seeks at his best to imitate the movement of life

2. George Eliot, "German Wit: Heinrich Heine," *The Works of George Eliot,* 10 vols. (Boston, 1890), IX, 219. This essay was originally published in 1856 in the *Westminster Review.*

rather than a preconceived idea of it. His moral force comes not so much from taking positions, but from widening and enriching the ground from which moral positions are taken.

But, of course, as all readers of Thackeray know, though he could be subtle and evasive, he could also be heavyhanded and obvious. If he could imitate the general flow and confusion of life, he could also mimic very specific mannerisms and habits of speech and, in so doing, make what appear to be emphatic, rapid, and sometimes ruthless moral judgments. Thackeray was a droll caricaturist, an expert at detecting buffoonery. The question is whether the arch, wicked, and sometimes silly side of him fits in with his concept of the humorist as compassionate moralist. Does he succeed at putting cap and bells at the service of an open mind and benevolent heart? Or is he merely another "quack" — as he sometimes claims — pretending one thing while doing something else?

Of course, the answers to these questions vary with particular works; but one general observation is worth making at the outset. For Thackeray the humorist, in contrast to the tragedian and philosopher, is a bold entertainer — one who snatches the attention of his audience by almost any means rather than earning it through patient reasoning or gradual development of character and situation. The tonal nuances and meditative digressions may come later, but first it is important to capture the spectator's fancy. For Thackeray beginnings are important and, in his own work, they are often filled with memorable displays of posing and face-pulling.

Despite his persistent references to the artificiality, the sham posturing of comedians, nothing was more natural to him than to play the mimic. One sees it everywhere in his writing, in letters, reviews, lectures, and journals as well as in novels, tales, and burlesques. Just as he could sketch while receiving visitors or attending an opera, so too his ear could apparently work away while the rest of his mind was on other things. Some of the early imitations are little more than aural doodles — fragments of tea-talk, diplomatic pronouncements, pedantic rumblings, odds and ends of a brogue. They do not represent carefully worked out or even very conscious attitudes. They are unguarded reactions, almost absentminded ways of seeing and hearing.

Readers are still irritated by his travel books because of his habit of mimicking accents and expressions, exaggerating modes of dress and social intercourse, in short, appearing to ridicule customs of every sort simply because they are not British. There is no denying that he had most of the prejudices of his nation and class. The *Irish Sketch Book* and *From Cornhill to Grand Cairo* tell relatively little about foreign places and a great deal about the middle-class Victorian baggage which the traveler was so often unable to put down and forget. But, like many tourists, Thackeray often felt an urge to become part of the very scenes which he could hardly describe without a cliché or a laugh. However, unlike the student abroad who thinks he can stop shaving and blend in, Thackeray was acutely aware of his unmistakable Englishness. When in his prose he does adopt a foreign guise, he seeks some of the pleasure of masquerade without, for any length of time, mistaking it for assimiliation.

Thackeray's foreign sketches are partial admissions of his own limitations as well as comments on strange places and people. The initial pleasure in imitation is no less genuine for being undercut by a sense of that aspect of the self which can never be other than that which it solidly and rather sadly is. The point is that even at his least supple and imaginative, Thackeray displays an irrepressible urge to try on voices, expressions, and styles other than his ponderous own.

One of the first characters introduced in the *Paris Sketch Book* is Sam Pogson, a young Englishman who is hardly in Calais before trying out French ways — or what he thinks are French ways — flirting with every woman in sight, drinking champagne constantly, and dropping fashionable phrases. Thackeray, unable to resist mimicking an Englishman trying to be French, quotes from a letter in which Pogson describes one of his successes to a friend:

> I'll tell you how it occurred. Everybody in France, you know, dines at the ordinary — it's quite distangy to do so . . . You know my way with women: champagne's the thing; make 'em

drink, make 'em talk — make 'em talk, make 'em do anything. So I orders a bottle, as if for myself; and 'Ma'am,' says I,
'will you take a glass of Sham — just one?' Take it she did
. . . Bob Irons told me that he had made some slap-up acquaintances among the genteelest people at Paris, nothing but by offering them Sham.   (II, 20)

Pogson's performance is a sham of class as well as of na-
tionality, and Thackeray enjoys ridiculing it. But, in a way, he
also understands the impulse behind it. Pogson's folly is not so
much in wanting to enter into the spirit of things by imitating
foreign ways, but in his adoption of a self-congratulatory tone in
the midst of his failure to see the difference between his copy
and the real thing. Pogson has no perspective on the world or
himself and therefore lacks the power of successful imitation as
well as the saving grace of irony.

Nothing so much preoccupied Thackeray — even in his
seemingly offhand criticism of society, literature, and art — as
the nature and value of imitation. He revered and wanted
originality, yet it was his peculiar gift to "take off" from what
others had already said and done. His nonfiction is a gallery of
borrowed poses, but his imagination never lodges very long or
happily in any single one. If we are searching for the author's
own voice, we can find it in the characters he chooses to imitate
so long as we recognize that there is a continual "trying on"
during which some parts seem to fit and others do not. Thackeray is not all Pogson any more than he is all Michael Angelo
Titmarsh or Pendennis. We can discover him — or, at least, his
imagination — only if we follow his movement to and from, in
and out of such creatures. Imitation, role-playing, even mimicry
are, for Thackeray, essential to humor; for, unlike the wit, who
continually distinguishes between himself and others, the humorist is one who seeks a common ground and risks, like Pogson, looking like a fool if he cannot find it.

The parallel between Pogson's problem — his inability to
distinguish between a true copy and a sham — and the humorist's
dilemma, though not explicitly drawn, is everywhere in evidence
in the *Paris Sketch Book*. The work is a journal and therefore
one does not expect much in the way of form, yet Thackeray is

continually searching in it for a meeting place between moral rigor, sympathy, and a light heart. One sees it in the typical pattern of his approach to French character. Stage one is the detached view (which usually means rather harsh criticism of French ways on moral grounds); stage two is an amiable warming to the color and vivacity of the subject (often accompanied by wishful ejaculations — "Would that we English had their wit, their museums, their elegance!"); stage three is a self-consciously exaggerated imitation of someone or something French in which the joke is double-edged because based on the incompatibility of the French and English temperaments; stage four is a return to the sensible and comfortable English voice, still moralizing, but less strident than at the outset.

Thackeray, the humorist, like Pogson, the tourist, wants somehow to enter into an unfamiliar life — to become, if only very briefly, that which he contemplates. He is able to see that Pogson's vulgarity and condescension, his lack of feeling and respect for French life, make his role-playing farcical; but that insight does not quite enable Thackeray to eliminate every trace of Pogson in himself. His solution, not a philosophical choice so much as a psychological compromise, is to keep his vulgar feelings of superiority separate from his moments of sympathetic identification. What results is a radical and rapid alternation of mood and perspective — usually regarded as a virtue in Thackeray's fiction, often looked on as a form of weakmindedness or hypocrisy in his travel writing and criticism.

It is certainly true that Thackeray was unable to work out a coherent system by which the two tendencies could be logically reconciled; but this is not an unfamiliar problem to the student of the nineteenth-century mind. If Thackeray's habit of shifting tone and distance is thought of as an aesthetic strategy based on psychological need rather than as a form of moral cowardice, it becomes apparent how much it resembles the strategy of many nineteenth-century writers, particularly the Romantics. To approach one's subject cautiously from a distance, to move closer to it, to unite with it imaginatively, and again to return to the remove created by habit is to express in sequential, dramatic terms an experience of the mind and heart which appears to defy coherent rational justification and intellectual consistency.

A striking example of the pattern can be seen in Thackeray's treatment of young French painters in the *Paris Sketch Book*. At first, he calls their existence "the easiest, dirtiest, merriest . . . possible" and makes it clear that he disapproves of their arrogance, vanity, and immorality. But as he proceeds to scorn their foppish ways, he becomes fascinated and then charmed by the very details he had seemingly been preparing for his own indignation. Their ingenious hairstyles and beards, their fancy jackets and incredible caps — at first taken up as objects of ridicule are suddenly used by Thackeray, despite his earlier reservations, as badges of honor. He seems to turn on his English reader and on the Pogson side of himself and, almost without warning, he is speaking, not as a disapproving tourist, but as a defender of French culture. He borrows French phrases and French sarcasm to pour out invective against an England where "a grocer's daughter would think she made a *mésalliance* by marrying a painter, and where a literary man . . . ranks below . . . the apothecary, the attorney, and the wine-merchant." Warming to his subject and to his sheer pleasure in role-playing, he imitates, not the English traveler trying to sound French, but the way a Frenchman might mimic an English conversation: " 'Who is that monstrous pleasant fellow?' 'Don't you know? . . . It's Asterisk, the author of so-and-so, and a famous contributor to such-and-such.' 'Good Heavens! a literary man! I thought he had been a gentleman!' " (II, 45).

But Thackeray, as usual, cannot keep up the pretense for very long. "To our muttons," he says, and returns to his sensible English voice. Calling himself back once again to the ostensible subject of the chapter — the French school of painting — he takes up neoclassicism and appears, by a shift in tone, to be avoiding the consequences of his own wishful thinking. In a broader sense, however, he does not change his real subject at all. He is still preoccupied with the artist's role and with the nature of imitation in art and life. He criticizes French classicism not because he thinks the ancients are unworthy of imitation but because he thinks the moderns are incapable of matching their achievement: "Because to these lofty heights giants had scaled, behold the race of pigmies must get upon stilts and jump at them likewise! and on the canvas, and in the theatre, the French frogs (excuse the pleasantry) were instructed to swell out and roar as much as possible like bulls. What was the consequence . . . ? In trying to make themselves into bulls, the frogs made themselves into jackasses, as might be expected" (II, 46).

Thackeray's language here is harsh and his English prejudice bursts unpleasantly to the surface (though the echo of Aesop and La Fontaine's "La Grenouille qui veut se faire aussi grosse que le Boeuf" suggests that even in this he was the mimic). But there is more at issue than national rivalry. Having abandoned a career as a painter, he knew what it was to try to scale the "lofty heights" and to realize that he, like all the rest, was a member of a new race of pigmies. Considering his own stylistic habits and indeed the paragraphs filled with posturing and role-playing which precede his discussion of neoclassicism, Thackeray's attack on imitative artists takes on a significance and even a poignancy beyond its value as a general critical statement:

> And yet we, O foolish race! must try our very best to ape some one or two of our neighbours, whose ideas fit us no more than their breeches! It is the study of nature, surely, that profits us, and not of these imitations of her. A man, as a man, from a dustman up to Aeschylus, is God's work, and good to read, as all works of nature are; but the silly animal is never content; is ever trying to fit itself into another shape; wants to deny its own identity, and has not the courage to utter its own thoughts.
> (II, 46)

Clearly, Thackeray is referring as much to his own problems as a writer as he is to the French school of painting. Once again, the rhetoric, at least, appears to be built upon Romantic formulations. One cannot assume that Thackeray meant the same thing that Wordsworth or Coleridge did when they spoke of nature; nonetheless, it would be a mistake to discount such passages altogether. One of Thackeray's basic objections to French classicism was that it perpetuated a myth of heroism which, if it ever had validity, certainly seemed in the nineteenth century to have it no longer. For Thackeray, as for many Victorians, the classical hero was a thing out of nature. The writer who wished to be true to nature (that is, to himself and his

times) wrote about common, ordinary people and was, therefore, in one very old-fashioned sense of the word, bound to be
a comic artist.[3]

But Thackeray recognized that a successful imitation of nature
depends on more than choice of subject matter and a will to tell
the truth. Supposing a writer does have the "courage to utter his
own thoughts," how does he shape these thoughts in such a way
that they will make sense to others? What are the stylistic resources, the formal conventions, the vocabulary, the syntax of
the honest man? These are questions which Thackeray often
posed, and sought in his roundabout way to get at.

One tends to remember the lectures on *The English Humourists* for their many outbursts of moral indignation, but the fact
is that Thackeray was willing to forgive almost anything in a
writer whose style struck him as somehow natural and authentic.
After condemning Swift's grossness, he praises his "elaborately
simple" style; he admires Congreve's "energy" despite his
"heathen immorality"; he says of Addison that "he came to that
artificial age, and began to speak with his noble, natural voice";
he admits that Steele was coarse, but praises the naturalness of
his writing too, which he says comes from the fact that "he wrote
so quickly and carelessly that he was forced to make the reader
his confidant, and had not the time to deceive him"; he calls
Gay "such a natural good creature"; and he excuses Fielding's
lapses in taste on the grounds of what he calls his "vast health."

Though Thackeray does not try to suggest that there is a
single key to the method by which all this naturalness is conveyed through language, he does make it clear that the public
display of private emotion is not what he had in mind. His
harshest criticism is reserved for Sterne and not, as is sometimes
supposed, primarily because of Sterne's bawdy humor, but because of his habitual parading of sentiment. "A perilous trade,
indeed, is that of a man who has to bring his tears and laughter,
his recollections, his personal griefs and joys, his private thoughts

---

3. Thackeray's "common man" was, of course, a middle-class creature, not a pauper or laborer. In *Roundabout Papers* he laughs at those
who would "portify" themselves, that is, pretend to be of better vintage
than they are. He calls himself *vin ordinaire,* but does not identify himself with those who have no wine at all.

and feelings to market" (XIV, 665). Thackeray had a horror of self-exposure which extended into his literary judgment. As he goes on to explain in the lecture on Sterne, the peril for the artist who is too intimate with his reader lies in one of two extremes: either he loses all control, all sense of the difference between art and life (Thackeray asks of Sterne, "Where did the lie begin, and did he know where?"), or else the control is so taut as to make the personal effusiveness part of a calculated hoax. In the former case, emotion is reduced to self-pity and art to self-indulgence. But it is the latter view which Thackeray finally adopts toward Sterne: "The humour of Swift and Rabelais, whom he pretended to succeed, poured from them as naturally as song does from a bird . . . But this man . . . is a great jester, not a great humourist. He goes to work systematically and of cold blood" (XIV, 666).

It is important to be sure that a post-Freudian conception of the distinction between wit and humor does not lead to a misinterpretation of Thackeray's point. In his 1928 essay "Humour," Freud argues that wit is the result of a "preconscious thought (being) given over for a moment to unconscious revision. A joke (witticism) is thus the contribution made to the comic by the unconscious. In just the same way, humour would be the contribution made to the comic through the agency of the superego . . . In bringing about the humourous attitude, the superego is actually repudiating reality and serving an illusion . . . It means, 'Look! here is the world, which seems so dangerous! It is nothing but a game for children — just worth making a jest about!' " [4]

For Freud, wit is amoral and, to some degree, discomforting *because* it is spontaneous, irrational, and born of a hidden reality. Humor, on the other hand, rationalizes, moralizes, comforts, and therefore falsifies reality. Thackeray's vocabulary is different from Freud's, and one cannot with precision equate "heart" with "unconscious" and "mind" with "superego." Still, it is clear that in an important respect his psychological assump-

4. Sigmund Freud, "Humour," *The Standard Edition of the Complete Psychological Works of Sigmund Freud*, gen. ed. James Strachey, 24 vols. (London: Hogarth Press, 1961), XXI, 165–166. This essay was written in 1927 and first published in 1928.

tions are the reverse of Freud's. Sterne is a mere jester, a false and immoral wit *because* his works are cool, cerebral calculations. What is good *and* true, in Thackeray's view, usually comes spontaneously and unsystematically from man's heart, not from his brain which is the real source of egocentricity. There is no necessary split between the "felt response" and a good conscience. Indeed, the humorist may be one who is willing to sacrifice logic, structural coherence, and even moral consistency to that principle.

But, of course, to repudiate the value of a systematic use of intellect — even lightheartedly — is to risk chaos or, at the very least, verbal confusion. For poets the risk has always seemed more adventuresome and heroic than it has for novelists, especially novelists with a sense of humor. Thackeray was never in danger of turning into a Blake or a Pound; he was very much in danger of turning into a Barthelme, celebrating his freedom from the extremes of confessional sentimentality and cool rationality by producing warmed-over trivia. What saved him was his great gift for mimicry. He did not have to have a mind and ideas of his own so long as he inhabited other people's. His range and depth may not have been Shakespearian, but his ability to observe human nature, coupled with his willingness to borrow whatever he found useful from other writers, saved him from maudlin egoism and incoherent abstraction.

Thackeray's imitative habits may at times seem in direct contradiction to his diatribes against neo-classicism. Yet, if one follows his circuitous argument closely, it becomes clear that his objections are to pretentiousness and static formalism rather than to imitation in general. He admitted, for example, that there were cases in which an author might truly find a mind congenial to his own among classical writers and therefore best be able to express himself in reference to the works of that writer. He praises Matthew Prior without claiming originality for him: "Horace is always in his mind; and his song, and his philosophy, his good sense, his happy easy turns and melody, his loves and his Epicureanism bear a great resemblance to that most delightful and accomplished master" (XIV, 582).

But, from Thackeray's point of view, few writers have Prior's luck in discovering a perfect soul mate in the past; for others to persist in headlong and solemn imitation was a masquerade of the most foolish and inadvertently farcical sort. Yet Thackeray's alternative was not quite mock-heroic either. He was not sufficiently sure of himself nor fixed in his opinion of ancient and modern writers to carry off a sustained and consistent piece of ironic imitation. His approach to other writers — like his approach to the characters in his novels — is a mixture of whimsy, compassion, respect, ridicule, and affection. According to his own definition, he was a humorist even in his criticism.

Thackeray prefers talking about men to talking about books, and he insists that the crucial question for the critical biographer to ask about his subject is not "what are his works like?" but "would we have liked to live with him?" In the early pages of *The English Humourists* he is up to his familiar trick of trying on various roles, imagining what it would be like to have been the friend of Swift, of Fielding, of Dr. Johnson. Warming to the idea, he writes: "I should like to have been Shakespeare's shoeblack — just to have lived in his house, just to have worshipped him — to have run on his errands." It is the sort of remark which seems to a modern reader to be neither biographical nor critical. One might almost conclude that, despite some misleading labels, all of Thackeray's works are fictions. But it would be more accurate to say that there is no clear boundary between fiction and criticism in Thackeray's prose, that the critic, like the novelist, is continually meandering between evaluation and collaboration, between detachment and sympathy.

The general impression of Thackeray's literary criticism is one of inconsistency and excess. He either praises or blames too much. One reason for this is that, though most of his critical pieces were written for public occasions, many of them are in fact conversations between the artist and himself, a kind of shoptalk in monologue. He may, as he says, go to the lives and works of other writers for moral uplift and so on, but he also goes, like any artist, to learn his craft. The results of such inquiries are more like an artist's sketchbook than like a sustained piece of academic criticism. It would be a mistake to interpret his denunciation of certain writers as a sign that he wished to disregard their work. There is a wonderful story in *Roundabout*

Papers about his being asked to admire the work of an American sculptor who had never seen a statue. Thackeray got himself in trouble with the American press for saying that looking at other statues would have done the man no harm.

For all his impatience with certain kinds of imitativeness, Thackeray most definitely believed in looking at other men's "statues." But if we wish to know what he thought of another writer's style, we should look not at what he says about it or its author, but at how he treats (and mistreats) it in his own prose. The quality and resonance of an echo must be considered, not the solidity of a critical formulation. *Novels By Eminent Hands* are humorous imitations rather than strict parodies, because in them Thackeray was studying his art as well as lampooning the habits of other writers. There is a warming to the very mannerisms which are selected for ridicule, even a kind of collaboration, because the humorist could not quite keep his curiosity and sympathy out of the picture.

It is therefore a mistake to dismiss the fictional burlesques as mere barbs aimed at authors whom Thackeray disliked. Though each author parodied by Thackeray obviously possessed traits which he found amusing, each also provided him with techniques he adapted to his own purposes in his fiction. The burlesques are entertainments, but they are also critical statements and laboratories in which Thackeray tested his powers. Among those parodied are Disraeli, Fenimore Cooper, Mrs. Gore, G. P. R. James, and Charles Lever. Two of the most distinctive pieces are one based on Bulwer-Lytton's *Eugene Aram* and one on *Ivanhoe* which, though much longer than any one of the group collected under the heading *Novels By Eminent Hands,* was begun in the same spirit.

Though always fascinated by the works of Bulwer-Lytton, Thackeray found much in them objectionable and silly. He disliked the snobbish Francophilia and forced elegance of *Pelham;* he disliked presumptuous inventions of dialogue between great historical and literary figures, as in *Devereaux* where Bolingbroke, Swift, Pope, Addison, Voltaire, and Condorcet are paraded before the reader in a series of "accidental" encounters with the hero; and he disliked the glorification of vice in the person of a glamorous criminal. All of these Bulwerisms are exaggerated and ridiculed in *George de Barnwell,*[5] but the most amusing and telling aspect of the parody is Thackeray's imitation of Bulwer's style which seeks at the same time to be dramatic and philosophical, sublime and picturesque, classical and modern — all things to all readers.

Thackeray opens his burlesque with a prefatory statement by the author explaining — as Bulwer often liked to — that the seemingly vulgar nature of his subject did not make it unworthy of epic treatment: "Is Odysseus less august in his rags than in his purple? Fate, Passion, Mystery, the Victim, the Avenger, the Hate that harms, the Furies that tear, the Love that bleeds, are not these with us still?" (VIII, 84).

Then, after a long catalogue of the passing parade on the streets of London, the narrator becomes reflective: "And the Philosopher, as he regarded the hot strife and struggle of these Candidates in the race for God, thought with a sigh of the Truthful and the Beautiful, and walked on, melancholy and serene" (VIII, 85).

Thackeray seizes upon Bulwer's inflated language, his meaningless strings of abstractions, his apostrophes and forced alliterations, and shows them as part of one long cliché. The implication is that Bulwer is writing in the mock-heroic vein without knowing it. He is another laughable, humorless Pogson, a maker of shams, except that his condescension is not restricted to the French. From Thackeray's point of view, Bulwer was a literary as well as a social snob. Despite his protestations about writing romances of "real life," he was not primarily interested in common experience or the broad types of human nature in which all men could recognize something of themselves. He explained in the preface to the 1840 edition of *Eugene Aram* that he chose to write about this supposedly benevolent and sensitive criminal because he "presents such an anomaly in human conduct so rare and surprising."

In an article in *Frasers,* Thackeray elaborated upon his objection to Bulwer's persistent quest for the rare and exotic. A young

5. Thackeray took the title and situation of this sketch from George Lillo's play *The London Merchant,* first performed in 1731. Like Aram, Barnwell was a decent man led by circumstances to committing a brutal crime.

English journalist had recently died, and Bulwer had published a long eulogy in which he attributed death to a fever brought on by the young man's refusal to take shelter in a rainstorm and getting "heroically wet through." According to Thackeray, Bulwer went about telling the tale in precisely the wrong way, enveloping "the chief personage in fine words, as statuaries do their sitters in Roman togas," rather than giving the episode fully and "in detail." What Thackeray means by "detail" is partly visual imagery — more of the storm and the color of the man's jacket — but also circumstantial material drawn from the character's life to that point. The situation is thus made interesting not because of any inherent or isolated quality, but because of the way it intersects with the rest of the character's life and the way the pattern of that life may resemble the lives of other men.

There is no doubt that Thackeray had a keen eye for Bulwer's faults, but he saw it as no contradiction for the critic to emulate what he found worthwhile in an imperfect model. The humorist-as-critic retains his notion that life and art are mixed affairs and that the careful observer may often find reason to praise and blame in very nearly the same breath. The true humorist is as wary of the perfect scapegoat as he is of the perfect hero. Thackeray admitted later in his life that he had learned much from Bulwer. But even if he hadn't said so, we might have guessed that his use of historical figures in *Henry Esmond* owes part of its success to a close and critical observation of Bulwer's attempt at the same thing.

Thackeray also enjoys ridiculing Bulwer's philosophical narrator meditating on the follies of humanity; yet, of course, the opening of *Vanity Fair* shows him resorting to the same convention. After describing the noise and confusion of the Fair, the narrator says:

> A man with a reflective turn of mind, walking through an exhibition of this sort, will not be oppressed, I take it, by his own or other people's hilarity . . . but the general impression is one more melancholy than mirthful. When you come home, you sit down in a sober, contemplative, not uncharitable frame of mind,

and apply yourself to your books and your business. I have no
other moral than this to tag to the present story of "Vanity Fair."
(XI, 7)

The relative simplicity of diction and the disclaimer of a
clear moral issue immediately distinguish this passage from a
comparable one by Bulwer. But a subtler and more crucial difference is reflected by the way in which Thackeray switches
smoothly from third person to first to second and back to first
again in such a short space. The narrator here, as throughout
the novel, changes his perspective and tone by slipping like a
salamander from role to role. He may be the stage manager who
manipulates the whole show, or a character as vain and helpless as the others, or an observer just watching the spectacle
with the reader. Bulwer lets himself become frozen in the convention of the melancholy philosopher while Thackeray darts in
and out of it like a quick-change artist.

Thackeray's way of avoiding a pose was to keep moving. He
admired but also mistrusted Scott's "big bow-wow strain," yet
could not sustain the controlled understatement of an Austen
either. His realm — and what he considered to be the realm of
the humorist — lay between heroic drama and comedy. The
humorist forever wavers between laughter and tears. Thackeray
never strikes an emotionally sublime note because his feelings
are continually qualifying and diluting one another. *Rebecca and
Rowena* is one of his most curious and, in some ways, most instructive critical imitations because it contains such an un-
coordinated mixture of modes and tones. It is part sequel, part
parody, and part meditation. The terms takeoff and put-on —
which sound like opposites, but aren't — suggest the nature of
Thackeray's peculiar approach to Scott. There is an air of
whimsy and fraud throughout the piece, which sometimes parallels and sometimes entangles itself with a serious putting on of
the very costumes and conventions which are being mocked. It
is a less successful variant on the puppet theater theme in *Vanity
Fair* which can, by contrast, make other episodes in the book
appear more like life.

Many of the reservations he had about Bulwer as a novelist,

Thackeray had about Scott as well. The static descriptions, the hero worship, the false archaisms struck him as being silly. Thackeray liked to think in terms of probabilities and demanded that even characters in novels should occasionally reveal a bit of common sense. If Ivanhoe had had any sense, for example, he obviously would not have settled for the bloodless and vapid Rowena but would have married the intelligent, virtuous, and beautiful Rebecca. The piece contains a good deal of fun at the expense of Scott and the fashion of Romantic medievalism, but it also contains many passages of straightforward adventure narrative, and it concludes on a pathetic note about the early deaths of the heroine and hero which is quite extraordinary for a so-called parody.

The work is so rich in itself that one might take it up at almost any point and learn much about Thackeray as a humorist. Of particular interest is the way it reveals Thackeray's use of humor in order to explore the possibilities of historical fiction. One of the major problems facing the writer of historical novels — and one which Thackeray did not think Scott had adequately solved — was to evoke the atmosphere of another era while, at the same time, making the characters and events credible to contemporary readers. Scott's habit of mixing archaic and pseudo-archaic language with colloquial expressions of his own time was to Thackeray a constant source of amusement. Rather than endowing the past with an authentic vitality, it created a stage setting peopled by characters who seemed to forget their lines from time to time and say things in their own words and accents. Even the prompter or narrator was often guilty, as can be seen in Thackeray's imitation of Scott describing Ivanhoe leaving his castle for battle:

> Then Ivanhoe's trumpet blew: then Rowena waved her pocket handkerchief; then the household gave a shout; then the pursuivant of the good knight, Sir Wilfrid the Crusader, flung out his banner (which was argent, a gules cramoisy with three Moors impaled sable): then Wamba gave a lash on his mule's haunch, and Ivanhoe, heaving a great sigh, turned the tail of his warhorse upon the castle of his fathers.
>
> As they rode along the forest, they met Athelstane the Thane.

powdering along the road in the direction of Rotherwood on his great dray-horse of a charger. "Goodbye, good luck to you, old brick," cried the Prince, using the vernacular Saxon. "Pitch into those Frenchmen; give it 'em over the face and eyes; and I'll stop at home and take care of Mrs. I."

(X, 509–510)

The humor here is a bit too obvious — but, among other things, Thackeray is playing with words and moods, making discord almost too easily but listening through it for the possibilities of harmony. One of the lessons Thackeray learned from Scott's successes as well as his failures was not to strive too feverishly for the antique effect. His reasoning is the same as that which we come upon again and again in his dissertations on the imitative possibilties of art. The imitation, however conscientiously attempted, will simply not match the original. The more earnest and exact the writer tries to be, the more awkward and apparent will be his failure. The artist must remain sufficiently conscious of the representational nature of his art so that he will not deceive himself into trying to make it do what it never can.

In accepting the limitations of language and of all literary conventions, the humorist is able to free himself from wasting his energy on the wrong problems — that is, the ones he cannot solve. Similarly, the historical novelist who realizes that he cannot "recreate" another age may free his imagination to play with its shadows, to hint and evoke rather than to repeat. The success of *Henry Esmond* is the result of many things, but surely one of them is the tactful and unobtrusive way in which Thackeray suggests the style of Augustan English without attempting an exact copy of it. One recognizes a tone, a cadence, here and there a word or phrase, but the attention is never stopped by it. One way to describe the achievement is to say that it would be impossible to parody.

One could go on citing the ways in which Thackeray put humor to work for him outside of the novels, but the pattern already emerges clearly enough. The humorous imitation — whether of a foreigner or a fellow novelist — is the epitome of the qualified response, the art of making up your mind and then changing it. Thackeray's criticism is nearly always tempered

by sympathy, his sentimentality undercut by irony. But everywhere in his work the voice of the mimic can be heard. In the
early sketches the fun seems to be for its own sake, but soon the
adoption and exaggeration of accents and gestures becomes a
way for the artist to draw near his subject without identifying
himself with it altogether. Thackeray came to see that a momentary flash of truth may be captured indirectly by edging up
to things and treating them obliquely. And the only way he
knew of keeping the approximation from absorbing and reducing the reality was continually to change it. In his criticism and
short sketches as well as in his novels, he threw exactness and
consistency to the winds and aimed, like most great humorists,
at the variety and energy of life — "the great aggregate experience" — rather than at its meaning abstractly conceived.

Thackeray's imitative mode is rarely simple or purely negative. Some of the traits he most enjoyed lampooning in Bulwer-
Lytton and Scott show up in altered form in his own novels.
But then, he would have been willing to admit that the humorist
must be a persistent and shameless scavenger if he is to keep
his devices varied and changing. Almost any old trick will do
if it is not allowed to stand so long as to become stale. Harlequin can console himself that his art is in a serious relation to
life only if he resists the rigidity which comes of growing too
fond of one mask. Then he can achieve what George Eliot called
"that wonderful and delicious mixture of fun, fancy, philosophy,
and feeling, which constitutes modern humour." [6]

6. *Works of George Eliot,* IX, 220.

JOEL PORTE

Transcendental Antics

I have long nourished a desire — shared, I suspect, by other students of Transcendentalism — to compile what might be called an irreverent anthology of Transcendental humor; to make a collection of writings by and about adherents to the school that would expose the light side of the movement and thus provide some hours of comic relief for sober students of intellectual history. But let me expand a bit on the possible value of such a compilation. I want to suggest that the light-hearted approach to Transcendentalism may be one of the best, as well as one of the most pleasant, ways to understand it. There is, of course, a certain measure of policy in the tactic I am adopting here, since I agree with Lord Bacon that "it is good in discourse and speech of conversation to vary and intermingle . . . jest with earnest, for it is a dull thing to tire"; and nothing indeed can be more tiresome than a large dose of Transcendentalism unrelieved by any glimmer of comedy. As Thoreau noted in his essay on Carlyle, "transcendental philosophy needs the leaven of humor to render it light and digestible."

But, policy aside, I would insist that the comic impulse is a significant component of Transcendentalism: for its abundant presence within the movement itself testifies to a self-awareness,

a self-criticism, an ability to see oneself in the round, a fundamental balance and sanity, which are important characteristics of
the great burgeoning of American consciousness we know as
Transcendentalism. And let me add that the susceptibility of
Transcendentalism to comic criticism from the outside is
equally important as a reminder that the beliefs and postures of
members of the group were frequently, nay usually, extravagant;
and extravagance — that quality which Thoreau prayed for —
easily lends itself to exaggeration and caricature. But it is also
a sign of passion and commitment, of fervent searching and
large need to express oneself loudly, and these things, I need
hardly say, lie at the heart of the Transcendental ferment. From
our point of view, moreover, the ease with which Transcendentalism lent itself to critical lampooning makes such comic
criticism an especially useful historical tool, since it brings many
of the salient characteristics of the movement into high relief.
But enough of prelude. "To use too many circumstances ere
one come to the matter," as Bacon observes, "is wearisome."
Let us turn directly to an antic portrait of Concord on the
Merrymake and environs.

I shall begin with the retrospective glance of a contemporary
— a portrait etched in acid from the pen of James Russell
Lowell in 1865. Casting his thoughts back some thirty years,
Lowell was reminded of the Boston publication of *Sartor
Resartus,* and he asserted that Carlyle's "sermon on Falstaff's
text of the miserable forked radish gave the signal for a sudden
mental and moral mutiny . . . On all hands with every variety
of emphasis, and by voices of every conceivable pitch, representing the three sexes of men, women, and Lady Mary Wortley
Montagues," Lowell continued — with a slighting allusion to the
birth of the American bluestocking — on all hands the cry went
out that the time of the Newness had come.

> The nameless eagle of the tree Ygdrasil was about to sit at last,
> and wild-eyed enthusiasts rushed from all sides, each eager to
> thrust under the mystic bird that chalk egg from which the
> new and fairer Creation was to be hatched in due time . . .
> Every possible form of intellectual and physical dyspepsia brought
> forth its gospel. Bran had its prophets, and the presartorial sim-

plicity of Adam its martyrs . . . Everybody had a mission (with a capital M) to attend to everybody else's business. No brain but had its private maggot, which must have found pitiably short commons sometimes. Not a few impecunious zealots abjured the use of money (unless earned by other people), professing to live on the internal revenues of the spirit. Some had an assurance of instant millennium so soon as hooks and eyes should be substituted for buttons. Communities were established where everything was to be common but common sense. Men renounced their old gods, and hesitated only whether to bestow their furloughed allegiance on Thor or Budh. Conventions were held for every hitherto inconceivable purpose . . . All stood ready at a moment's notice to reform everything but themselves.[1]

Lowell's description, despite its personal animus and precisely because of its splendid if splenetic sense of comedy, brings clearly before us some of the major impulses, as well as some of the important problems, involved in the ferment of the 1830's and forties. Crusaders burning to remake the world pinned their hopes on dietary reform or the removal of restrictions in dress; others saw the crass commercialism of the State Street bankers as the chief evil of the time. "The Americans have little faith," Emerson told his audience in 1841; "they rely on the power of a dollar" [2] — and five years later this lament was expanded into Theodore Parker's thundering jeremiad, "A Sermon of Merchants." Lowell also reminds us of the strength of the communitarian impulse, the hungry search for meaningful society; and his facetious mention of Thor and Budh only underlines what scarcely needs emphasis — namely, that the Transcendental movement had its birth in a profound religious upheaval.

Here I should like to draw a parallel that I think is too often overlooked by historians of Transcendentalism. I want to suggest a connection between the seriocomic religious fervor of Transcendental reform and that passionate wave of religious

---

1. "Thoreau," in *The Shock of Recognition,* ed. Edmund Wilson (New York: Modern Library, 1955), pp. 229–230.

2. See "Man the Reformer," in *Nature, Addresses, and Lectures* (Boston, 1890), p. 237.

revival which characterized American religion at large during the first half of the nineteenth century. I believe that both impulses were radically allied, equally expressive of forces deeply rooted in the American character, and equal sources of native American humor. "The dominant theme in America from 1800 to 1860," writes Perry Miller in *The Life of the Mind in America,* "is the invincible persistence of the revival technique . . . We can hardly understand Emerson, Thoreau, Whitman, Melville, unless we comprehend that for them this was the one clearly given truth of their society." [3] The "revolution" of 1800–1801, writes Alan Heimert — referring to the Second Great Awakening — "reawakened the evangelical hope of the great community . . . a nineteenth century in which humanity's social arrangements would be perfected." [4]

This hope, of course, was also that of the Transcendental reformers; and their community of aspiration and attitude with the Awakening — the connection between revival and reform — is nowhere better illustrated, and its problems suggested, than by a section of Constance Rourke's classic study of *American Humor.* I should like to quote at length a passage which seems to me worthy of the widest currency and which points expertly in the direction of some of the notions I am attempting to develop in this essay. The movement of revivalism, writes Miss Rourke, "was away from creeds and close formulas, toward improvisation, rapturous climaxes, happy assurances, and a choral strain. In the revivals of Methodism and the other free new faiths all was generic, large, and of the crowd; in the end all was wildly hopeful. Rhapsody was common; the monologue in the experience meeting unfolded those inner fantasies toward which the native mind was tending in other, quite different aspects of expression, not in the analytic forms of Calvinism, but as pure unbridled fantasy and exuberant overflow." And she continues:

The pattern of comedy appeared again in the innumerable cults which sprang up in the '30's and '40's as from some rich and

3. *The Life of the Mind in America: From the Revolution to the Civil War* (New York: Harcourt, Brace and World, 1965), p. 7.
4. *Religion and the American Mind: From the Great Awakening to the Revolution* (Cambridge, Mass.: Harvard University Press, 1966), p. 544.

fertile seeding-ground. Religious and social traditions were flung to the four winds. The perfectionists declared that the bondage of sin was non-existent and that the Millennium had already begun. At Oneida the bonds of earthly marriage were broken. Spiritualism proposed to break the bonds of death. The theme of death, which had been a deep preoccupation in the life of the pioneer, was repeated by these cults, with a fresh and happy outcome. Life was to be prolonged, the Millennium had arrived; in the state of perfection death might never come at all. Most of the new religious communities created almost overnight in the '30's and '40's agreed to release mankind from sin, poverty, or mortal care. They all possessed formulas, religious, economic, or social; and they all anticipated conclusions such as the world had never known. Triumph was their note . . . Hysterical, wrapped in a double sense of national feeling and religious conviction, the believers passed into moods of wildest exaltation. "New, new . . . make all things new." The enchanting cry resounded through all this ecstasy of faith.[5]

Here I want briefly to break off my quotation from Miss Rourke's book to juxtapose some sentences from Emerson. Explaining in his lecture "The Transcendentalist" what were called "new views" in New England, Emerson said that "Transcendentalism is the Saturnalia or excess of Faith" and announced that newness was to be the order of the day: "I do not wish to do one thing but once. I do not love routine." [6] These mingled themes of newness and ecstasy had already been iterated and reiterated gaily by Emerson and Margaret Fuller in their high-spirited introduction to the first number of the *Dial*. Announcing a "new design" in their opening sentence, they called theirs "a Journal in a new spirit," the voice of those making "new demands on literature," eager to express "new views." Drawing on "the conversation of fervid and mystical pietists," on a faith "earnest and profound," the *Dial* would express "a new hope," open "a new scope for literature and art," and ultimately through its perpetually innovational criticism cast "a new light on the whole world." [7]

5. *American Humor* (Garden City, N.Y.: Doubleday Anchor, 1953), pp. 111–112.
6. In *Nature, Addresses, and Lectures,* pp. 320, 330.
7. The *Dial,* 1, no. 1 (July 1840), 1–4.

Thus does the cry of the cults described by Miss Rourke —
"New, new . . . make all things new" — echo through Transcendental writing. And she continues:

> Among all these cults a latent humor broke out; this was clear
> in the names which they chose or accepted, such as the placidly
> humorous variations on Harmony and the grotesque nomencla-
> ture of the Shakers, Groaners, Come Outers, New Lights, Hard
> Shell Baptists, and Muggletonians . . . A wide level of comic
> feeling had been established, sometimes infused with pliant
> hope, most often with exuberance. Frequently it was hard to
> tell when burlesque was involved, when fakery, when a serious
> intention. The basic feeling was romantic, but it crested into a
> conscious gaiety which raced beyond the romantic. Even in the
> most ponderous of these assertions there was something light-
> hearted.[8]

Now this comic extravagance inherent in and common to
American revivalism, religious cultism, and Transcendentalism
clearly assumes in Miss Rourke's discussion the character of a
perennial national habit or mood, the expression of something
fundamental in the American spirit. First, of course, there is the
idea of how necessary has been the cultivation — indeed, the
exaggeration — of hope in a land where almost everything had
to be done from scratch, whether because of the actual thinness
of American culture and tradition or because of the programmatic assertion that life in the new world had to be purely self-
defined and self-generating. Great hope was needed to sustain a
perpetually unrealized and perhaps unrealizable dream of social
and religious perfectability; and perhaps just such a great and
constantly renewed hope was the almost conscious counter-
weight to a gnawing fear that the needful energy or spirit might
flag or disappear. Secondly, the humor associated with religious
and spiritual movements in America since the declension of the
true Bible commonwealth — since the loss, that is, of the
Calvinistic ideal — suggests an anxiety that is being shuffled off
in nervous, if not hysterical, laughter: an anxiety about losing
the true faith, an anxiety about traducing one's forefathers,
one's traditions, those institutions and beliefs that one still half

8. *American Humor*, pp. 112–113.

believes in. The American genius for creating new religions and cults and for throwing oneself into them with exaggerated intensity is matched by a characteristic comic awareness that incessant newness, the perpetual casting off of yesterday's ideas and institutions, is a near-relation to faddism and folly. The impassioned American cry is for something ever new and better, and the American comic response to that answered prayer represents an awareness that the promised perfection is and must always be short of its promise. But the possibility that foolishness or even fakery may crown the irrepressible American effort to regenerate or reform must not be taken as a sign of failure or loss of heart. On the contrary, as Miss Rourke suggests in her statement about how the comic exuberance of American revivalism and cultism "crested into a conscious gaiety which raced beyond the romantic," the very consciousness of gaiety is a final mark of sanity — a guarantee that wild improvisation and romantic delusion are always being counterbalanced and corrected by amused self-awareness. Thus, the ultimate value of American spiritual experimentation may lie in precisely the kind of sharpened perspective and insight that its comedy foments.

There is probably no better example of this sort of fruitful interplay between extravagant action or thought to which one is committed and a simultaneous awareness of comedy than that provided by the Transcendental ferment. Here, finally, American religious fervor broke the mold of formalized religion, and the passion for reform exhausted the available channels of reformation. The result, at its best, was a literature of witty observation and reflection that has scarcely been surpassed since. And having said that, I must return to Emerson, one of the great American masters of combining participation with ironic detachment. A good place to begin is his own *Dial* essay, "The Comic":

If the essence of the comic be the contrast in the intellect between the idea and the false performance, there is good reason why we should be affected by the exposure. We have no deeper interest than our integrity, and that we should be made aware by joke and by stroke of any lie that we entertain. Besides, a perception of the comic seems to be a balance-wheel in our metaphysical structure. It appears to be an essential element in a fine character. Wherever the intellect is constructive, it will be found. We feel the absence of it as a defect in the noblest and most oracular soul. . . . The perception of the comic is a tie of sympathy with other men, is a pledge of sanity, and is a protection from those perverse tendencies and gloomy insanities into which fine intellects sometimes lose themselves.[9]

Emerson himself offers us many pledges of his own sanity, examples of how he attempted to enforce the integrity of his being by dissociating himself — now slightly, now pointedly — through gentle humor or mild satire, from some of the more egregious follies of the Transcendental brotherhood. But what is to be noticed is the sharp distinction between Lowell's ill-tempered lampoon of what he considered to be little more than a spiritual disease, and Emerson's delicately managed comic portraits. For Emerson, the perception of the comic side of Transcendentalism was indeed a way of re-asserting his ties of sympathy with other, non-Transcendental men; but he clearly had no intention thereby of denying the bonds of mutual affection and concern that allied him to those fine, though occasionally extreme, intellects among whom he would always be numbered. Leaving the Transcendental club, Emerson could sometimes hear, as others of the group perhaps could not, the voice of nature whispering, "So hot? my little Sir." [10] But this perception of the disparity between the placid calm of nature and the fret and fume of Transcendental disputation, and the comic statement to which such perception gave rise, would not usually cause Emerson to forget or disparage the moral, artistic, or spiritual fervor that produced the heat.

But lest my argument grow too solemn, let me offer some good examples of Emersonian comedy playing over the vagaries of Transcendental reform. Reporting in the *Dial* for July 1842 on "a Convention of Friends of Universal Reform" (otherwise known as the Chardon Street and Bible Conventions), Emerson noted the presence of "men of every shade of opinion, from the

9. In the *Dial,* 4, no. 2 (October 1843), 250.
10. See "Spiritual Laws," in *Essays First Series* (Boston, 1884), p. 129.

straitest orthodoxy to the wildest heresy, and many persons whose church was a church of one member only" and then allowed himself to sketch a consciously humorous portrait of the gathering: "A great variety of dialect and of costume was noticed; a great deal of confusion, eccentricity, and freak appeared, as well as of zeal and enthusiasm. If the assembly was disorderly, it was picturesque. Madmen, madwomen, men with beards, Dunkers, Muggletonians, Come-Outers, Groaners, Agrarians, Seventh-day-Baptists, Quakers, Abolitionists, Calvinists, Unitarians, and Philosophers, — all came successively to the top, and seized their moment, if not their *hour,* wherein to chide, or pray, or preach, or protest." [11]

Carrying the idea of Democratic equality (one man one vote) to its comic conclusion, Emerson has Calvinists and madmen rubbing shoulders — through subtle inference and comic juxtaposition reducing them, as it were, all to one level. In this "Anacharsis Clootz deputation," to use Melville's phrase, tradition and eccentricity have equal rights, but neither has any special privilege. All have the same right to rise momentarily out of the disorderly assembly and try to be heard, but does *this* — Emerson's comic voice seems finally to say to us — constitute an example of the great community? Or of any community at all? A few well-known sentences from *Moby Dick* are especially apposite here: "They were nearly all Islanders in the Pequod, *Isolatoes* too, I call such, not acknowledging the common continent of men, but each *Isolato* living on a separate continent of his own. Yet now, federated along one keel, what a set these Isolatoes were!" What a set indeed is Emerson's nineteenth-century American circus of opinion, and his humor quietly expresses the same uneasiness that laces Melville's sentences. Is this unstable federation really an ecumenical council, or simply a grotesque collection of isolated individuals — "persons whose church was a church of one member only" — who have come to speak but not truly to listen, and who will depart as separate and alone as they have come? Emerson's description of the Chardon Street Convention continues, it must be admitted, in a generally optimistic fashion, but it is surely no exaggeration

11. "Chardon Street and Bible Conventions," in the *Dial,* 3, no. 1 (July 1842), 101.

to see in his humor here a clear sign of that growing distrust of Transcendental reform and ebullient hope that was increasingly to characterize his writing, as well as Thoreau's and that of such demi-Transcendentalists as Hawthorne and Melville. For all of these men, the humor of Transcendentalism became a judgment on the extravagance of its promises — and, perhaps, on the promise of American life generally.

The growth of Emerson's distrust, at all events, is not hard to document. Scarcely two years after reporting on the Chardon Street Convention, he delivered a lecture on "New England Reformers" in which his humor, now sharpened into mild satire, had grown into a pervasive mood of bemused detachment. Speaking of those who had attended the many reform meetings and conventions, he wrote: "They defied each other, like a congress of kings, each of whom had a realm to rule, and a way of his own that made concert unprofitable." The democratic picturesqueness of Chardon Street has become the despotic determination of each to have his own way; and Emerson now views the zeal and enthusiasm of New England reformers as almost pure folly. He continues:

> What a fertility of projects for the salvation of the world! One apostle thought all men should go to farming, and another that no man should buy or sell, that the use of money was the cardinal evil; another that the mischief was in our diet, that we eat and drink damnation. These made unleavened bread, and were foes to the death to fermentation. It was in vain urged by the housewife that God made yeast, as well as dough, and loves fermentation just as dearly as he loves vegetation; that fermentation develops the saccharine element in the grain, and makes it more palatable and more digestible. No; they wish the pure wheat, and will die but it shall not ferment. Stop, dear Nature, these incessant advances of thine; let us scotch these ever-rolling wheels! Others attacked the system of agriculture, the use of animal manures in farming, and the tyranny of man over brute nature; these abuses polluted his food. The ox must be taken from the plough and the horse from the cart, the hundred acres of the farm must be spaded, and the man must walk, wherever boats and locomotives will not carry him. Even the insect world was to be defended — that had been too long neglected, and a

society for the protection of ground-worms, slugs and mosquitos was to be incorporated without delay. With these appeared the adepts of homeopathy, of hydropathy, of mesmerism, of phrenology.[12]

On and on goes Emerson's list of the things that were attacked as being the source of all evil — law, trade, manufacturing, the clergy, academia, marriage — but the conclusion of his wonderfully witty thrust is surprising indeed: the result of this "din of opinion and debate" which he has so wonderfully made sport of he claims to be good, for it asserts "the sufficiency of the private man." The reader, it seems to me, has more justification for feeling that Emerson's treatment of this din of opinion and debate insists rather on the sufficient foolishness of private idiosyncrasy and group hobbyhorses. And so it turns out to be, for the body of his lecture expresses a deep disillusionment with most methods of reform and a belief only in individual *character*. Not the excesses he has pilloried, but rather the humorous detachment — exemplified by his own handling of these things — which sees the world in perspective truly asserts "the sufficiency of the private man." "They are partial," Emerson argues of reformers further on in the lecture; "they are not equal to the work they pretend. They lose their way; in the assault on the kingdom of darkness they expend all their energy on some accidental evil, and lose their sanity and power of benefit. It is of little moment that one or two or twenty errors of our social system be corrected, but of much that the man be in his senses."

Clearly, the only method of reform that Emerson believes in, the only way of forcing men back into their senses, is the use of his own special brand of literary drollery — that Emersonian voice of near-comic exhortation: "Do not be so vain of your one objection. Do you think there is only one? Alas! my good friend, there is no part of society or of life better than any other part. All our things are right and wrong together. The wave of evil washes all our institutions alike. Do you complain of our Marriage? Our marriage is no worse than our education, our

12. This and other quotations below from "New England Reformers," in *Essays Second Series* (Boston, 1897), pp. 240–270.

diet, our trade, our social customs. Do you complain of the laws of Property? It is a pedantry to give such importance to them. Can we not play the game of life with these counters, as well as with those?"

I suppose there is no denying that Emerson's posture of comic detachment here verges on something close to existential discouragement or even despair. It seems that the habitual perception of humor had itself become Emerson's major defense and the only method of Transcendental reform he still believed in: a conscious gaiety that transformed Transcendental crotchets into whimsical insights and Transcendental querulousness into valuable, if painful, satiric thrusts. "What is it we heartily wish of each other?" Emerson continues. "Is it to be pleased and flattered? No, but to be convicted and exposed, to be shamed out of our nonsense of all kinds, and made men of, instead of ghosts and phantoms. We are weary of gliding ghostlike throughout the world, which is itself so slight and unreal. We crave a sense of reality, though it comes in strokes of pain." Emerson's comic unmasking of folly is his ultimate Transcendental weapon — painful to the point of existential anguish — as it is the major weapon of other great Transcendental writers. This passage from "New England Reformers" clearly looks forward to another satiric thrust, that almost morbid twist of Thoreau's knife in *Walden,* which is meant to impart life though its antic maneuvers toy with death: "If you stand right fronting and face to face to a fact, you will see the sun glimmer on both its surfaces, as if it were a cimeter, and feel its sweet edge dividing you through the heart and marrow, and so you will happily conclude your mortal career. Be it life or death, we crave only reality. If we are really dying, let us hear the rattle in our throats and feel cold in the extremities; if we are alive, let us go about our business." [13]

Well, the chief business of much Transcendental writing and of the criticism which it directly — indeed, defiantly — inspired was precisely that of convicting and exposing folly, of shaming the world out of its nonsense. And such reform had of course to begin at home. Time and time again, the Transcendentalists, and

13. From the penultimate paragraph of "Where I lived, and What I lived for."

those who remained warily on the fringes of the group, lampooned the extravagances that they mostly all shared — as if to demonstrate that imaginative excess coupled with the ability comically to deflate one's own excesses were the twin characteristics which, precisely through their inseparability, defined the special quality of the intellectual spirit of the times. Melville, for example, alternately attracted and repelled by Transcendentalism, embodied his ambivalent attitude toward the movement in the wide spectrum of his comic response to the Newness — broadly humorous in *Mardi, Moby Dick,* and *Pierre,* but poignantly — almost despairingly — funny in "Bartleby the Scrivener" and savagely satiric in *The Confidence-Man.* Melville chided these "new-light" Apostles, with their "Pythagorean and Shelleyan dietings on apple-parings [and] dried prunes," who "went about huskily muttering the Kantian Categories through teeth and lips dry and dusty as any miller's, with the crumbs of Graham crackers"; but his humor was explicitly meant as a tribute. "Let me here offer up three locks of my hair," Melville exclaimed with gently mocking praise in *Pierre,* "to the memory of all such glorious paupers who have lived and died in this world. Surely, and truly I honor them — noble men often at bottom — and for that very reason I make bold to be gamesome about them; for where fundamental nobleness is, and fundamental honor is due, merriment is never accounted irreverent. The fools and pretenders of humanity, and the imposters and baboons among the gods, these only are offended with raillery." [14] Despite his decidedly irreverent pun on "bottom," Melville had no fear of offending the true Transcendental masters because he knew that what was valuable and noble in them was finally beyond the reach of raillery. Besides, *their* comic self-awareness of folly often easily overmatched his own efforts at friendly satire.

What, in fact, was Transcendentalism at its best, if not a willingness to risk hyperbolic foolishness in the service of truth? Hawthorne could complain good-naturedly of Concord that "never was a poor country village infested with such a variety of queer, strangely dressed, oddly behaved mortals," but he as-

14. *Pierre: Or, the Ambiguities,* ed. Henry A. Murray (New York: Hendricks House, 1949), p. 314.

serted equally: "It was the very spot in which to utter the extremest nonsense or the profoundest wisdom, or that ethereal product of the mind which partakes of both, and may become one or the other, in correspondence with the faith and insight of the auditor." [15] Emerson certainly knew, when he published that first, momentous book in 1836, that his description of himself as a transparent eyeball was comically overdone; but the risk of self-mockery was the price — indeed, the guarantee — of making a serious point with sufficient emphasis. Emerson's object was to convince his audience that spiritual rebirth was contingent on their opening their eyes, literally, to the great new world which was their birthright. Needing more than anything else to behold God and nature face to face, they had — like Emerson — to become transparent eyeballs and *see all*. Then, and only then, would their true *prospects* (the title of the last section of *Nature*) come into focus. "So shall we come to look at the world with new eyes," he concluded headily, insisting that unclouded perception — both *sight* and *insight* — could perform the miracle of turning visions into reality.

Because Emerson's major purpose was to force the sluggard intellect of America to "look from under its iron lids," he had to enact the meaning of his essay by becoming a metaphoric eyeball, even at the risk of seeming silly. Or perhaps becoming metaphorically foolish was the only way of underscoring — indeed, publicizing — his point. Christopher Cranch's now well known and splendidly funny caricature of Emerson as a wide-eyed visual organ on legs takes the author up on his own implicit offer to seem ridiculous. But in this case, to Emerson's ultimate advantage, exaggeration and truth enforce one another, and Emerson's meaning is made certain. Indeed, he would later, in his *Poems* of 1846, reiterate and make further use of this comic self-portrait, ironically allegorizing himself as Uriel, the archangel of the sun, whose "piercing eye" with its "look that solved the sphere" made the stern old Unitarian war gods shudder and helped destroy their bland and complacent Paradise.

Few readers may have noted and truly appreciated the significant comedy of Emerson's eyeball humor, but it was not lost

15. See "The Old Manse," in *Mosses from an Old Manse*.

on Henry Thoreau, who continued the jocular tradition in his first book. James Russell Lowell must have been in a particularly dour mood when he wrote, with surprising imperceptivity, that "Thoreau had no humor." [16] But I wonder how many readers of *A Week on the Concord and Merrimack Rivers* have noticed that Thoreau turned Emerson's own favorite literary device against his master when he waggishly "attacked" Emerson in the "Sunday" section of the book:

What earth or sea, mountain or stream, or Muses' spring or grove, is safe from his all-searching ardent eye, who drives off Phoebus' beaten track, visits unwonted zones, makes the gelid Hyperboreans glow, and the old polar serpent writhe, and many a Nile flow back and hide his head! [Then Thoreau broke into a mock-heroic paean.]

> That Phaeton of our day,
> Who'd make another milky way,
> And burn the world up with his ray;
>
> By us an undisputed seer—
> Who'd drive his flaming car so near
> Unto our shuddering mortal sphere,
>
> Disgracing all our slender worth,
> And scorching up the living earth,
> To prove his heavenly birth.
>
> The silver spokes, the golden tire,
> Are glowing with unwonted fire,
> And ever nigher roll and nigher;
>
> The pins and axle melted are,
> The silver radii fly afar,
> Ah, he will spoil his Father's car!
>
> Who let him have the steeds he cannot steer?
> Henceforth the sun will not shine for a year;
> And we shall Ethiops all appear.

From *his* [quoting Emerson's poem "The Problem"]

> "lips of cunning fell
> The thrilling Delphic oracle."

16. "Thoreau," *Shock of Recognition*, p. 238.

And yet, sometimes,

> We should not mind if on our ear there fell
> Some less of cunning, more of oracle.

"It is Apollo shining in your face," Thoreau concluded. "O rare Contemporary, let us have far-off heats. Give us the subtler, the heavenlier though fleeting beauty . . . Let epic trade-winds blow, and cease this waltz of inspirations."

It is hard to know where to begin unraveling the complications of Thoreau's wit here. He starts, of course, by hyperbolically verifying the justice of Emerson's metaphoric representation of himself as an "ardent eye," but then Thoreau's humor turns into an expression of anxiety over the danger that this "undisputed seer" may permanently outshine all other Concord literary lights; whence Thoreau accuses the local Apollo of being too clever and smooth in his inspirational music. "Let epic trade-winds blow," exclaims the younger man with over-inflated metaphoric grandeur, commencing to aim his wit against himself as his attack on Emerson turns into a comic advertisement for Ulysses D. Thoreau on the way up — since, naturally, an excellent example of the kind of rough heroic literature being advocated is Thoreau's book itself, an oracular chronicle of Henry the Navigator's brave voyage up these mysterious inland rivers. But, of course, the joke is quite obviously and consciously on Thoreau himself, for his epic journey is no more than a gentle jaunt from Concord to Concord; and the joke will once again be on this self-styled great adventurer when his next contribution to the world's heroic literature documents an errand into the wilderness of Walden Pond — otherwise identifiable as neighbor Emerson's woodlot. Thus, in the very act of lampooning Emerson's own comic literary tactics, Thoreau continues the Transcendental tradition of shrewd and effective self-parody learned from his mentor.

Examples could be multiplied, but I trust my point is sufficiently clear. The Transcendental persuasion, as I see it, was very largely an antic persuasion — an American Renaissance and Reformation of the spirit that owed much of its force to humor. It was a romantic movement endowed with a conscious gaiety that raced beyond the romantic into that supernal realm where the silly and the solemn meet and merge to produce something that begins to resemble truth. Although the comedy of Transcendentalism has often been represented as little more than a merely parochial humorous outburst — Henry James called it "a kind of Puritan carnival" that "produced no fruit" [17] — it was the kind of inevitable comedy that arises from the tensions of a deeply serious human debate. In this case, the debate itself was carried on largely in the spirit of revel. Much of its fruit was therefore unusually sweet — or bittersweet — and it has not all been harvested yet.

17. "Emerson," in *The Art of Fiction and Other Essays* (New York: Oxford University Press, 1948), p. 236.

WALTER BLAIR

"A Man's Voice, Speaking": A Continuum in American Humor

After spending nearly four years in various sections of the country, Frances Trollope reported in *Domestic Manners of the Americans* (1832) that she had found gaiety nowhere. Saturnine natives begrudged pennies they had to pay to see comedies; humorous publications failed; she looked in vain for "keenly cutting satire" which amputated bad taste and dullness. But updating her book in 1839, the lady inserted a footnote warning that her accusations "must never be repeated": America at last had produced writings that "prove, much beyond . . . contradiction, that humour, rich and original, does exist in the United States, and . . . when such a treat is given them, the people know how to enjoy it." [1]

Mrs. Trollope forecast a pattern: time and again American humor would be declared nonexistent or defunct, only to hop from its deathbed and discredit mourners. E. C. Stedman in 1873 announced the funeral; James T. Thurber did the same

1. Ed. Donald Smalley (New York: Alfred A. Knopf, 1949), pp. 209–210, 305, 324.

in 1962 and Melvin Maddocks in 1970.[2] Looking back, one
sees that often viewers-with-alarm simply failed to recognize
our humor in some new guise. In 1832 it had an unfamiliar
look because it was being Americanized; in 1873 a Funny Man
school was emerging; in 1962 and 1970 black humor was mus-
cling in.

But a remarkable fact is that through demises and rebirths
one form not only endured but thrived: the comic narrative
modeled upon the oral tale. This hardy continuum which survived changes for more than a century and a half merits detailed
consideration.

Scholars have cited abundant evidence that the manner and
matter of oral stories were seminal to much of the best American humor from its beginning to the Civil War; they have particularly stressed the impact upon antebellum humorists of the
old Southwest. Their emphasis obscures the fact that elsewhere
— in New England, the South, and the Far West — much oral
humor was reincarnated in print.[3] Too, postwar humorists
through 1900 were active in every region producing comedy
derived from oral storytelling — Mrs. Stowe, Sam Lawson's
Yankee yarns; Joel Chandler Harris, the Uncle Remus fables;
Mark Twain, Mississippi River and Far Western tales — to
name a few among scores.

Oral origins and influences were clearest when a humorist
pictured a storyteller spinning his yarn and his audience reacting, and enclosed within his framework a directly quoted
traditional anecdote or one resembling it in substance and form
(T. B. Thorpe's "The Big Bear of Arkansas," 1841; *Sam Lawson's Fireside Stories,* 1871). Indebtedness was only a bit less
clear when the author transcribed allegedly oral tales, but

2. *Life and Letters of Edmund Clarence Stedman,* ed. L. Stedman,
G. M. Gould (New York, 1910), I, 447; James T. Thurber, "The
Future, If Any, of Comedy," *Harper's Magazine,* 223 (December 1961),
40–45; Melvin Maddocks, "We Are Not Amused — and Why," *Time,*
20 July 1970, pp. 30–31.

3. Norris W. Yates, *William T. Porter and the Spirit of the Times*
(Baton Rouge: University of Louisiana Press, 1947); Richard M. Dorson, *American Folklore* (Chicago: University of Chicago Press, 1959),
pp. 39–73.

omitted the framework (W. T. Thompson's "A Coon Hunt; or, A Fency Country," 1851; Mark Twain's *Adventures of Huckleberry Finn*, 1884).[4] Although both the "framework story" and the "mock oral tale" underwent changes, as described above they won warm affection or critical praise — often both — of Americans from 1900 to the present. Even a highly selective survey suggests their remarkable persistence.

As the century turned, Edward Noyes Westcott's *David Harum* (1898, 1900) was amassing sales of half a million copies (rough equivalent today: one and a third million) in twenty months. It sold briskly for decades — about a million and a quarter copies by 1965 — thanks largely to many tales in rustic dialect told by horse-sensible David and his sister. Central New York was the setting; but the decade 1900–1910 was a great one for Far Western oral tales — or facsimiles — in frameworks. Owen Wister's *The Virginian* (1902), reprinted fifteen times in nine months, was not only a bestseller (a million seven hundred thirty-six thousand copies by 1965) but also the source of a play performed for decades, three cinematic versions, and recently an interminable television series. The most amusing parts were based upon oral stories, and three crucial chapters detailed a tall-tale-telling contest between the villain and the hero. Between 1897 and 1913, Alfred Henry Lewis published six popular volumes of discursive tales told in dialect by one "Old Cattleman" about Arizona. And between 1903 and 1905 Andy Adams published three novels that served as a framework for yarns — twenty-nine in all — spun by cowboys resting after their labors. Adams followed these with *Cattle-Brands* (1906), subtitled "A Collection of Western Camp-fire Stories" — boxed narratives enclosing tales in which "the sound of the voice and the turns of everyday speech . . . racy and full of localisms," are heard. Adams still is admired and re-

4. It is incorrect to claim, as some scholars have, that "most" antebellum stories took this form. Actually, even in the Southwest, most did not. Nevertheless many did, including some of the best ones. See Walter Blair, *Native American Humor* (New York, 1937; rev. ed. San Francisco, 1960), pp. 79–101, which dealt with oral influences and initiated discussions of framework stories and mock oral tales in Southwestern humor.

printed as both an artist and the most authentic portrayer of Texas cowmen.[5]

Texas was long the home of O. Henry, who won fame during the same decade and continued to be popular and respected as a master of the short story until 1930 or so. During three years in prison, he launched his career by retelling stories told by fellow prisoners; and until his death in 1910, he utilized oral anecdotes. One group of stories still admired are framed reminiscences of wandering confidence man Jeff Peters, most of them included in *The Gentle Grafter* (1908).[6] Similar stories, many of them tall tales, about and by other characters were included in books which sold several million copies, and the esteem in which he was held was indicated by the establishment of the O. Henry Memorial Award Prizes in 1919.

Authors of the 1920's tended to neglect framework stories; but they produced mock oral tales which were popular and critical successes — Don Marquis' Old Soak and biblical stories; Roark Bradford's Negro dialect legends about "ol' man Adam and his chillun" (which inspired a Pulitzer Prize play); Ring Lardner's highly praised short stories in Midwestern dialect. The form migrated to urban settings in some of Lardner's cynical dramatic monologues, John V. A. Weaver's free verse narratives "in American," and Anita Loos's *Gentlemen Prefer Blondes.*

The same decade produced the best vernacular retelling of tall tales about Paul Bunyan — that by Esther Shephard. This heralded rediscovery, in the 1930's, of several similar heroes and the publication of stories, mostly in dialect, about them — John Henry, Mike Fink, Davy Crockett, and Febold Feboldson. The 1930's also produced Stephen Vincent Benet's esteemed tales about Paul Revere, Dan'l Webster, the Fool-Killer, the Cape Cod Sea Serpent, and others he called "our own folk-gods and giants and figures of earth"; most appeared in America's most popular magazines. Dorothy Parker wrote dramatic monologues of big blondes and brunettes with big problems. H. L.

5. Wilson M. Hudson, *Andy Adams: His Life and Writings* (Dallas: Southern Methodist University Press, 1964), p. 71 and *passim.*

6. O. Henry's own favorite, "The Atavism of John Tom Little Bear," first published in 1903, is in *Rolling Stones* (New York, 1912), pp. 34–52.

Davis' Pulitzer Prize *Honey in the Horn* spaced many tall tales through a meandering narrative about pioneer Oregon. Thornton Wilder's *Heaven's My Destination,* a monologue by that legendary figure the traveling salesman, exploited the author's skill with dialect — a skill used best in the 1938 Pulitzer Prize play, *Our Town,* by the Stage Manager, an old-fashioned Yankee sage.

During the 1940's Jesse Stuart's *Taps for Private Tussie* — a story, humorous for the most part, told by a teen-age Kentucky farm boy — was cheered by critics and sold a million copies. William Saroyan's *Adventures of Wesley Jackson* had a similar, somewhat older, vernacular narrator. Beginning in World War II years, Jesse B. Simple spoke for blacks in monologues recorded by Langston Hughes; these continued into the 1960's.

The 1950's brought J. D. Salinger's greatly admired *The Catcher in the Rye,* which has attracted five million buyers; H. L. Davis' *Winds of the Morning,* a book club selection sprinkled with vernacular anecdotes; several novels in the same mode by Mark Harris or (their title-pages claimed) by illiterates whose grammar and punctuation Harris edited; Eudora Welty's admirable *The Ponder Heart,* honored with the Howells Medal for Fiction; and Vance Randolph's five volumes of homespun Ozark anecdotes. Mac Hyman's *No Time for Sergeants* (1954), was a book club choice, a bestseller for two years (two million four hundred thousand copies), and the source of a Broadway hit, a motion picture, and a durable television series. The 1940's, in addition, were the decade which brought forth Robert Louis Taylor's *The Travels of Jaimie McPheeters,* which many reviewers recognized as a book in the mode of *Huckleberry Finn.*

The success of this book (bestseller, Pulitzer Prize) encouraged Taylor to follow it during the 1960's with two other novels with teen-age narrators. During the same decade, William Price Fox's *Southern Fried* stories followed the tradition; Thomas Berger's *Little Big Man,* with an elaborate framework, and Charles Portis' mock oral *True Grit,* Westerns, were bestsellers. Racier successes used vernacular narrators in substantial comic stretches — Robert Gover, *The $100 Misunderstanding* (Kitten's monologues) and Gore Vidal, *Myra Breckenridge* (Buck Loner's tape recordings). The 1970's continued the trend in more sanitary narratives: David Wagoner's Andrew Jackson Holcomb, Jr., in *Where Is My Wandering Boy Tonight?* (1970) told the story of his maturing in Wyoming; in 1970 Eudora Welty's *Losing Battles,* nominated for a National Book Award, consisted largely of stories told by Granny Vaughn's multitudinous descendants at a Mississippi family reunion. As recently as the summer of 1971, David Freeman's *U. S. Grant in the City* mounted to comic pinnacles in a Bowery bum's sagebrush tall tales; and in Jose Brown's *Addie Pray* an adolescent orphan girl told a picaresque story which became a book club selection.

This listing omits much fiction the inclusion of which might be questioned because its narrators, though they use the vernacular, may be too educated or too hard-boiled to be accepted without an argument (Pal Joey, Lardner's and Edward Streeter's letter-writers, Augie March, Todd Andrews, Alexander Portnoy, private operators whose amanuenses were Hammett, A. A. Fair, Mickey Spillane, and others). But it must not conclude without mentioning books which unquestionably belong high on the list — books by the most admired of all American writers extensively using framework narratives and mock oral tales, William Faulkner. His works employing these forms span four decades and include, notably (though far from exhaustively) *The Sound and the Fury* (Jonas' segment), *As I Lay Dying* (which may be called a series of mock oral narratives), the Snopes trilogy, and the bestselling *The Reivers.*

Thus, though eighty-eight years ago many would have agreed with Henry Watterson that humor of the sort represented by all these works had survived only because it effectively pictured a bygone race of country folk,[7] it has continued to flourish not only for nostalgic evocations but for narratives with very different aims. Why, one may well ask, did it continue to thrive long after America had lost its frontiers and become urbanized?

Scotsman Andrew Lang in 1889 remarked that Americans, contrasted with Britons, eternally swapped stories. These stories he called "the subsoil of American literary humour, a rich soil in which the plant . . . grows with vigour and puts forth fruit

---

7. Preface to *Oddities in Southern Life and Character* (Boston, 1883), pp. vii–viii.

and flowers." [8] If these truly are the soil, today it is far from depleted. The railway smoking cars and steamboat social halls which Lang mentioned as scenes for swappings are no longer much frequented. But bars, his third setting, flourish, and potential storytellers converge on restaurants for coffee breaks, four-martini lunches, and expense account dinners. In night clubs, amateur raconteurs at tables are regaled by professionals on platforms such as Myron Cohen, Sam Levinson, Bill Cosby, David Steinberg, Joan Rivers, and Phyllis Diller. Introduced by masters of ceremony who lace monologues with anecdotes, these entertainers and others such as Alexander King and Selma Diamond spin yarns for millions of listeners to radio or viewers of television. Even those recurrent guests on conversation shows who are not thought of as storytellers thrive by "ad libbing" humorous anecdotes. The professionals' oral narratives are immortalized on records or in briskly selling books. One outstanding performer, Jean Shepherd, has supported his claim: "I'm a story-teller; a story-teller can work any medium." [9] For a decade and a half Shepherd has spun leisurely yarns on a New York radio station; he published many in magazines and collected several in *In God We Trust: All Others Pay Cash* (1967); and in 1971 he appeared in a subsidized educational television series, "Jean Shepherd's America."

Sixty years ago, pondering reasons why "the vernacular [is] the natural vehicle for the most persistent and most popular variety of American humor," Joel Chandler Harris suggested that the comic oral lore it embodies "is based upon [the people's] unique experience; it is part of their personality; it belongs to their history; and it seems, in some ways, to be an assurance of independence and strength, of sanity and wisdom, of honesty and simplicity." [10] He perhaps had in mind the fact that since Americans often distrust smart alecks, wits, or book-read men, a narrator may disqualify himself by using highfalutin language while another wins trust by using vernacular phrasings. So canny politicians often deliberately mutilate their grammar, and

8. "Western Drolls," in *Lost Leaders* (London, 1889), pp. 186–187.
9. John Kronenberger, "Jean Shepherd Tells It Like It Was, Maybe," *New York Times*, 6 June 1971.
10. "Humor in America," in *American Wit and Humor,* 5 vols. (New York, 1909), I, xxi–xxii.

when Edgar Guest and Rod McKuen write idiomatically they even overcome widespread prejudices against poetry. Moreover, the vernacular is useful for comic effects because: (1) It exploits a conviction that Americans long found hilarious — that there is no necessary relationship between a man's formal learning and his knowledge or even his wisdom. (2) It nurtures indirect statements, and these are better than direct ones for satire; a throwaway comment can be funny when a frontal attack cannot.

Harris quite probably had in mind the appeal of the substance of humor based upon what he called "the pungent and racy anecdote, smelling of the soil" and capturing a vital "memory or tradition." In the discussion cited above he spoke also of the way "the dramatic manner" of an oral rendition gave "an added perfection" which, unhappily, the writer misses. "It's the despair of the writing man who has known the best storytellers," wrote J. Frank Dobie in 1961, "that he cannot translate the oral savor into print." The lament was recurrent. In 1834, eulogizing John Wesley Jarvis, whose oral stories had a prodigious impact on early American humor, William Dunlap found himself incapable of reproducing them "dressed in cold black and white." Lincoln's hearers made similar complaints. Mark Twain felt that some of his best anecdotes, based upon "outrageously funny" yarns told by pocket miner Jim Gillis, became "mild and pale" when he put them on paper; and reporters often despaired of capturing in print the charm of Twain's platform presentations.[11]

Today's raconteurs offer proof that such disparities still exist. Myron Cohen and Harry Hershfield have been praised by peers and by night club, radio, and television audiences as superb tellers of stories. But when, respectively in *Laughing Out Loud* (1958) and *Laugh Louder Live Longer* (1959), they

11. J. Frank Dobie, "Storytellers I Have Known," in *Singers and Storytellers* (Dallas: Southern Methodist University Press, 1961), p. 61; Dunlap, *History of the Rise and Progress of the Arts of Design in the United States* (New York, 1834), II, 90; Richard M. Dorson, "Oral Styles of American Folk Narrative," in *Folklore in Action*, ed. H. P. Beck (Philadelphia: University of Pennsylvania Press, 1962), pp. 93–98; *Mark Twain in Eruption*, ed. B. DeVoto (New York: Harper, 1940), pp. 358–366; Fred A. Lorch, *The Trouble Begins at Eight* (Ames: Iowa State University Press, 1968), p. 236.

parade their favorite anecdotes, only a few retellings compare in excellence with oral tellings. Equally inferior to skilled oral recitals are printed versions of anecdotes in twenty-five other volumes compiling them during the last thirty-six years (many of the stories included have been newly unleashed by modern tolerance of sexual frankness and now await classification in motif indexes by folklorists who enjoy performing heroic drudgeries).[12] A revealing fact is that three such collections are generally more amusing: H. Allen Smith, in *Buskin'* (1968) and *Rude Jokes* (1970), and Leo Rosten, in *The Joys of Yiddish* (1968), rather consistently manage to impart to their printed narrations the appeals such tales have in oral tellings. Possibly they succeeded because they prepared for their chore by cultivating considerable skill as creative writers. The moral — one that Harris, Twain, and others articulated — is that effectively translating oral lore into written humor requires craftsmanship and care.[13] I suggest that the very nature of oral storytelling caused both skill and assiduity to come into play and that this was greatly to the advantage of the style, the structuring, and the characterization in written humor.

How the style is shaped is indicated by many who have heard stories told well, who remark upon the witchery of their rendition, and who discuss reasons for it. Jarvis' auditors, for instance, suggested that he was a master because "some of his humour was . . . manual" and because he was an expert mimic of dialects, gestures, and facial expressions, and neither the postures nor the mimicry was communicable in print. Something of a caricature, James H. Delargy's sketch in 1945 of an Irish storyteller in action indicates other uncommunicable elements: "His . . . limbs are trembling, as, immersed in his story . . . he puts his very soul into the telling . . . he uses

12. G. Legman has started a classification which includes a number in *Rationale of the Dirty Joke* (New York: Grove Press, 1968), vol. I. A second volume is planned. As the title indicates, the book omits cleanly jokes — and the author has not classified a great number of less antiseptic anecdotes which have been included in other compilations.

13. Twain discusses this fact in *Eruption,* pp. 216–224, and sets down a platform version of "His Grandfather's Old Ram" that differs greatly from the version printed in *Roughing It,* chapter 53.

a great deal of gesticulation, and by the movement of his body, hands, and head, tries to convey hate and anger, fear and humour, like an actor in a play. He raises his voice at certain passages, and at other times it becomes almost a whisper." An obvious inference, as Vivian Mercier suggests, is that this raconteur was giving a skilled dramatic performance.[14]

John Ball, in "Style in the Folk Tale," offers an impressive list of play-acting ingredients which elude print — "intonation, voice rhythm, continuity, speaking rate, pitch, voice intensity, pauses, facial expressions, gestures, pantomime or re-enactment . . . voice imitation (even of the opposite sex or of animals), methods of reacting to audience response — in fact the whole delicate and complex process of participating with the audience in the story-telling situation." Richard M. Dorson adds items to this catalogue — chanted phrases, onomatopoeia, eye contact with the audience, and the use of props — "all adding up to a small theatrical performance." Dorson notices that Vance Randolph, realizing that some oral tales depend upon pauses, and that literally transcribed texts take no account of these, at times feels compelled to edit tales that he has recorded.[15] To compensate not only for lost pauses but also for other lost play-acting devices, skilled writers of humor based upon oral storytelling constantly employ a great many expedients.

Some of course are used to give a vernacular sound to the quoted story. The late Frank O'Connor, reading for radio audiences, was "horrified to see how . . . generations of skilful stylists from Chekhov to Katherine Mansfield and James Joyce had so fashioned the short story that it no longer rang with the

14. James H. Delargy, *The Gaelic Story-Teller* (London: British Academy, 1945), p. 16; Mercier, "The Irish Short Story and Oral Tradition," in *The Celtic Cross* (Lafayette: Purdue University Press, 1964), p. 113. Mercier suggests that "attitudes and techniques based on oral literature can revivify written literature in a period of sterility" and that this happened at the beginning of the Romantic movement.

15. Ball's article appeared in *Folk-Lore,* 56 (December 1954), 170; Dorson's is "Esthetic Form in British and American Folk Narrative," in *Medieval Literature and Folk Studies,* ed. J. Mandel and B. A. Rosenberg (New Brunswick: Rutgers University Press, 1970), p. 308. Dorson has described the varying dramatic performances of a number of storytellers in "Oral Styles," pp. 79–92.

tone of a man's voice, speaking." To restore the ring he omitted passages or even "departed altogether from the script," eliminating "carefully arranged scenes and balanced sentences." [16] Mark Twain took additional measures. He knew that "the best and most telling speech is not the actual impromptu one, but the counterfeit of it, [one that] will seem impromptu," also that "written things have to be limbered up, broken up, colloquialized, and turned into the common forms of unpremeditated talk" and that "a touch of indifferent grammar flung in here and there, apparently at random, has a good effect." At best a writer did what William Dean Howells did — combined "clearness, compression, verbal exactness" with "seemingly unconscious felicity of phrasing." [17]

Paradoxically, the effort becomes too evident when the writing is either too far from the vernacular style or too close to it. Messrs. Bellow, Roth, Barth, and Vonnegut in first person narratives as a rule do not catch the quality of talk because they use too many Latinate words, because they characterize too complexly, and because they scorn simple chronology. At an opposite extreme is George Washington Harris (1814–1869). This Tennessee humorist, even his severest critic concedes, is one of America's great writers. But modern readers bog down in a passage like the following one in which Harris' Sut Lovingood pictures a frightened mare which has been mounted by a Yankee with a huge clock tied to his back:

> " 'Yu git up, yu pesky critter,' sed he, a-makin his heels meet, an' crack onder her belly. Well she did 'git up,' rite then and thar, an' staid up long enuf tu lite twenty foot further away, in a broad trimblin squat, her tail a-tween her thighs, an' her years a dancin a-pas' each uther, like scissors a-cuttin. The jolt ove

16. *Stories* (New York: Vintage Books, 1956), p. vii.

17. The quoted phrases are from "William Dean Howells," *Works*, 37-vol. definitive ed. (New York, 1922–1925), XXVI, 228–238; and "On Speech-Making Reform," *Mark Twain's Speeches,* ed. A. B. Paine (New York, 1923), pp. 2–3. Mark Twain praised novelist E. W. Howe for writing "as a man talks" in a letter of 1883 — "Mark Twain's Criticism of *The Story of a Country Town*," ed. C. E. Schorer, *American Literature,* 27 (March 1955), 110. A perceptive summary is that by Sydney J. Krause, "Twain's Method and Theory of Composition," *Modern Philology,* 56 (February 1959), 166–177.

the litin sot the clock tu strikin. Bang-zee-bang-zee whang-zee. She listined pow'ful 'tentive tu the three fus' licks, an' they seem'd to go thru an' thru her as quick es quick-silver wud git thru a sifter. She waited fur no more, but jis' gin her hole soul up tu the wun job ove runnin frum onder that infunel Yankee, an' his hive ove bumble bees, ratil snakes, an' other orful hurtin things, es she tuck hit tu be . . . An she jis' tried tu run outen her sorril hide."

Compare a passage about another frantic horse by Mark Twain's Simon Wheeler in the Jumping Frog story:

"Thish-yer Smiley had a mare — the boys called her the fifteen-minute nag, but that was only in fun, you know, because of course she was faster than that — and he would win money on that horse, for all she was so slow and always had the asthma, or the distemper, or the consumption, or something of that kind. They used to give her two or three hundred yards' start, and then pass her under way, but always at the fag end of the race she'd get excited and desperate like, and come cavorting and straddling up, and scattering her legs around limber, sometimes in the air, and sometimes out to one side among the fences, and kicking up m-o-r-e dust and raising m-o-r-e racket with her coughing and sneezing and blowing her nose — and *always* fetch up at the stand just about a neck ahead, as near as you could cipher it down."

A third horse cavorts in Faulkner's vernacular "Spotted Horses" after a Texas dealer corners three or four of the pranksome creatures:

Then he jumped into them, and then we couldn't see nothing for a while because of the dust. It was a big cloud of it, and them blare-eyed, spotted things swoaring outen it twenty foot to a jump, in forty directions without counting up. Then the dust settled and there they was, that Texas man and the horse. He had its head twisted clean around like an owl's head. Its legs was braced and it was trembling like a new bride and groaning like a saw mill, and him holding its head wrung clean around on its neck so it was snuffing sky. "Look it over," he says, with . . . his neck swole up like a spreading adder's . . . Then it was all dust again, and we couldn't see nothing but spotted hide and mane, and that ere Texas man's boot-heels like a couple of walnuts on two strings, and after a while that two-gallon hat come sailing out like a fat old hen crossing a fence.[18]

Harris' attempt to render dialect unselectively (with some cacography thrown in) renders his passage more obviously artful and less spontaneous — in appearance — than the other two: the contrast suggests that this great humorist would profit by some modernization. But the passages share stylistic traits — homespun diction, peccable grammar, informal but rhythmical sentences, onomatopoeia (Bang-zee-bang-zee), mispronunciations (pow'ful, m-o-r-e), portmanteau coinage (swoaring), assorted tropes (similes, metaphors, hyperboles, synechdoche), clarity and precision such as Twain lauded in Howells.

But any compression results from omitting descriptions and interpretations: there is no skimping of ludicrous imagery. These passages typically mingle the circumstantial and the precise with the outrageous and the imprecise. Though meticulous about dates, dimensions, and techniques, the storyteller unashamedly introduces men and animals that are impossible monsters. Often vernacular passages mingle the vulgar with the poetic. Typically, the narrator of "The Big Bear of Arkansas" is squatting to defecate at the very instant when he has a highly poetic vision of a supernatural beast, and seconds later he loses his pants. An unhurried savoring of details, like that of yarnspinners entertaining loafers in bars, by firesides, or on shaded porches, characterizes quoted stories.

Three plot patterns that thrive in oral storytelling recur in written retellings: one meanders scandalously, one details a conflict in which a weak character defeats a strong opponent, and one soars to a comic climax. Mark Twain notes in "How to Tell a Story" that, whereas "a witty story" rushes to a point,

18. George Washington Harris, "The Widow McCloud's Mare," *Sut Lovingood's Yarns,* ed. M. Thomas Inge (New Haven, 1966), p. 46; Mark Twain, "The Notorious Jumping Frog of Calaveras County," in *Selected Shorter Writings of Mark Twain,* ed. Walter Blair (Boston, 1962), p. 15; William Faulkner, "Spotted Horses," *Scribner's Magazine,* 89 (June 1931), 587–588. A third person version in *The Hamlet* (1940), IV, offers an illuminating contrast.

"the humorous story may be spun out at great length . . .
wander around as much as it pleases, and arrive nowhere in
particular." Stephen Leacock also contrasted an anecdote in
which "there is no fun . . . until the end is reached" and one
"amusing all through." Max Eastman felt these differentiations
were between the technique of practical jokes and that of
"poetic humor," which involves "the playful enjoyment of a
mess, the messier it is, within the limits of patience, the better":
so many humorous stories make "slow progress, or no progress
at all, or progress backwards." [19] This picaresque meandering
is recurrent in our humor: witness *Huckleberry Finn* and *Little
Big Man*.

Some humorists follow what Axel Olrik called "Epic Laws of
Folk Narrative" in 1909: no subplots, two chief characters in
conflict, a peak tableau. Another folklorist, Max Lüthi, in
"Parallel Themes in Folk Narrative in Art and Literature"
(1967), notices that a common conflict of this sort ends with
"the defeat of the great by the small, the mighty by the apparently powerless." Pondering these generalizations, Dorson remarks, brings to mind "the triumphs of Brer Rabbit over the
bear and the fox, . . . of Davy Crockett over b'ars, panthers,
and armies," and "the perilous odyssey of Huck Finn." [20] The
list can be greatly extended. Our humor throngs with tricksters:
crafty Yankee peddlers and gamblers of antebellum years; confidence men such as the duke and the dauphin in the 1880's,
O. Henry's Jeff Peters in the 1900's, and Addie Pray's Long
Boy in 1971; Stuart's Tussies of 1943 and Hyman's Will Stock-
dale of 1954, who outwit government agencies. Again, there
are boasters who are defeated and deflated by quiet opponents
— little Davy, for example, in *Life on the Mississippi*, who
makes the rampaging Child of Calamity and Bob the self-
styled Corpse-Maker "own up that they are sneaks and cow-

19. Eastman, *Enjoyment of Laughter* (New York: Simon & Schuster,
1936) cites Leacock's statement and comments upon it, pp. 305–306.
One of the most popular antebellum stories was Hamilton C. Jones's
"Cousin Sally Dilliard," which continually digressed; beginning in the
1830's, it was reprinted often. "Colonel Wanderwell," by *Delta*, published in the *Spirit of the Times* in 1833, utilized the same pattern; so
did Frances Whitcher's "Hezekiah Bedott," in *Widow Bedott Papers*
(1855), frequently reprinted in newspapers and periodicals.
20. "Esthetic Form," p. 321.

ards." A character's vernacular speech, in fact, may suggest that he is an underdog, especially if he is having trouble with more assured or more sophisticated folk.

A third recurrent pattern was described by Norris Yates, in *William T. Porter and The Spirit of the Times,* which provides a fine history of the magazine that published the best pre-Civil War vernacular stories. In many stories in that magazine, *The Spirit of the Times,* says Norris: "Event is piled on event and detail on detail, each taller than the last, until the apex, the tallest incident of all, is reached." This climactic ordering was used in tales which Yates particularly admires, including the most widely praised and reprinted comic narrative *The Spirit* ever published, "The Big Bear of Arkansas." [21] It was used again and again by Mark Twain. In *The Innocents Abroad,* he utilized it in practically all of the most famous passages such as the one about the bedeviling of the guide, the one about Da Vinci's "Last Supper," and Twain's cogitations by the Tomb of Adam. Again in *Roughing It,* he used it to picture the fright-prone jackass rabbit and the omnivorous camel; Bemis' buffalo story; the yarn about the Mexican plug. It provided the overall organization for "Old Times on the Mississippi" and for his best framework story, "Jim Baker's Blue-Jay Yarn." Owen Wister had Trampas and the Virginian use the climactic tall tale form in their confrontation, and of course the same form is the standard one still for lying contests. When a liar tells a series of stories that fill a whole book, naturally they pile up higher and higher. As the man who has recorded Jack Crabb's yarns in *Little Big Man,* Ralph Fielding Snell, remarks: that one man experienced a third of Jack's adventures is "unlikely," half "incredible," the whole lot "mythomaniac."

At best the style and the structuring of the quoted story create not merely the vernacular character but a particularized narrator. When you recite a story to an audience, said Twain, "you absorb the character and presently become the man himself." Elsewhere Twain speaks of so writing a story as to let the imagined character "tell his story *himself* and let me

21. *William T. Porter,* pp. 161–163. For an analysis of Thorpe's story, see Walter Blair, "The Technique of 'The Big Bear of Arkansas,'" *Southwest Review,* 28 (Summer 1943), 426–435.

merely act as his amanuensis." Twain seems to have sensed a subtle difference between the written and the oral procedures, but unfortunately he never managed to formulate it, and regardless, the procedures clearly were analogous. That this is true is indicated in Twain's praise of a performance by James Whitcomb Riley, "about the funniest thing I have ever listened to," during which Riley tells a story in such a way as to simulate perfectly the character of a simple, innocent, sincere old farmer who perfectly reveals himself by the telling. In this performance, as in many written works, the most important disclosures are unconscious ones. The delightful revelation of "The Old Soldier's Story," completely unbeknownst to the old man, is that he is constitutionally incapable of telling a funny story well.[22] Twain cherished Robert Browning's dramatic monologues because they too provided illuminations of monologuists — "a splendor of stars and suns" that filled "the whole field with flame" — and believed that by simulative interpretations he could "read Browning so Browning himself can understand." [23] Huck Finn, like the English poet's dramatis personae, acquainted readers with a rather complex character by uttering a monologue.

Unconscious revelations by means of monologues have continued to appeal to Americans: witness those of Lardner's narrators in "Haircut," "The Love Nest," and other stories; of Dorothy Parker's battered womenfolk; of Jason Compson in Part Three of *The Sound and the Fury*; and of Holden Caulfield, who tells perceptive readers much more than he himself knows about his mental state.

George Brush, monologuist in *Heaven's My Destination*, left even discerning critics unsure whether he was a saint or a fool:

22. *Eruption*, pp. 224, 243; How to Tell a Story," *The Complete Works of James Whitcomb Riley* (New York, 1916), X, 2670–2673. In the same volume, p. 2662, Riley has a vernacular character discuss the reading of monologues.

23. Albert Bigelow Paine, *Mark Twain: A Biography*, 4 vols. (New York: Harper, 1912), III, 846–847; *Mark Twain to Mrs. Fairbanks*, ed. Dixon Wecter (San Marino: Huntington Library, 1949), pp. 260–261; DeLancey Ferguson, *Mark Twain: Man and Legend* (Indianapolis: Bobbs-Merrill, 1943), p. 207.

by surrounding his narrative with a framework, Thornton Wilder might have made clear his creator's conviction, expressed elsewhere, that he was both. Thus, by describing a storyteller and his background, an author may clarify and enlarge his characterization of the raconteur. Thorpe's Jim Doggett gains vividness because he is shown swaggering confidently as he enters the steamboat cabin, then putting his feet on the stove, "his eyes . . . as sparkling as diamonds, and good-natured to simplicity." Twain's Simon Wheeler is helpfully shown "dozing comfortably by the barroom stove of the decayed mining camp of Angel's . . . fat and bald-headed, and [with] an expression of winning gentleness and simplicity upon his tranquil countenance." It is useful to know that as Simon told his story "he never smiled, he never frowned, he never changed his voice from the gentle-flowing key to which he tuned his initial sentence." H. L. Davis generalizes to the advantage of the reader about old Flem Simmons: "he could take the measliest little episode . . . and string it out and wool it around and supple it and driddle it along for hours as joyful and preoccupied as an old squaw tanning a stolen buckskin . . . He had to start with the way the weather had looked when he woke up and what he thought about it, what fuel he had started the fire with . . . and the most infernal rigmarole of particulars . . . [He] told a story that began with his getting his boots wet so he had to grease them with tallow before he could put them on . . . It wasn't very easy on the ears." [24]

Writers of framed tales, as Richard Boyd Hauck suggests, often are enabled to focus attention upon the psychology of a storyteller who is more complex, indeed more ambiguous, than casual readers realize.[25] As revealed by Twain's comments as well as his blue jay yarn, Jim Baker is an opinionated, deranged, and overcomplicated misanthrope. Faulkner was able to sense under the horseplay of Sut Lovingood a character whom he ranked with Don Quixote, Falstaff, and other great fictional creations because "he had no illusions about himself, did the

24. H. L. Davis, *Honey in the Horn,* 1935 (New York: Avon Books), p. 143.

25. *A Cheerful Nihilism* (Bloomington: University of Indiana Press, 1971), pp. 51–63.

best he could; at certain times he was a coward and knew it and wasn't ashamed; he never blamed his misfortunes on anyone and never cursed God for them." [26] Faulkner himself in "Bear Hunt" and the Snopes trilogy gave his best storyteller, V. K. Ratliff, wisdom, compassion, and irony that deepened meanings of yarns entrusted to his telling.

Revelations in the framework of what happens to the storyteller and to his audience can add a second plot of sorts to the one in the quoted narrative. As early as 1829 in "Otter-Bag" John Neal has an auditor, warmed with flip, find a tale enchanting at first, then become increasingly bored until finally he hurries away to avoid a retelling. Much the same thing happens in 1865 when Simon Wheeler blockades his auditor in a corner and forces him to listen to a frog story that the man finds so long and tedious that, at the first chance, he too escapes. Flem Simmons, it eventuates, is stringing out his "infernal rigmarole" to keep his two auditors from squabbling. This framework tale therefore is one of hundreds involving a hoax. Such a subplot still is attractive in *Little Big Man,* where Jack Crabb dies leaving his pedantic editor uncertain whether Jack is a forgotten hero or a prodigious liar. Or the plot of the framework may initiate and terminate a climactic development that mounts toward a peak in the enclosed story ("The Big Bear of Arkansas"). The framework plot may be contrapuntal, antithetical, or both to that of the quoted story ("Baker's Blue-Jay Yarn" and parts of the Snopes trilogy.)

The framework language usually contrasts with the vernacular of the quoted story to stress comic aspects: Homer Wilbur's sesquipedalian words and Latin quotations incongruously introduce Hosea's Yankee doggerel; Ralph Fielding Snell's prissy "Foreword" and "Editor's Epilogue" bracket a narrative in the informal style of Jack Crabb. Interruptions of a vernacular account by more pretentious stretches serve the same end: a "gentlemanly" English huntsman intrudes upon Jim Doggett's narrative; letters in fustian are inserted every now and then in Jaimie McPheeters' story.

26. Interview with Jean Stein, *Paris Review,* 1956, in *William Faulkner: Three Decades of Criticism,* ed. F. J. Hoffman and O. Vickery (Lansing: Michigan State University Press, 1960), p. 79.

Clearly humor rooted in oral storytelling traditions persists partly because it can be modified to serve many purposes. Brief looks at two novels in which it plays very different but quite important roles — one by William Faulkner and one by Eudora Welty — will support this claim.

Although Faulkner's affection for oral humor and of published humor based upon it, and his indebtedness to them, have been well documented,[27] critics seemingly have not considered reasons why he embedded vernacular narratives in *Light in August* (1932) at two important points. At the end of chapter 15, then at the very end of the book (chapter 21) he abruptly relinquished a style often empurpled by rhetoric and had vulgar storytellers take over.

The earlier anecdote, about the meeting of Uncle Doc and Mrs. Hines with Joe Christmas following his capture, is told by clerks, loafers, and farmers around family tables and in shadowed yards. It thus becomes a community's commentary on an important event, and as such it shows the community's deep prejudices, which are critically relevant.[28] The contemptuous picturing of Hines is achieved in part by verbs which show the old man hollering, hobbling, screeching, slobbering, shaking and flopping, in part by homely similes that liken him to a hypnotist's victim and a runaway from a crazy house. His wife too is caricatured — as squat and dowdy — looking like a toy balloon on which Katzenjammer kids have painted a funny face; so when this weird female completely shuts up the bombastic little gaffer, plants him in a chair, and forces him to stay put, the humiliating deflation contributes a great deal to Faulkner's sustained assault upon the man's fanaticism.

A furniture dealer who has helped hitch-hiking Lena Grove and Byron Bunch on their journey tells the second story to his

27. *Lion in the Garden: Interviews with William Faulkner 1926–1962,* ed. J. F. Meriwether and M. Millgate (New York, 1968), pp. 11, 38–39; H. M. Campbell and R. E. Foster, *William Faulkner: A Critical Appraisal* (Norman, 1951), pp. 99, 102–107; M. Thomas Inge, "William Faulkner and G. W. Harris," *Tennessee Studies in Literature,* 7 (1962), 47–59.

28. The community attributes each of Joe's actions to either his black or his white blood. Lawrance Thompson, *William Faulkner* (New York, 1963), p. 79, notices that, ironically, highly educated Gavin Stevens reveals precisely the same prejudices.

ardent young wife as they lie abed between couplings. The pair's earthy quips about their relish of sex starkly contrast with the man's story about Byron's timid try at seducing Lena, her disdainful but unperturbed refusal, and his hangdog return to her side. Set in such an incongruous frame and stressing ludicrous details, the account enforces a comparison between Lena's and Joe's biographies that runs through the novel and adumbrates the central theme. Its placing as the very last chapter gives it a particular emphasis.

In *Losing Battles,* three generations of the descendants of Granny Elvira Jordan Vaughn gather to celebrate her ninetieth birthday at a home in the hill country of northeastern Mississippi. A few events which occur during the two days and a night of the reunion are recounted by the third person narrator, but practically all the telling of the narrative takes the form of familial talk, endlessly discussing current events and telling leisurely stories about what happened in the past. The lifelike vernacular style characterizes the speakers as individuals and as members of a clan, evokes ways of living, feeling, and thinking, and in the end works verbal magic of a sort that compassionately deals with evil and suffering — even with the loss of battles by major and minor warriors. Overall the tone is comic, and the end result — like that of most rituals — is propitiation. Miss Welty's impressive achievement provides proof (if any is needed) that narratives based upon oral storytelling are alive and well and living in Mississippi. As they are in other parts of the country.

The *Titanic* Toast

Shortly before midnight, 14 April 1912, the White Star liner *Titanic*, on its maiden voyage from Southampton to New York, sheared its side on an iceberg 1,300 miles from its destination; the next day, along with over 1,500 of its passengers and crew, the *Titanic* sank in the icy waters of the North Atlantic. The rising star of modern technology had a sudden loss of magnitude as that sleek and enormous ship that could not be sunk tore its hide and collapsed. It was the major disaster of the era, and it struck the imaginations of the rich, who lost friends and relatives on the ship (among the dead were Benjamin Guggenheim, George D. Widener, Isidor Straus), and the poor, for whom the ship represented the great shining and glistening world forever denied them and anyone they would ever know.

That shipwreck produced a million words of prose, several motion pictures, a few songs — and one poem.

The poem has been heard by a very small number of white Americans and by several million blacks. That is either curious or ironic, for not only were there no blacks on the *Titanic*'s passenger list, but neither were there any blacks on the staff. The ship was lily-white, but the one item in American folklore that widely documents its sinking is in a genre performed almost entirely by blacks, a genre of oral narrative poetry called the *toast*.

One version of the *"Titanic"* toast goes like this:

A. RECORDED 24 MARCH 1966, HUNTSVILLE, TEXAS
All the old folks say the fourth a May was a hell of a day.
I was in a little seaport town and the great Titanic was goin' down.
Now the sergeant and captain was havin' some words
when they hit that big iceberg.
Up come Shine from down below,
he said, "Captain, captain, you don't know,
we got nine feet of water over the boiler room floor."
And the captain said, "Go on back and start stackin' sacks,
we got nine pumps to keep the water back."
Up come Shine from down below,
he said, "Captain, captain, you don't know,
we got forty feet of water all over the boiler room floor."
He said, "Go on back and start stackin' sacks,
we got nine water pumps to keep the water back."
Shine said, "Your shittin' is good and your shittin' is fine,
but there's one time you white folks ain't gonna shit on Shine."
Now a thousand millionaires was lookin' at him
when he jumped in the ocean and he begin to swim.
Rich man's daughter came up on deck
with her drawers around her knees and underskirt around her neck.
Like a long day clock Shine stopped
and his eyes stood dead on that cock [*vagina*].
She says, "Shine, oh, Shine," says, "save me please,"
say, "I give you all the pussy that your eyes may see."
He said, "I know you got your pussy and that's true,
but there's some girls on land got good a pussy as you."
She said, "Shine, oh, Shine, please save my life,"
say, I'll make you a lawfully wedded wife."
He said, "Your shittin' is good and your shittin' is fine,
but first I got to save this black ass of mine."
Now there was another fella by the name of Jim,
he jumped in the ocean and he began to swim.
Another girl ran up on deck
with her drawers around her knees and underskirt around *her* neck.
Like a long day clock Jim stopped
and his eyes fell dead on that cock.
Now she had long black hair that hung from the crown of her neck

to the nape of her belly,
she had a twenty-pound pussy that shook like jelly.
She said, "Shine, oh, Shine," says, "save me, please,
I'll give you everything that your eyes may see."
Now before the last word could fall from her lip,
Jim climbed his black ass back up on that ship.
Up come a shark from the bottom of the sea,
said, "Look what godamighty done sent to me."
Shine bowed his neck and bent his ass,
said, "Get out the way and let a *big* shark pass."
And after old shark seen that Shine had him beat,
he said, "Swim, black motherfucker, 'cause I don't like black meat."
About four-thirty when the Titanic was sinkin',
Shine done swimmed over in Los Angeles and started drinkin'.
Now when he heard the Titanic had sunk,
he was in New York damn near drunk.
He said, "Ladies and gentlemen," say, "when I die don't ya'll bury
    me at all,
soak my balls in alcohol
and lay my old rod up across my breast,
and tell all the peoples old Shine has gone to rest."

I intend to discuss here some important variant texts of the *"Titanic"* toast and what they might do for the people who recite them or listen and laugh when the recitations are done by others.

Roger D. Abrahams, in *Deep Down in the Jungle,* his fine book on urban black folklore from Philadelphia, says about the genre: "The toast is a narrative poem that is recited, often in a theatrical manner, and represents the greatest flowering of Negro verbal talent. Toasts are often long, lasting anywhere from two to ten minutes. They conform to a general but by no means binding framing pattern. This consists of some sort of picturesque or exciting introduction, action alternating with dialogue (because the action is usually a struggle between two people or animals), and a twist ending of some sort, either a quip, an ironic comment, or a brag." [1]

1. Rev. ed. (Chicago: Aldine, 1970), p. 97. Most of the book is a study of toasts, toast tellers, and themes in one small neighborhood, but the book's theoretical implications are relevant to urban black folklore in general. Abrahams includes texts and discussion of *"Titanic,"*

The poems are recited in a variety of situations: while hanging around street corners, at parties (much as someone might sit down to play the piano or sing a song or tell a joke), among inmates in jails with long hours to consume and not much to do in them. Toast-telling sessions are similar to joke-telling sessions (and sometimes mixed with them), in that a person might recite "Stagolee," the toast about the sociopathic badman, and someone else might respond with another version of "Stagolee," saying, "The way *I* heard it was . . ." or with another toast, such as "Signifying Monkey," "Dance of the Freaks," or *"Titanic."* The toast is a social genre.

The toasts, like much folk literature, have to do with problems of human relationships, but they deal with them in a special, highly filtered, and exaggerated way. There is much violence in them, some of it sexual. There are homiletics about good men and trustworthy women, about the wages of sin; there are short narratives — often highly obscene — close in form and content to the better known drinking toast, and there are the longer narratives about badmen, tricksters, and other heroes. Some derive from schlock-literary tradition, such as the Robert W. Service poems found in paperback recitation books, but in the main the poems are from black oral tradition. The actors are heroes, pimps, fools, tricksters, prostitutes, hustlers, squares; the characters often deal with the same threats and problems dealt with by the listeners, but unlike them the toast protagonists deal with these difficulties with style and grace, and when they fail their failures are spectacular. Folk literature is often like that.

In the toast world values are unambiguous: one wins, one loses, one has sex, one is denied sex, one is a hero, one is not a hero. Sexual relationships in the toasts are invariably affectionless and usually affectless: the female exists there as a device for exercise and articulation of male options, not as an integral member of a bilateral relationship.

pp. 101–103, 120–129. Abrahams and I have discussed the toasts, corresponded about them, and read each others' writings about them, published and unpublished; my debts to him are far more extensive than these notes might indicate, and I want to generally acknowledge them here.

The three toasts heard most frequently in the United States are "Stagolee," "Signifying Monkey," and *"Titanic."* [2] "Stagolee" is about an irrational badman who engages in gratuitous violence and joyless sexuality, a man who fires his gun a lot but is almost totally nonverbal; "Signifying Monkey" is about a jungle trickster who by clever lying manages to send his archfoe, the Lion (whose roaring renders him impotent), off to be stomped and mangled by the stately Elephant, and who gloats from his high perch when the Lion comes back through the jungle "more dead than alive." And there is *"Titanic,"* about the black man named Shine, who combines the agility of the physical hero (swimming the wide sea, which none of the whites can do) with the verbal skill of the trickster hero (flinging back several witty rejoinders as he swims away, and besting in repartee sea creatures like the shark and the whale who would like to capture him).

All three poems are about making it, making do, but they treat that subject in very different ways, and the heroes are totally different from one another. Stagolee is the archetypal bully; he strikes out blindly, articulating or decathecting his rage on any passing object or person (in one version of the poem he kills a bartender, another badman, a pimp, he swives into loyal submission a passing hooker, then he hurls invective at the judge and jury); his sheer strength and his large-caliber pistol bring him fame, but there are for him no solutions, only occasional valve-openings. Signifying Monkey uses wile and cleverness to accomplish what he cannot accomplish with brawn: his mode is a verbal judo, he uses the enemy's ego against him and he does it all with words. In many of the poems he falls out of his tree while gloating and jumping up and down, and the Lion pounces on him, but he usually tricks the Lion into stepping back to permit him to "fight like a natural man," whereupon he again leaps back to his tree. There is another sequence of poems about him as a cardsharp or poolsharp, beating the dull-witted Baboon at cooncan or rotation pool.

Both Stagolee and Signifying Monkey (and, to a lesser degree, the Poolshooting Monkey) are exaggerations of roles

2. See *Deep Down in the Jungle, passim,* for texts and discussion of "Stagolee" and "Signifying Monkey."

known on the street: the type that makes it with brawn and the type that makes it with brains, the type that takes what is there and sees if he has a use for it and the type that knows what he wants and cleverly figures out a way to acquire it.[3]

But the one hero of the folk toasts who perfectly mediates between those two extremes — Shine, who is smart enough to jump ship when the whites aboard still trust its purported infallibility, strong enough to swim past several natural obstacles, and sexual enough in many versions of the poem to finish by a grand encounter with a mob of women — is the one toast hero who does it against a foil of white men. What is rare about *"Titanic"* is that the argument is largely put in terms of white and black, and it even includes a statement of how all the white man's wealth and machinery is worthless if he can't get his "ass in the water and swim like me." [4]

Among the three hundred toast texts I have collected in the field, the various papers and collections done by students in

3. Ulf Hannerz, in the best study of American black ghetto culture to date, *Soulside* (New York: Columbia University Press, 1969), questions Abrahams' distinction of toast heroes as " 'trickster' and 'badman' types." This, he says, "may be misleading, for smartness and toughness are only facets of a single if somewhat amorphous conception of ghetto specific masculinity which both Stagolee and the monkey serve. That is, most street-corner men would be able to recognize both of them as cultural models for their own role, although they may personally emphasize one or the other" (p. 115). But most social models are extremes — these two certainly are — and behavior suited to survival needs modulating devices because steady extremism is usually socially intolerable. It may well be that the men of the street corner society can see in both types of hero aspects with which they identify; but they too — in their folklore at any rate — make a clear distinction between them. We must respect that distinction if we are to be able to deal with the folklore at all.

4. Abrahams, after describing the style of heroism Shine embodies, says: "Here is a Negro story that overtly pictures the enemy as white. The white man has been one of the authority figures against whom he has been rebelling. But here he achieves that greater act of rebellion, the turning of his back.

"This is then something of a declaration of independence" (*Deep Down in the Jungle,* p. 81).

I find that somewhat excessive: the white man may be Shine's foil in this poem, but he is hardly his enemy. That the white man is *not* presented as an enemy but only as someone rather opaque and clumsy is part of what is startling about the toast.

my folklore classes at Harvard and Buffalo, and various papers
and books that have published toast texts, I have found only
two that explicitly deal with whites and blacks: "Up on the
Farm," a poem I collected only once, in Texas, about a black
man who refuses to work for a white farmer because he knows
he will have difficulty collecting his wages, and *"Titanic." "Titanic"* articulates a black rejection of white bribes and status
symbols; and in the toast canon that is a rare rejection indeed.
Although *"Titanic"* is one of the three best known toasts, and
it is a poem whose themes seem compelling and clear, it has
nevertheless spawned no thematic analogues. One doesn't wonder that the theme of the black rejection of white turns up in
"Titanic," but rather that it turns up almost nowhere else in
the toasts.[5]

It can hardly be accidental that the protagonist is named
Shine, a white man's term for Negro that is unambiguously de-
rogatory. "Shine" never had "nigger's" casual currency among
some blacks (one still hears in parts of the South lines like "all
us niggers . . ." and, in the North and the South, the expression "he's a *bad* nigger," a term approving of someone's toughness). A character named Shine appeared in some early nineteenth-century minstrel routines, but he never became a character in black prose narratives. Even so, only one of the
performers of the various texts included here feels any need to
identify him: the *D* text says he is "a fella called Shine, / he was
so dark he changed the world's mind." The only other such
identification I've heard is in a tape of a performance of Rudy
Ray Moore, a nightclub performer: "Up stepped a black man
from the deck below that they called Shine." The folklore of
color among American blacks is too complex to deal with here,
but one should note that "black is beautiful" is a recent perception, and there are many blues praising "high yellow" women
and complaining about black women; also that in much folk-

5. The theme does sometimes turn up in folksong, however, including Leadbelly's blues ballad about the sinking of the *Titanic*, which has
a stanza about the captain rejecting heavyweight champion Jack Johnson as a passenger because "I ain't haulin' no coal" (in John A. and
Alan Lomax, *Negro Folk Songs as Sung by Lead-Belly* [New York:
Macmillan, 1936], p. 182).

lore the "coal-black nigger" was often portrayed as dumber, meaner, and tougher than mulattoes — blacks were not free of the white stereotypes.

Consider the *A* text of *"Titanic."* After a beginning which sacrifices chronology for euphony ("fourth a May" is far easier to rhyme and vocalize than "twelfth of April"), the narrator situates himself far away from the action; we hear no more of him. The action proper begins with those in command — the captain and the sergeant in this version — "havin' some words," that is, squabbling like fools when they should be tending to the ship. Shine tells them what is going on, but they reject his data. He in turn rejects them: "but there's one time you white folks ain't gonna shit on Shine." He leaves the ship with "a thousand millionaires lookin' at him," but money is not his first temptation; it is rather the rich man's daughter, standing there clumsily with her drawers around her knees and her underskirt around her neck. She offers him sex, which he rejects, then marriage, which he also rejects. Another black leaves the ship — Jim — and he sees another girl on the deck who makes Shine the same offer. "Jim climbed his black ass back up on that ship," and we hear no more of him: he is the kind of fool Shine isn't, he can't delay gratification, and so presumably drowns along with the rich whites. Shine meets the shark, whom he outswims, and there is a sulking line I've heard in no other versions: "Swim, black motherfucker, 'cause I don't like black meat." While the *Titanic* is going down, Shine is in Los Angeles; by the time it has gone under he is across the country "damn near drunk." The poem concludes with a quatrain that is really a separate piece, one that not only has an independent existence as a drinking toast, but is on occasion appended to other poems.

Each version of the toast, except the short *B* text, has for an ending a group of lines that is detachable, lines that often are from another poem. It is almost as if when Shine reaches dry land he is no longer the same man he was at sea and must therefore be given another identity, a more familiar one, an identity appropriate to a cool stud on dry land.

Except for the second black man, Jim, and the Shark's sulking line, neither of which appear in any other versions, the text follows the general pattern of the toast. In most versions, Shine is propositioned by two women or by one woman twice; the first offer has to do with sex, the second with marriage, and he always rejects both.

The *E* version is interesting because of its use of uncoupled lines ("So John jumped and begin to swim," and "So John said, 'I want me some cock'"), which demonstrates that the poem is perceived in structural blocks; but more important is the narrator's confusion of Shine the swimmer with John the trickster. John is the clever slave in antebellum Negro folktales, the man who in one way or another outwits his brutal or clumsy or naive master (he is occasionally caught, but rarely); after Emancipation John becomes the hero of John / boss stories, many of which are the John / master stories altered to fit the new situation. He is the hero who by his wit and acuteness time and again outwits the boss — and sometimes other blacks — and manages favors or privileges otherwise denied him, or manages to get off scot-free for deeds that should have gotten him in trouble.[6]

But Shine is not a trickster; he has the verbal ability, the obvious pleasure in *saying* things, but he tricks no one, his mode is common sense. He is practical to the extreme. In all versions, it is not until the very end of the narrative, when he is safe on dry land, that he ceases to be busy and becomes silly or foolish or exhibitionistic. So why should this narrator — and some others not cited here — confuse him with John?

The link may be this: John is the man who again and again outsmarts the white man; Shine is the man who outswims him. At one very obvious level the toast is a response to a number of racial indignities: there is great pleasure for the audience hearing about Shine paddling away and refusing the white man's two favorite toys — his women and his money. In white folklore, the black man is supposed to be oversexed and incapable of handling money; there is even a pejorative term for a person who spends too freely, "nigger rich." Shine says he understands those things have their place: money is good only on shore,

6. See Richard M. Dorson, *American Negro Folktales* (New York: Fawcett, 1967), for many examples of John tales.

which is where *he* is going; as for sex, he is obviously able to get quite enough of that on dry land, where it is safer to do that sort of thing anyway.

I suspect it would be a mistake to view this toast in racial terms only. The paucity of overt racial themes in other toasts (what might be worked out subconsciously is another argument, moot here) suggests that if we want to know what this particular toast is about we should consider other interpretations in addition to the racial ones. Furthermore, the racial matter has always been so frustrating, and the audience knows that the humor is always terribly hollow.

In all the toast texts here except *B*, Shine finishes in a joint of some kind, with a prostitute, or having a massive sexual encounter. *B* is the shortest text — Shine comes up from below only once, and the offer of money in that version is combined with the response to sex, for the captain's daughter offers him money but he responds in terms of preferring other women. It is a good example of how a mediocre performer can recite the basic structure of the poem. *B* text is bare, lacking the modular units, the extra exchanges in couplets with people on the ship, and the extensions at the end. In the *C* text, for example, "The captain and the major was havin' a few words / and the old Titanic hit the first iceberg," then a little later, "Captain and the major had a few more words, / and the old Titanic hit the second iceberg." Such incremental repetition is the mark of a better folk poet, one who understands the genre and knows how to manipulate his audience and has a stanzaic repertory large enough to effect such manipulation. Notice that the temptation sequence in the *C* text begins with the captain's offer of money (while four thousand millionaires watch), then a thousand whores offer Shine sex, and then the captain's daughter offers him marriage. The *C* text has a line similar to the end of the *B* text — "I just left that big motherfucker fifteen minutes ago" — but it adds another quatrain.

The *C* text and Rudy Ray Moore's nightclub performance (not printed here) present the captain's daughter as being pregnant. I'm not sure about the meaning of this, unless it is a way of suggesting that she is hardly the nice virgin a captain's daughter is supposed to be, that trading sex for favors is nothing new to her, that the only thing new is the big step of offering the trade to a black man. But Shine knows any fool can get pregnant and he will have no part of it.

Written literature can outlive its maker and its original audience, so students tend to see written literature as existing on its own, independent of the maker and the user, and there are even pejorative terms used by literary critics for one who seriously examines what the maker intended or the respondent responded — the Intentional Fallacy and the Affective Fallacy. But the study of folk literature does not allow such luxury; we cannot forget that an item of folk literature has an ephemeral existence, it is transitory and idiosyncratic; the artist's perception of the audience's response and interest influences length and decoration and design. The telling situation of an item of folk narrative, the context, is as important as the text itself. A folktale told by a television wit and the same tale told the same way by an Ozark farmer are not the same thing, however much the words may sound alike.

Students of written literature must concern themselves with meaning, but students of folk literature must also consider function. The joke, for example, is a powerful genre: it puts all listeners in a dependent condition. That is why shaggy-dog stories elicit such frustration, and why interruption of a joke by a listener with the punch line so infuriates the teller and the failure of a punch line to elicit laughter so deflates him. In any joke-telling situation — and the recitations of toasts like "*Titanic*" are joke-telling situations — there are a number of dynamics occurring simultaneously. The individual listeners are responding in terms of their aesthetic to the manner of performance by the teller, but they are also responding in terms of their own concerns (their fears or anxieties are being exercised or decathected); and they must also respond to the social situation engendered by the telling between them and the teller, and between them and the other listeners.

Another problem is that there may be within the narrative certain notions or roles having particular significance for the group using the narrative but which are by no means constant. When we consider the bravery of a folk hero, we do well to consider what the culture at that time thought of bravery, and whether or not the perception of heroics changed over the time the folk narrative was in active repertory, and if so how that change influenced performance of the tale or how different perceptions were permitted by the same narrative structure.

The toast genre, for example, no longer serves the same safety-valve function it once served for black youths, and there has been a marked decrease in toast telling by younger blacks. The emergence of the toast as part of a nightclub act only verifies that; for the population in nightclubs is older, and their reactions to the stilted and stylized performances of someone like Rudy Ray Moore is at least partially informed by nostalgia for the days when *they* told the things themselves.

I would like to extend the symbolic action by Shine beyond the white/black conflict. It should take no great Freudian commitment to see Shine's leaving the ship and its captain as a rejection of more than mere white authority. The captain is the agent of all power at sea, he is the repository of all authority, the ship is his extension, the sea his medium; Shine rejects the first two and masters the dangers of the third. Not even the sexual temptations offered by members of the captain's (father's) entourage are sufficient to draw Shine back to that drowning fold. He cuts loose, strikes out on his own, his own man now. His silly reversion at the end — he is either drunk or trying to recover from an orgy — is no reversion in a temporal sense: he is childish, perhaps, but he is not childlike, and that is what is humorous about his role (a child, by the way, cannot be childish, the adjective is redundant). He has earned the right to be childish if he wishes, for earlier he was practical, the only one aboard the ship practical enough in time to save himself (the others do not, in the poem, even man their boats), unsentimental enough to refuse to try to save the others. The father, the authority, are gone; he has refused serious offers of sex in trade and now he may casually trade in sex. Shine is solidly on dry land, and he may now play the childish game without fearing revocation of his status. The one thing no one can take away from him is the fact that he has grown up.

Variant Texts

B. RECORDED 23 AUGUST 1965, OTEY, TEXAS.

It was sad indeed, it was sad in mind,
April the 14th of 1912 was a hell of a time,
when the news reached a seaport town
that the great Titanic was a sinking down.
Up popped Shine from the deck below,
says, "Captain, captain," says, "you don't know."
Says, "There's about forty feet of water on the boiler room floor."
He said, "Never mind, Shine, you go on back, and keep stackin'
    them sacks,
I got forty-eight pumps to keep the water back."
Shine said, "Well, that seems damned funny, it may be damned fine,
but I'm gonna try to save this black ass of mine."
So Shine jumped overboard and begin to swim,
and all the people standin' on deck watchin' him.
Captain's daughter ran on the deck with her dress above her head
    and her titties below her knees,
and said, "Shine, Shine, won't you save poor me?"
Say, "I'll make you as rich as any shine can be."
Shine said, "Miss, I know you is pretty and that is true,
but there's women on the shore can make a ass out a you."
So Shine turned over and began to swim,
people on the deck were still watchin' him.
A whale jumped up in the middle of the sea,
said, "Put a 'special delivery' on his black ass for me."
Shine said, "Your eyes may roll and your teeth may grit,
but if you're figurin' on eatin' me you can can that shit."
Shine continued to swim, he looked back, he ducked his head, he
    showed his ass,
"Look out sharks and fishes and let me pass."
He swimmed on till he came to a New York town,
and people asked had the Titanic gone down.
Shine said, "Hell, yeah." They said, "How do you know?"
He said, "I left the big motherfucker sinkin' about thirty minutes
    ago."

C. RECORDED 24 JUNE 1964, JEFFERSON CITY, MISSOURI.

In the year of 1812 [*sic*]
so many lives were lost it's hard to tell.
Now the story's true in every way,

but the third of May was a hell of a day.
The captain and the major was havin' a few words
and the old Titanic hit the first iceberg.
Shine come up from the decks below,
he said, "Captain, captain, don't you know:
there's forty foot a water on the boiler room floor."
Captain say, "Shine, Shine, that can't be a fact,
I got too many pumps to keep that water back.
Go back and get another blow."
Captain and the major had a few more words,
and the old Titanic hit the second iceberg.
Shine come from below the deck
with a lifesaver around his neck.
He say, "Captain, captain, I can't work no more.
Don't you know there's forty foot a water on the boiler room floor."
Captain say, "Shine, Shine, that can't be a fact,
I got four hundred pumps to keep that water back.
Go back and hit another blow."
Shine said, "Captain, captain, can't you see,
this ain't no time to bullshit me!
I'd rather be out on the big ocean going 'round and 'round
than to be on this big motherfucker slowly sinkin' down."
Shine jumped in the water and commenced to swim,
four thousand millionaires watchin' him.
Captain said, "Shine, Shine, save poor me,
I'll make you richer than old John D."
Shine turned around and took another notion,
say, "Captain, your money's counterfeit in this big-assed ocean."
Then from below the deck came a thousand whores
with their drawers in their hands and their tits around their neck.
They say, "Shine, Shine, save poor me,
I got the best white pussy you ever did see."
He says, "I'm sorry, ladies, but I gotta go,
but there's better pussy on yonder shore."
Then from below the deck came the Captain's daughter
with her drawers in her hand and her tits around her neck.
She said, "Shine, Shine, save poor me,
I'll make you the best white wife you ever did see."
He say, "I'm sorry, lady, but you 'bout to have a kid,
so jump and split the water like old Shine did."
Shine took a overhand stroke
that carried him five miles from that sinkin' boat.

Up popped a whale with a slimy ass,
say, "You a long time a-coming, but you here at last."
Shine said, "You swallowed old Jonah and you spit him on dry land,
but you'll never swallow me 'cause I'm a hell of a man."
Folks on the land were singin' "Nearer my God to Thee,"
The sharks in the ocean were singin', "Bring your ass to me."
Shine split the water like the battleship Maine,
the way he hit that New York harbor was a goddamned shame.
He spread it around town
that the Titanic was slowly sinking down.
They say, "Shine, how you know?"
He say, "I just left that big motherfucker fifteen minutes ago."
When the news reached Harlem that the Titanic had sunk,
Shine was in a whorehouse damn near drunk.
He said, "Now, whore, don't sit there with your mouth poked out,
'cause I'm a swimmin' motherfucker and a water trout."

D. 24 JUNE 1964, JEFFERSON CITY, MISSOURI. PERFORMED BY
SOMEONE ELSE IN THE SAME GROUP IMMEDIATELY AFTER C-
TEXT ABOVE WAS RECITED.
I don't know, but my folks say,
eighth a May was a hell of a day.
News reached the little seaport town
that the old Titanic was about to go down.
They tell me on board was a fella called Shine,
he was so dark he changed the world's mind.
Shine came up from the bottom deck below,
he said, "Captain, there's water runnin' all in the firebox door,
and I believe this big motherfucker's gonna overflow."
Captain said, "Shine, you go back down,
I got forty horsepower to keep the water pumped down."
Shine went down and came up with a teacup in his hand,
He said, "Look here, captain, I'm a scared man.
I'd rather be out there on that iceberg goin' around and 'round
than to be on this big raggedy motherfucker when it's goin' down."
Shine hit the water and he began to swim,
with ninety-nine millionaires lookin' at him.
Captain came out on the second deck, he said, "Shine, Shine, if you
    save poor me,"
say, "I'll make you as rich as any black may can be."
Shine said, "There's fish in the ocean, there's whales in the sea,
Captain, get your ass overboard and swim like me."

Now the captain's daughter came out on the second deck,
she say, "Shine, Shine, if you save poor me,"
say, "I'll give you all this white ass your eyes can see."
Shine say, "One thing about you white folks I couldn't understand:
you all wouldn't offer me that pussy when we was all on land."
Now Shine was swimmin', he was screamin' and yellin',
his ass was kickin' water like a motorboat propeller.
Swim on down by the Elbow Bend,
there he met the Devil and all a his friends.
Shark told Shine, say, "A bite a your ass would be a wonderful
    taste."
Shine said, "Man, it sure be a motherfucken race."
Then a stewardess came out on the second deck,
in her hand she held a book a check.
"Shine, Shine, if you save poor me,
I'll make you as rich as any black man can be."
Shine says, "Your money's good, it's good as gold,
but there's other shit on the other shore."
Say, when the news finally got around
that the old Titanic had finally gone down,
there was Shine on Main Street, damn near drunk,
tellin' every motherfucker how the Titanic sunk.
Now a whore said, "Shine, darlin', why didn't you drown?"
Said, "I had a cork in my ass, baby, and I couldn't go down."

E. RECORDED 17 AUGUST 1970, AT THE CONNELLY MIGRANT
CAMP NEAR BARKER, NEW YORK. THE PERFORMER IS PART OF A
GROUP OF MIGRANT WORKERS WHO MAKE THEIR PERMANENT
HOMES IN NORTHERN FLORIDA, WHICH ACCOUNTS FOR THE
REFERENCE TO JACKSONVILLE NEAR THE END OF THE POEM IN
A STRUCTURAL SLOT USUALLY FILLED BY NEW YORK OR HARLEM.
ALL THE FLORIDA VERSIONS I HAVE COLLECTED HAVE SHINE'S
SEXUAL MASTER FEAT AT THE END, BUT THIS VERSION ALSO HAS
TACKED ON IT A SLIGHTLY GARBLED VERSION OF ANOTHER TOAST,
ABOUT A SEXUAL HERO WHO LOSES HIS TESTICLES AND PENIS
BECAUSE OF VENEREAL DISEASE.
The tenth of May was a hell of a day
when the great Titanic was sinkin' away.
Hit the iceberg, that's what Richard [the performer] heard.
Shine on the fifth floor, captain on the sixth floor.

Shine come up from the deck below,
big old black dick all over the floor.
Saying, "Captain, this here gonna sink."
He say, "John, oh, John, fear no doubt,
I got forty-nine pumps to keep the water out.
So go and pump a little more."
Shit! Shine come up from deck below,
draggin' big old black dick all over the floor.
"Captain," he say, "we gonna sink."
He say, "John, oh, John, fear no doubt,
I got forty-nine pumps to keep the water out."
John say, "Yeah, captain, your word might be true,
but here's one goddamned day your word won't do."
So John jumped and begin to swim
with all those millionaires looking after him.
A millionaire's daughter came up on deck,
had her drawers around her neck.
She had nips on her titties sweet as plums,
she had hair on her cock make a dead man come.
She said, "Shine, oh, Shine, please save me,
I give you more pussy than a motherfucker see."
Shine say, "A nickle is a nickle, a dime is a dime,
get your motherfucken ass over the side and swim like mine."
Shine made two strokes
and water shot out a his ass like a two-ton motorboat.
So Shine begin to swim, runnin' with a shark.
Shark say, "Shine, oh, Shine, you better swim fast,
I got thirty-two teeth in the crack of your ass."
Shine say, "I outswim the white man, I outswim the Jew,
I know motherfucken well I can outswim you."
The little baby shark say, "Mama, mama, fear no doubt,
he swim like a fish and he taste like a trout."
Say when the great Titanic had sunk,
John was in Jacksonville damn near drunk.
So John said, "I want me some cock.
Now I'm gonna line a hundred whores up against the wall,"
say, "I'm gonna fuck 'em all in an hour's time."
So John fucked ninety-eight and he thought he was through.
He said, "Beat it, whore, I'm gonna get me a oyster stew."
He come back and fucked the other two.
He went to the doc, said, "I'm stupid like a goddamned fool."

Doctor cut his nuts off up to his dick.
He said, "Doctor, doctor, are you through?"
He said, "Hell, no, motherfucker, your nuts' goin' too!"

F. 10 AUGUST 1970, WILSON, NEW YORK. THIS INTERESTING
TEXT WAS COLLECTED FROM A TWELVE-YEAR-OLD BOY BY JUDY
KOLBAS, A STUDENT IN ONE OF MY FOLKLORE CLASSES AT BUF-
FALO. MOST OF THE NARRATIVE IS RECITED AS PROSE; ONLY THE
LINES WITH A DOUBLE INDENTATION WERE RECITED WITH VERSE
STRESS. THE TERM "JELLY" IS A EUPHEMISM FOR SEXUAL IN-
TERCOURSE.

This is about Shine O Shine. The captain was on his boat and he
was white. Shine runnin' around, he say, "Captain, water on the
first floor!"
"I don't give a damn if it's on the second floor."
He say, "Captain, water on the second floor!"
"I don't give a damn if it's on the third floor."
"Captain, captain, water on the third floor!"
"I don't care if it's on the fourth floor."
"Captain, captain, water on the fourth floor."
So the ship sunk. Everybody started strokin' out. Shine O Shine,
he strokin' on. So Shine met up with the captain. He say,
    "Shine O Shine, please save me,
    I give you more money than your eyes can see."
Shine O Shine say,
    "Money on land, money on sea,
    Money on land is just for me."
Shine kept on a strokin'. He met up with the captain's wife. She
say,
    "Shine O Shine, please save me,
    I give you more jelly than your eyes can see."
    He say, "Jelly on land, jelly on the sea,
    Jelly on the land is just for me."
And here go the captain's daughter, same age Shine is, and,
    "Shine O Shine, please save me,
    I give you more than your eyes can see." [Miss Kolbas said,
"More what?" and the narrator and two friends, also twelve, burst
out laughing.] He met up with a shark. He say,
    "Shine O Shine, you're strokin' fine,
    miss one stroke, your ass is mine."
That's what the shark say. Shark took after Shine O Shine who was
strokin' out. So Shine got on land. So Shine say,

"I lay a hundred womens against the wall,
I fucked ninety-eight, my balls turned blue,
I bet you a hundred dollars I fuck the other two."

G. 17 MARCH 1966, HUNTSVILLE, TEXAS. THIS VERSION OF THE
SONG WAS COLLECTED FROM A MAN IN HIS SEVENTIES WHO TOLD
ME HE HAD LEARNED IT IN TEXAS IN 1918. THE SINGER USES THE
CHORUS, AND LATER SOME OF THE STANZAS, FROM QUITE AN-
OTHER SONG, ONE ABOUT THE FAMOUS GALVESTON FLOOD OF
1900.

Chorus:
God moved on the water, God moved on the water, lord,
God moved on the waters, lord, and the people had to run and pray.

It was in the year of nineteen and twelve, about April the thirteenth
    day,
When the great Titanic was sinking down, while the peoples had to
    run and pray.
(*Chorus*)

When the great Titanic was sinking down, they throwed lifeboats
    around,
saying, "Save the womens and the childrens, and let the mens go
    down."
(*Chorus*)

When the lifeboats got the landin', the womens turned around,
Cryin, "Look way 'cross that ocean, lord, at my husband drown."
(*Chorus*)

Well sun stood still, refuse to shine, silence in Heaven for a space
    of time,
The rock did burst, the tempest begin, and my Father, forgive the
    sinful men.
As the nation suspended, three o'clock,
At the foot of that cross, it was the gambling flock.

Galveston with her sea wall, to keep the waters down,
But the high tide from the ocean, put water all over that town.
(*Chorus*)

Once there was a old time gambler, he gambled to the break of day,
Well he rose up from the table, throwed the dice and cards away.
(*Chorus*)

ROGER ROSENBLATT

The "Negro Everyman" and His Humor

White men have always supposed that black men do a great
deal of laughing, perhaps in the hope that the tag of good humor,
like the tag of a sense of rhythm, might imply happiness and
effect a kind of absolution. Many of America's earliest comedians
were black, or in blackface, or sometimes both, and it did not
seem at all contradictory to the audiences of the Georgia Min-
strels that the same people who had been forced to provide
everything else for their masters should be called upon to provide
hilarity as well. The caricature of the happy darky may be one
of the reasons why black authors have put so few comic characters into black writing. There are good-humored characters
in black fiction such as Jimboy in *Not without Laughter* and
Tea-Cake in *Their Eyes Were Watching God,* a few witty ironists
such as Bob Jones of *If He Hollers Let Him Go,* characters such
as Augie March (*God Sends Sunday*) who get caught in comic
situations, clowns such as McKay's Zeddy the Bear (*Home to
Harlem*) who are funny unintentionally; and there are pitchmen
and tricksters such as William Kelley's Cooley (*dem*), Ellison's
Ras (*Invisible Man*), and, in a way, Claude Brown (*Manchild
in the Promised Land*). But, with one exception, black literature
has produced no full, self-sustaining humorous hero, either out

225

of the desire to avoid reproducing end men, or because end men
seem out of place in the depictions of a nightmare.

The exception is Langston Hughes's Jesse B. Semple, called
Simple, who was stronger and more important than any nightmare in which he functioned. Modeled on a factory worker
Hughes met in a Harlem bar in the early forties, he became
known as the Negro Everyman, and during the twenty years of
his prominence his commentary filled over a hundred and fifty
columns of the *Chicago Defender* and the *New York Post,* five
books, and a Broadway musical. He was the embodiment of an
ideal intelligence, at once shrewd, generous, irreverent, resilient,
contemptuous of hypocrisy, inconsistent, manly, unrefined, and
frighteningly sane. He held opinions on everything which were
rarely encumbered with facts, and he had no formal learning to
choke on. In the Simple sketches Hughes pits his own college
education against Simple's native sense, and as is always the
case in such literary battles, the college education comes in
second. The name, Jesse B. Semple, was a combination of advice and imperative, and in his so-called simplicity Simple
joined the corps of American folk hero humorists — Uncle
Remus, Josh Billings, Mr. Dooley and others — who drew
laughter out of the shock and novelty of common sense. Simple
may not always have been as funny as his predecessors, but he
was richer and much more complicated.

He was an urban folk hero, equipped with city tastes and a
city vocabulary, yet he was as ardent a regionalist as Sam Slick,
Jonathan Oldstyle, Hosea Biglow, or any of the rural American
humorists. It made no difference that Simple's region was Harlem
and that his dialect was Harlem argot; his attitude toward his
section of the country was as elaborately loyal as a Westerner's
or Down Easter's, and he was just as purely a home-grown
philosopher. He was brash, as are all literary regionalists, he
was anti-authoritarian, and in spite of his critical stance and
occasional doomsday visions, he was an optimist at heart.
Where he differed from his fellow regionalists is that his region
was continually under attack, because in a larger sense than
Harlem his region was blackness; and so the criticisms he leveled
at the nation were often informed by a sense of urgency and
frustration which, until the emergence of contemporary black

comedians such as Dick Gregory and Godfrey Cambridge, was unique in American humor. There was also the difference between a cracker barrel and a bar stool. The fact that Simple did his philosophizing from a local dive was designed to be one of his comic properties, but it also suggested that in order to sustain his hopeful view of the world it helped to be high, if only on beer.

Above everything, he was a race man: " 'you certainly are race-conscious,' I said. 'Negroes, Negroes, Negroes! Everything in terms of race. Can't you think just once without thinking in terms of color?' 'I am colored,' said Simple." [1] In the middle of an essay on feet ("Feet Live Their Own Life," *Mind,* p. 3) he gives a list of the places where his feet have stood — at lunch counters, WPA desks, hospitals, graves, welfare windows, craps tables, kitchen doors, social security railings, soup lines, and the draft — all of which make up the Harlemite's itinerary. When his companion asks if there is anything truly special about his feet, he tells of a night in a Harlem street riot when one of his feet was used to kick in a store window, while the other was getting set to make a run for it. Inside the playfulness there is terror and indignation, yet the playfulness prevails. He composes poems about Jim Crow, feels the beating of Emmet Till as if it were happening to himself, and still can joke about a Second Coming in which Christ kills all the whites except for Mrs. Roosevelt. He can also poke fun at his own, mocking the kinds of articles that characterized black magazines of the fifties, and vowing that if he were in charge of one of such rags he would put out a three-part series, the first installment to be called *Can Sex Pass?* the second *Sex Seized in Passing,* the third *Please Pass the Sex.* Simple could make his readers feel angry, giddy, and abashed simultaneously and remain totally invulnerable to their feelings, like a good magician. His carapace was his honesty, not his humor, and when he said something like "I am colored," one smiled, not because the statement was funny, but because it was sublimely true.

1. Langston Hughes, *Simple Takes a Wife* (New York: Simon and Schuster, 1953), p. 22. Other Simple books quoted in this essay are *Simple Speaks his Mind* (New York: Simon and Schuster, 1950) and *Simple's Uncle Sam* (New York: Hill and Wang, 1967). References to these, abbreviated *Mind* and *Sam,* will hereafter be given in the text.

It was this sense of the sublime in him rather than his own sense of the ridiculous which accounted for Simple's effect. The laughter his pieces inspire springs from two absolutely antithetical impulses. One is the classical state of our feeling superior to him, not because he is silly or duped — he is rarely duped — but because he has been through a mill that most of his readers are safe from, at least at the moment of reading. Yet the other side of our laughter comes from sheer admiration and wonderment, out of our recognition that Simple is thoroughly superior to the things which have declared his inferiority. He is endurance itself. In his time, he boasts, he has been "laid off, fired, and not rehired, Jim Crowed, segregated, insulted, eliminated, locked in, locked out, locked up, left holding the bag, and denied relief . . . but I am still here" ("Census," *Sam,* p. 1). Throughout the sketches he repeats "I am still here" as if in defiance of a roll call which expected silence at his name. In a way, his humor derives from our perception that his obstinate desire to survive and flourish in the face of overwhelming odds is an absurd consistency, endurance being his humor in the Jonsonian sense. Yet we laugh more at the magnificence of the consistency than at its foolishness, as we would at the sight of something stunningly beautiful, the hah.

To create a character whom we laugh up to and down on at the same time takes an acute sense of balance. Hughes's method in the sketches was the standard one of setting up conversations between Simple and his friend, Boyd, which would serve as springboards for Simple's opinions and flights of imagination; but Hughes deviated from the pattern by giving Boyd a developed personality and a personal history. Ben Franklin's Silence Dogood, Seba Smith's Jack Downing, and other such characters who used the gimmick of letters addressed either to editors or imaginary relatives merely implied the existence of a third-party listener when they were confronting the reader directly. George W. Harris used an actual narrator for Sut Lovingood, but only as a kind of cattle prong, injecting "who"s and "why"s into Sut's monologues the way that Edgar Bergen would set up Charlie McCarthy for the punch lines. Mark Twain used a narrator in "The Celebrated Jumping Frog of Calaveras

County" who, like Boyd, was more of a gentleman than the main attraction; but Twain's speaker was only a straight man, created to heighten the humor by incongruity. Mr. Dooley had his Hennessy, but Hennessy functioned solely as an interviewer who was no more educated, and a good deal duller, than his friend. In contrast to these Boyd is a lively, intelligent, likeable, and completely believable man. Simple trusts and admires him, and is responsible for our doing the same. That he outshines and gets the better of Boyd only says so much more for Simple.

Occasionally, as in "Lynn Clarisse" (*Sam*, p. 83) where Boyd is trying to pick up Simple's cousin, Hughes lets his narrator out on his own, but he cannot afford to do this often for fear of dividing the reader's attention. Because Simple is the wiser and more clever of the two it is essential that he dominate the sketches, yet the interesting thing about Boyd is that Simple would not be half so effective a critic without his companion's presence. Susanne Langer points out (in *Feeling and Form*) that we tend to laugh at things in the theater which we might not think to be funny in life because we are not laughing at what the jokes mean to us, but what they mean to the play. There is a kind of two-man play being performed in all the Simple pieces, a play that progresses nowhere, has no beginning, middle, and end, but that nevertheless contains a number of distinguishable players (albeit most offstage), a distinct setting, a major character, a minor character, and a series of scenes. If, when we laugh at Simple's humor, we are merely laughing at the exercise of a comic spirit within a theatrical (unreal) framework, then none of Simple's social commentary can be too painful or outrageous. But neither can it be meaningful or effective. This is clearly one reason for minimizing Boyd's time "on stage," to avoid diminishing Simple's prominence and therefore increasing the power of his direct address to the reader.

But there is also a special sense of timing in operation here. Simple rarely starts any of his protest pieces with a protest. Usually he begins griping about something inane and irrelevant, and then only after a while does he strike his theme. He cons his reader in an obvious and expectable way; but the real trick is Hughes's, because by allowing just enough dialogue to go on between Simple and Boyd before the protest theme is reached he lets his reader think he is watching a play throughout. We laugh, then, at what the humor means to the play, and we continue to laugh long after the play construction has been dropped, after Boyd has dropped out, and right on into Simple's speech (on segregation, personal ethics, or national brutality), which is not spoken to any character but ourselves. If we do not laugh outright, we are at least pleased, and it is no easy feat to please people in their own instruction.

Like every comic realist, Simple is at heart a dreamer. Boyd, who is much more of a realist, takes him up on this fact often, and Simple admits it freely. There is a connection in his mind between dreaming and optimism, yet his comic fantasies are usually ominous and baleful. His sense of the fantastic is the satirist's sense. Commenting obliquely on black people as invisible men, he envisions a demonstration in which every black in the country, including Martin King, Adam Powell, "every waitress in Chock Full o' Nuts," and the Black Muslims, would take off his clothes so that "America would be forced to scrutinize our cause" ("Pose-Outs," *Sam*, p. 109). In another piece he worries that as yet there are no Negro astronauts in space, "because if one of them white Southerners gets to the moon first, 'Colored Not Admitted' signs will go up all over heaven as sure as God made little green apples, and Dixiecrats will be asking the man in the moon, 'Do you want your daughter to marry a Nigra?" ("The Moon," *Sam*, p. 28). His gazes into the future foresee exaggerations of the present by which the present is itself held up to ridicule. What he accomplishes with them is a projection of logical consequence, as if to say that if you doubt the craziness of the world we have now, let me show you how it will look done to a turn. Despite his fantasies, however, Simple can be as practical as Boyd. When his friend asks him if he would be the first to volunteer for the black "nude-out," Simple answers, "that honor I would leave to you."

The other device that Hughes puts to use is dialect, and Simple handles the device in a conventional way. Hughes did not indulge in the idiocy, which one often sees elsewhere, of misspelling words that his character pronounces correctly (for example, *luv*), and therefore making it appear as if the character is an illiterate writing the sketch rather than a speaking participant in it. Simple, however, does misplace *s*'s, add *-ations*, say "do" for "does," make verbs out of nouns, and generally mispronounce what is formally considered to be correct English. Such defects of language are traditionally supposed to be comic because they make the reader feel as if he possesses a higher culture and more education than the speaker. This is a particular trap for a portion of the white audience who — beneath the condescension it took to be amused by the sketches in the first place — believes all blacks to be ignorant and wants them to sound like it. One of the things that made *Amos and Andy*'s Kingfish, Rochester of the *Jack Benny Program,* and Mantan Moreland and Willie Best of the movies so hilarious to whites was the way they spoke. Accordingly, dialect was a peculiarly touchy device for Hughes to employ because he knew how his black readers would resent anything that smacked of stereotype. (In "Summer Ain't Simple" he digs at certain white representations of black life by having Simple observe that his papa wasn't rich, nor was his mama good looking). What Hughes did with dialect was what Twain had done with Huck and Henry Shaw had done with Josh Billings; he made it an integral part of his hero's intelligence. All the mistakes of diction which Simple makes are subsumed in that intelligence, are neutralized by it, and indeed are transformed. Not only does Simple dignify dialect, he makes the King's English seem awkward in comparison.

Under the surface of Simple's way of speaking is the implicit American contempt for education, which is both black and white and is attached vaguely to the Romantic conception of a free man. As a folk hero, humorist or otherwise, Simple is expected to outwit Boyd because Boyd is only "colleged," while Simple has had his education where it counts, in the streets. Although this feeling runs high and deep in American literature it has a particular quality when a black author expresses it, because for black people the question of the value of a formal education has less of a mythic and more of a practical base. For blacks in this country neither education nor the lack of it has provided much opportunity for advancement or freedom. The only reason for opting for street schools over colleges may be that the former take less time and effort to arrive at the same place, which is usually nowhere. Hughes handled this theme in his novel *Not Without Laughter,* where at the end the bright and promising Sandy is going to head for college and save his soul. But the ending seems tacked on and unconvincing. There is a much more realistic conclusion earlier in the book when Sandy takes a job running an elevator, just as Richard does in Baldwin's *Go Tell It on the Mountain* before he kills himself, because an elevator like a formal education is the perfect vehicle for providing the illusion of progress without the fact. When Will Rogers used "ain't" for "isn't" he was implying that moral and wise men have an eloquence of their own, but when Simple does the same thing he is not so much saying that the wrong words are better than the right ones as he is pointing to the futility of worrying about the problem.

I am beginning to refer to black and white readers under the assumption that Simple's audiences are distinct and show distinguishable responses. This assumption would not be true for "serious" black writing, either poetry or fiction, because in those cases the writer writes for an inner audience which is largely colorblind. In *Native Son,* for example, Wright may have considered the effects of his story on white and black readers separately, hoping for different kinds of awakening in each, but one still feels that such consideration was secondary to the professional and private exercise of his craft. With Hughes, however, the question of audience becomes more pertinent because in writing humor one must always theoretically be facing outward in order to court the laughter which is the only sort of approbation available. Simple is a black man, not making fun of black life, yet making fun out of it. When a white man laughs at this fun, is it the guilty laugh, the sympathetic laugh, Beckett's "dianoetic" laugh (*Watt*), or is it punitive? When the black man laughs, is it nervousness, embarassment, revenge, or magnanimity?

At one point in the "Census" sketch Simple complains that, because the census taker was white, he did not understand when Simple was making a joke. It is not true that white readers do not understand when Simple is joking, but the problem is what they understand those jokes to mean. For a black reader the impulse to laugh at "Feet" may be informed by commiseration or by a feeling of exhilaration in sharing the episode vicariously. For the white reader the reasons may be similar, but they can never be the same, and it is more likely that he laughs out of shame than anything else. The black reader too may feel shame, but it is the shame of what has happened to him, not at what he has caused to happen. Yet it also may be that no group feeling is present at all.

Bergson believed that the act of laughter suggests a complicity with other laughers, but in reading Simple it is questionable whether such complicity is felt. It seems more often than not that Simple is addressing the private best in our black or white selves, which we always assume to be in opposition to the public (or group) worst. Whenever he indicates that the nation is made up of fools, we read "the rest of the nation." He often does not appeal to fellow feeling in his readers as much as he does to the personal and isolated situation and, in a sense, to individual vanity, which is an educable element. Whether or not there is a color line in his audience it is fascinating, and a credit to Hughes, to note that as a character Simple does not seem to care in the least who his readers are or what they think. With most humorists, literary or real, we always get the sense of how fragile they are, that after three consecutive jokes without raising a chuckle they would disintegrate. But Simple seems entirely careless of our appraisal. He may appeal to our vanity, but he sustains himself on pride.

In *The Book of Negro Humor,* which Hughes edited, Roi Ottley records an anecdote about Robert S. Abbott, the founder and editor of the *Chicago Defender.* A judge named Abernathy in a small Georgia town was running for re-election on a hate-Negro platform. Blacks in the town sent Abernathy's campaign literature to Abbott, who instructed his staff to pillory Abernathy in an editorial. Abbott then sent five hundred copies of the editorial back to Abernathy's town for distribution, but when Abernathy's opponent reprinted the editorial for one of his own pamphlets, and acknowledged the source, Abernathy was re-elected by a landslide. The would-be heroes of the story, Abbott and the *Defender* staff, are hoist with their own petard, a classically comic circumstance. The unexpected occurs, Abernathy

turns the tables on his enemies, and as in cartoons where the
chased outwits the chasers, the audience is supposed to laugh
at the triumph of a lucky scoundrel. Yet, all the humor in the
anecdote derives from hatred: the judge's hatred of blacks, the
town's hatred of blacks and their Northern newspaper, Abbott's
hatred of Abernathy, and our own hatred of hatred as well.
What we are laughing (or more likely smiling) at is only partly
the irony of the judge's good fortune. That is a reflex laugh, the
situation demands it. But we are laughing primarily at our disappointment in humanity generally, and in ourselves. The anecdote is a pathetic story. It is funny largely because of its pathos,
which we appreciate because of our confidence in the inevitable
perseverance of human idiocy. In a sense our reaction defies the
Bergsonian rule, because instead of laughing at the unexpected
in the tale, we laugh at the all too readily expected. But the all
too readily expected can be as much of an aberration as total
surprise. Given enough time even the consistency of bigotry
becomes laughable.

Nobody understood this phenomenon more fully than Hughes,
who continually drew laughter from the unlaughable. Hazlitt
("On Wit and Humour") has said that humor makes the
ludicrous lead us to the pathetic, and in his choice of subject
matter this is precisely what Simple does. He jokes about poll
taxes, segregation, governmental corruption and neglect, dis-
enfranchisement, unemployment, hunger, ignorance, ghetto living conditions, the Ku Klux Klan, in short, about everything
that is inherently unfunny. Hughes himself said that "humor is
what you wish in your heart were not funny." [2] To Simple there
was nothing so terrible in the world that it could not be made to
seem ridiculous. He is purely and unrelentingly a social critic.
As Benchley took his humor from the upper reaches of the
middle class, from the perils of tennis games and hotel suites,
Simple took his from the harassment of his people and the con-
tinuation of their servitude. Surprisingly for a literary figure,
he only rarely deals in literary jokes — in "Matter for a Book"
(*Mind*), he wants to follow on Frank Yerby's success with
The Foxes of Harrow by writing *The Wolves of Harlem* — and

2. Langston Hughes, *The Book of Negro Humor* (New York: Dodd,
Mead, 1966), p. vii.

even more rarely is he witty or ironic. Nor will he indulge in savage or cruel comedy; the episode of the street riot is a joke about escape, not destruction. What he cares about exclusively are the troubles of being black, and like some of Synge's Wicklow and West Kerry men he makes laughter out of his own mistreatment.

Yet, along with being an ordinary man of his people, there is also an evangelical strain in Simple, a strain which is evident in the low-key preaching he does, and in the structure of the sketches themselves. Each of these pieces is built as a sermon. Not all of them deal with references to religion, though many do; but every one of them is modeled on the revivalist pattern of the preacher making an opening statement, which is followed by a pause in which the congregation says "amen" or an equivalent, which is in turn followed by the preacher's expansion of the topic at hand using examples usually drawn from his own experience. The use of this structure for comic rather than devotional purposes has been part of American stand-up comedians' routines for a long time. When Red Buttons began his act with "strange things are happening," or when Rodney Dangerfield starts out by saying "nobody gives me any respect," the idea was, and is, for the audience to think "amen," and then gear itself for the jokes to follow. Twain said that he was always preaching when he wrote, that if the humor emerged as part of the sermons, fine, but that he would have written the sermons in any case. We get something of this feeling with Simple. His sermons are part of himself and so they are humorous naturally, but because like Twain he is first a moral man, then a humorist, we realize that amusement is not the most important reaction intended.

There is a complication, however, in Simple's use of the religious framework which would probably not exist if he were white. Whenever he cracks jokes or fantasizes about heaven or angels or God, he is working within the convention of gently irreverent, folksy, and familiar humor, the kind that *Green Pastures* is made of. The main difference is tone, and Simple's tone on this subject is affected by his suspicion that he may be joking about someone else's God, a white one. There is a sketch called "God's Other Side" (*Sam*) in which Simple says that he would prefer to sit at the left hand of God instead of the right, like everyone else, so as to get more attention; but light-hearted as this piece is, underlying it there is the intimation that Simple and all blacks must always pay court to God's other side. In "Empty Houses" he recalls wondering if the white Jesus he had learned to pray to as a child "cared anything about a little colored boy's prayers" (*Sam,* p. 15). In all the sketches the religious joking lacks confidence, and without confidence the jokes develop an edge. Similarly his religious satires can sound heavyhanded, as is the case with "Cracker Prayer" (*Sam*), which when compared to something as finely controlled as John Betje-man's "In Westminster Abbey" seems ominous and seething.

No single aspect of black life in America has affected black literature as deeply as religion. In *Another Country* Ida, who is bent on revenge against the white world, remarks that she "learned all [her] Christianity from white folks." [3] She speaks bitterly because the God acquired was a God imposed, and along with the acquisition came a thousand crimes committed in His name. There is no major black author who has not grappled with the ambiguity of trying to believe in a religion which was trans-fused as a mollifying instrument for slaves, which promises future salvation while contributing to present isolation and tor-ment (Bigger Thomas noticed that the crosses burning outside his jail were no different from the one hanging around his neck), and which may, for all its promises, contain a heaven for whites only and be a hoax. This is the background to Simple's religious humor. When he speaks of St. Peter and the Pearly Gates it is not the voice of a man who trusts what he's making fun of, but of a man who is making a joke of something because he is supposed to trust it, yet does not. By poking fun at heaven Simple is partly poking fun at himself and all black people for whom heaven may be unattainable. There is fear behind this humor, but there is safety too; for if heaven and God do not exist for him after all, laughter may create the perspective to anticipate the loss.

The most remarkable thing about Simple is that he can be edgy or shaky in his humor or opinions, he can be grumpy or

3. James Baldwin, *Another Country* (New York: Dell, 1968), p. 237.

sour, digressive, illogical, wrong-headed, he can even be dull
without losing our affection or attention or anything in himself.
There is so much fluidity and grace in his makeup that the
subjects he discusses and the tricks he employs roll on and off
him like water beads, always leaving him to seem larger than the
sum total of his effects and defects as well. At the end of a
piece called "Dog Days" he simply runs out of ideas, but instead of stopping neatly he suddenly switches the topic from
dogs to a dogwood tree and a girl whom he once kissed under
it. When the consecutive-minded Boyd asks, "why did you bring
that up," Simple says "to revive my remembrance" (*Sam,* p.
106). The feat of these touches is that they regularly remind
us that Simple is more of a human being than a pundit. In this
he comes much closer to a folk hero like Davy Crockett
(though luckily he did not have a crazy living model to depend
on) than to a closet wit such as Jonathan Oldstyle, because he
has a life apart and distinguishable from his sense of humor. If
one were to imagine an instance when Mr. Dooley were pub-
licly proven wrong in his judgment of an important issue, it is
likely that Mr. Dooley's reputation would suffer because his
whole being relies on the accuracy of his wit. This is not the
case with Simple. He is more interesting than his intelligence,
and he outlives it. Nothing can shake him, no mishap and no
mistake.

He is, first of all, a completely honest man, about himself
particularly; and because his brand of honesty is so scarce it
becomes one of his comic attributes. As deeply as he is committed to the causes of civil rights, it is not an ethereal subject
with him, and he shows nothing but melancholy derision for
senseless martyrdom. In "Swinging High" he comments upon
the death of a white Cleveland minister who, as part of a protest against racial discrimination, lay down behind a bulldozer:
"I gather there are some things you would not do for a cause,"
said Boyd. "I would not lay down behind a bulldozer going
backwards," (*Sam,* p. 7) said Simple. His candor also extends
to the way he makes his points, loosely and without apparent
premeditation. The sketch on "Bomb Shelters" (*Sam*) deals
with the inanity of planning shelters for a Harlem tenement
whose quarters are so cramped that the shelters would not be

able to accommodate all the tenants, and which is probably
about to collapse anyway. Simple imagines a situation in which
he is battling his neighbors to get inside the shelter, a notion
which undoubtedly would have appealed to James Thurber.
But what Thurber would have done with it would have been
to invent a fable (riotous, of course) in which would be ex-
hibited all the selfishness people, or animals, are capable of,
selfishness akin to the evil that creates the necessity of bomb
shelters in the first place. Simple's style, on the other hand, is to
avoid the moral. He builds his theme haphazardly, letting the
laughs arise where they may, creating a full scene. By this he
suggests that nothing is funny or sad in isolation, himself included.

The honesty Simple uses to aid his humor works for other
effects as well. When he feels prejudiced, he says so directly (he
is unquestionably one of the most diehard male chauvinists in
literature). When he feels sanctimonious or sentimental he is
equally open. He gets away with total candor because he is
recognizably a good man, good enough even to laugh at his own
virtue: "now me, my specialty is to walk on water" ("Soul
Food," *Sam,* p. 111). His goodness is intimately bound to his
simplicity — which, at its conventional level, merely takes the
shape of wanting to strip the frills from things, of disliking high
tone and preferring soul food to French cooking, natural hairdos
to wigs, gospel to Italian opera, the Apollo Theater to the Met,
and so on. But in a more fundamental way Simple's simplicity
represents his effort to discover who he is and where he has
come from. It is the classic circumstance in black literature of the
hero's search for roots. By giving Simple his name Hughes implies that for a black man to be simple is a most difficult achievement. It means holding on to a sense of self and manhood in
a strange land that conspires daily against your doing so.

In the piece "Concernment" Simple and Boyd have a rare
squaring off, triggered when Boyd gets bogged down trying to
remember the exact word in a quotation. Simple says, "Boyd,
your diploma is worth every penny you paid for it. Only a man
who is colleged could talk like that. Me, I speaks simpler myself"
(*Sam,* p. 152). Boyd counters by observing that sometimes
simplicity can be more devious than erudition, to which Simple

answers, "of course." As usual Simple gets the last word, but by agreeing with Boyd he also makes a point. The reason Simple maintains his simplicity is not because he cannot fathom complications. Indeed, he gives the impression of already having been through the complications of a subject which have allowed him finally to arrive at his simple conclusion. What comes through instead of a contempt for complexities is a weariness of talking about them, of devising subordinate clauses and qualifying phrases which diffuse the energy of the central thought. The kind of maxim Simple coins is "greater love hath no man than that he lay down his life to get even" ("Junkies," *Sam,* p. 98). The kind of wisdom he lives by is that "there is no way for a man to commit bigamy without being married" ("Simple on Women," *Book of Negro Humor,* p. 146). If there are exceptions to his rules he takes them up one by one, but he refuses to be caught with the all-encompassing thesis on anything because such things carry a complacency which is alien to his nature and also impose a rigidity of their own.

Unlike the pseudo-innocent boy observers of American humor, Simple is a full-fledged grownup. He has been married and separated, is seeking and eventually obtains a divorce (which on principle he refuses to pay for), is courting one respectable woman while having an occasional fling with another less respectable one, has been, as he says, "cut, stabbed, run over, hit by a car, tromped by a horse, robbed, fooled, deceived, double-crossed, dealt seconds" ("Census," *Sam,* p. 2), can hold his liquor, believes very little he hears, and is beginning to go gray. As an adult he is not burdened by demands that his behavior or thinking be consistent. In separate sketches he toasts Harlem as paradise and condemns it as hell. He deplores warfare, composes a beautiful prayer against it, but admits "I would not mind a war if I could win it" ("A Toast to Harlem," *Mind,* p. 34). On the race issue he can, in different moods, sound like Ghandi or Rap Brown. He lives most of his time in a dream world and yet values nothing as highly as money and possessions. Having no use for education himself, he nevertheless would establish a fund to send all the young people in Harlem to college. He is a confirmed capitalist, yet fantasizes about the coming of a socialist millennium. At one point he brags to Boyd, "I am

the toughest Negro God's got" ("Family Tree," *Mind,* p. 26).
In a quieter spirit he confesses that he drinks because "I'm
lonesome inside myself" ("Conversation on the Corner," *Mind,*
p. 20).

There is a moment in the movie *Humoresque* when Oscar
Levant turns to John Garfield or Joan Crawford, I forget whom,
and says, "don't blame me, I didn't make the world; I barely
live on it." The sense Simple gives us is just that: of a man who
can take anything, who can roll with the punches, bounce back,
punch back if aroused, and at the same time who seems to be
living on a better and cleaner plane than the world he contends
with. In his "Character Notes" to the play *Simply Heavenly,*
Hughes describes Simple as Chaplinesque. Nothing could be
more apt. Like Chaplin, Simple was the complete humorous
creation. There has never been a character in black literature
like him, nor is there likely to be another in the future. For all
his combativeness Simple was a standard American dreamer who
believed in progress within the system, and his optimism would
have been incompatible with the present day mood. Moreover,
in a time of real and verbal militancy humor is judged to be a
harmful distraction, or "counterproductive." Yet he could not
have been born in a period earlier than he was, either; not in
the late twenties and early thirties when black writers were bent
on producing serious books and establishing the Harlem Renaissance, and certainly not before then, when whatever black writing existed was done by apologists. Simple came, flourished,
and went at just the right time. Even a few years before Hughes's
death in 1967 he was beginning to sound a little out of things,
a little forced.

Everyone knows that humorists perish rapidly, that unlike
tragedy, which endures from age to age, humor generally thrives
only within the lifetime of a particular taste. If Simple turns out
to be the exception to this rule it will not be because the jokes
he made held their flavor, but because the image of man he
represented was important to hold on to. On the level of vital
statistics no one could have stood further from the packaged
ideal of American heroism. He was disqualified from this designation by his loose love life, his upbringing, his habits, his
age, his physique, his disrespectful attitude, his friends, his

absence of prospects, and especially his color. Yet from a no less idealistic viewpoint Simple was more the embodiment of the all-American boy than a dozen Frank Merriwells or Jack Armstrongs. He was the fighter who knew when to quit, the resourceful, canny mind which could wax poetic on an impulse, the man unencumbered by possessions, the free man, the generous Joseph, the stumbler who admitted his mistakes, the survivor and the dreamer. To Schiller "the aim of comedy [was] the same as the highest destiny of man," [4] which was a liberation from all violence, cruelty, and stupidity. If Simple was more skeptical about such liberation being man's destiny, at least he felt it was worth a try. For himself he sought nothing but human decency between the races. When so simple a wish was persistently denied, he had to laugh.

4. Friedrich Schiller, "On Simple and Sentimental Poetry," in *The Comic in Theory and Practice,* ed. John Enck, Elizabeth Forter, and Alvin Whitley (New York: Appleton-Century-Crofts, 1960), p. 23.

W. M. FROHOCK

The Edge of Laughter: Some Modern Fiction and the Grotesque

The subject of these observations is not so much humor itself as the geography of that ill-defined border region that separates humor from the grotesque. That the territory is not exactly virgin anyone who remembers such landmarks as G. Wilson Knight's "*Lear* and the Comedy of the Grotesque," in *The Wheel of Fire,* will readily testify. As a matter of fact, only a feeling that the merit of Knight's thesis is not for me to contest inhibits suggesting that what I propose here could be taken as a sort of diffident footnote to his essay.

It seems to me plausible that, as Knight says, Shakespeare's triumph in *Lear* does consist of using the grotesque to exploit the parallel between the "Gloucester-theme" and the "Lear-theme" until, at the climax, they join in one mighty current of tragic emotion. On the other hand, I find his conviction that the play is in constant danger of slipping over the line from the grotesque into the ludicrous, or into what is currently called black humor, hard to share. I am not sure that one idiot bray of laughter could, in any event, be enough to let in the "salutary" light and air of comedy and empty *Lear* of all tragic substance, and still less persuaded that, even if it could do so, the danger of stirring uncontrollable laughter is at all real. But let this pass.

Assuming that Knight's contention is correct, and that the danger is indeed clear and present, he still fails to raise a question that would seem very proper in the instance: *how* does Shakespeare avoid such a collapse? Or rather, Knight raises it and then answers it so rapidly that it never gets off the ground: it is all a matter, he says, of controlling "perspective." As brief answers go, this one is unassailable, but it leaves us, since perspectives are in their turn a matter of contexts, knowing little more than that Shakespeare is Shakespeare and *Lear, Lear.* We may be left asking also what makes the achievement so very great.

If Knight had chosen to pursue the subject further he would have been forced to admit that lesser writers than Shakespeare have worked the shadowy area between the grotesque and the laughable, not only controlling perspective so as to avoid unwelcome effects but also manipulating it for purposes carefully contrived. The pursuit would have led him to consider a number of modern, and still current, novels. The choice of Céline's *Mort à crédit,* Ellison's *Invisible Man,* and Grass' *Blechtrommel* as illustration is prompted by the international character of the phenomenon and also by the fact that all three have heroes who could appropriately join Lear in his prayer to be kept in temper.

The following occurs early in *Mort à crédit*:

> L'oncle Edouard et son tricycle, c'est lui à présent que filait mon père, il surveillait de si près l'asphalte que sa bicyclette en pliait. Un gros caillou s'était logé dans sa narine. Le moteur tout doux roucoulait comme un amoureux ramier, mais les yeux d'Edouard traînaient au bout de deux ficelles, à même sur la route pour être bien certain de rien oublier.[1]

The image of the man leaning so far forward on his bicycle that the machine threatens to collapse under him, with his eyes dangling on strings almost to the surface of the street, and a pebble in his nostril, should qualify as grotesque: elements of ordinary, workaday reality have been dissociated into something

1. Paris: Editions de la Pléiade, p. 318.

incongruous and, since we do not know how to respond to the incongruity, enigmatic. But let the immediate context be restored and the enigma evaporates. The rider is following close behind his own primitive and decrepit but greatly cherished automobile, which someone else is driving. He is leaning over, with his eyes lowered to the asphalt, the better to observe the departure of various essential nuts and bolts. We have begun to suspect an explicit meaning: this could be a captionless and deadpan joke — in spirit not unlike the famous *New Yorker* drawing of the ski tracks separating to pass on opposite sides of a firtree — and on a subject extremely familiar to an era when automobiles were rare and properly functioning ones rarer. The grotesque would seem to have toppled over into humor.

In turn, the joke seems to become only richer and deeper when the passage is related to an earlier episode in which bicycle, rider, and automobile have also figured. Uncle Edouard, somewhat vaingloriously, invites the family to a jaunt in the new three-wheeler he has just bought. Grandmother, mother, and the narrator (at that writing a small child) crowd in; father follows, keeping pace with derisive ease, on his bicycle. Edouard's problem, once he has started the motor, is one of keeping the machine from disintegrating as it bumps and puffs along. His hands fly from one loosening part to another in a crescendo of frantic dexterity until, trying to cover the multiple leaks in a hose, his fingers race as if he were playing a flute.

The humor here is Chaplinesque: Edouard is in the position of the little tramp trying to cope with a difficulty too complex for him — and perhaps for anyone. And remembering this earlier sequence, the reader may interpet the later one — in which uncle and father have changed places — as an allusion intended to revive the mood of movie comedy. But he would discover his mistake in short order.

Beyond doubt, humor is plentiful in the sequence, but the use Céline makes of it is absolutely unhumorous. In the interval between the two episodes, the child who will become the narrator has started school. He has been brought home from class violently ill, fallen into fits of vomiting, and begun to run a high fever. Uncle Edouard's dangling eyes are part of his delirium; as the sequence proceeds the image will give way to one of a doctor embracing a thermometer four times as tall as the child.

I have dwelt so long upon this example because the nature of the novelist's strategy is so conveniently apparent. The raw material in both images is certainly humorous. The first one, reported by a presumably healthy, normal mind, retains its humorous quality. Taken out of context, the second is a textbook example of the device of treating a metaphor literally: in the instance, "keeping an eye out." The wild, losing struggle against the machine continues, unreal but madly logical. But with the full context restored, the reader is of course aware of having been forced to adopt a perspective not of normal health but of grave illness.

Habitual readers of Céline need no reminding of the importance of this strategy to his two early novels. From this point on, through the childhood of *Mort à crédit* and the adult years of *Voyage au bout de la nuit,* the narrative will waver between health and sickness, between the use of a "dependable" narrator and one whose illnesses overlie a chronic paranoia. A case is easily made for attributing the peculiar effect of Céline's fictions upon his reader to the latter's uncertainty about the narrator's vision at any moment of the story: are we, or are we not, sharing a hallucination? In episodes like that of the "Spanish Galleon" in *Voyage* we know the answer, but what about the pages about the Ellis Island louse-counting system which follow directly upon it? And when, subsequently, does sanity return?

Ralph Ellison's use of the grotesque toward the end of his novel is recognizably similar; acting as his own exegete, he reports needing a "naturalistic" style for the early part of his novel, an "impressionistic" one for the middle section, and a somewhat "surrealistic" one for the conclusion.[2] Doubtless he oversimplifies to make a point: the difference in treatment between the parts is not so distinct as he suggests. Yet one sees what he means. The hallucinated pages on the race riot in Harlem contrast markedly with, say, the report of the battle royal that opens the story. The following is from the final chapter of the narrative proper:

2. *Shadow and Act* (New York: Random House, 1964), p. 178.

The moon was high now, and before me the shattered glass glittered in the street like the water of a flooded river upon the surface of which I ran as in a dream, avoiding by fate alone the distorted objects washed away by the flood. Then suddenly I seemed to sink, sucked under: Ahead of me the body hung, white, naked and horribly feminine from a lamppost. I felt myself spin around in horror and it was as though I had turned some nightmarish somersault. I whirled, still moving by reflex, backtracking and stopped and now there was another and another, seven — all hanging before a gutted store front. I stumbled, hearing the cracking of bones underfoot and saw a physician's skeleton shattered on the street, the skull rolling away from the backbone, as I steadied long enough to notice the unnatural stiffness of those hanging above me. They were mannequins — "Dummies!" I said aloud. Hairless, bald, and sterilely feminine. And I recalled the boys in the blond wigs, expecting the relief of laughter, but suddenly was more devastated by the humor than the horror. But they are unreal, I thought: *are* they? What if one, even *one* is real — is . . . Sybil? I hugged my brief case, backing away, and ran . . .

They moved in a tight-knit order, carrying sticks and clubs, shotguns and rifles, led by Ras the Exhorter become Ras the Destroyer upon a great black horse. A new Ras of a haughty, vulgar dignity, dressed in the costume of an Abyssinian chieftain; a fur cap upon his head, his arm bearing a shield, a cape made of the skin of some wild animal around his shoulders. A figure more out of dream than out of Harlem, than out of even this Harlem night, yet real, alive, alarming.[3]

Even more clearly than in the episode of Uncle Edouard on his bicycle, links with waking reality, however severely strained, are not completely severed. Ellison's man does recover himself, even though on the very brink. We are in Harlem, not in some "other landscape" that never was. Human behavior here still presupposes rational motives, however obscure. What feels like a dream is still not one: the mannequins *look like* human bodies but with effort may be identified as what they are; the oneiric nature of the events is not absolute.

3. *The Invisible Man* (New York: Random House, 1952), pp. 419–420. This and the following passage from *The Invisible Man,* copyright 1952 by Ralph Ellison, are reprinted by permission of Random House, Inc.

Until the running man catches himself and reorients his vision, however, the procedure is identical with the one Céline uses: this is another case of metaphor treated literally. For a long moment hallucination commands the mind and actions of the protagonist. The glass-strewn surface of the street becomes a river and he feels himself being sucked under. And not only does the glass turn the asphalt to water, but the water is somehow strewn with dead men's bones while over it dangle the pseudo-corpses in their ghastly parody of a lynching. The enigmatic, disquieting incongruity characteristic of the grotesque is indisputably present — as in Céline: with minor allowances for modern elements in the context, this man could be running through a painting by Hieronymus Bosch.

What may not be immediately apparent, of course, is what change in perspective — what manipulation of context — would be required to reveal its content of latent humor.

Ellison lays the groundwork for such a change, to serve a purpose only gradually disclosed, in the picture of Ras the Exhorter. After the abrupt hiatus in the text, the reader's eye must take in, and his mind absorb, the spectacle of the mad street corner orator, who has been seen before only in his role of rabble-rouser, now emerging in his outlandish costume as a commander of men. He is out of place in space and time; and here again, in the mind of the beholder, dream and reality compete. More clearly than in the preceding picture, the incongruity is outrageous.

One's first, sanity-saving impulse, when confronted by such a vision, is to explain it away. It must be identified as a political gesture, an advertising trick, a bid for publicity, or almost anything of the sort so long as an understandable motive presents itself. The cost of failing to rationalize the spectacle, and thus tame it and restore it to its place in normal reality, can only be bewilderment and mental discomfort. So long as it remains enigmatic there can be no therapy of laughter.

Too much has happened to Ellison's man for him to be capable of such therapy. Especially since the defection and death of his friend, Clifton, he has been bombarded by more experience than he can absorb. His search for his own identity has been frustrated. For days he has been on the verge of physical flight. On this last evening, his drinking with his friend Sybil has been interrupted by news of the race riot in Harlem, for which, in a way, he is responsible. A ludicrous error — he gets on the wrong line uptown — delays his arrival on the scene. He moves about through a chaos of destruction until it comes home to him that what he has suspected is true: his life is literally in danger. Panic overtakes him, and is only increased by his encounters with the mannequins and with Ras. He simply takes to his heels.

Just what the total experience has done to him, how great the damage is, is of course the moral focus of his story. To solve the problem of revealing traumata that are of necessity internal, it is here that Ellison manages the radical change of perspective I have mentioned. His strategy consists of reviewing the meeting with Ras, which we have seen only as it has struck the hero's distraught mind, as it now has appeared to another character, who has been completely uninvolved and invulnerable to neurosis. Ellison makes his man go to ground behind a hedge, where he can hear two unidentified voices just beyond. Their dialogue takes up something more than two full pages.

A sample:

"You think *you* seen something? Hell, you ought to been over on Lennox about two hours ago. You know that stud Ras the Destroyer? Well, man, *he* was spitting blood."

"That crazy guy?"

"Hell, yes, man, he had him a big black hoss and a fur cap and some kind of old lion skin or something over his shoulders, and he was raising hell. Goddam if he wasn't a *sight,* riding up and down on this ole hoss, you know, one of the kind that pulls vegetable wagons, and he got him a cowboy saddle and some big spurs."

"Aw naw, man!"

"Hell, yes! Riding up and down the block yelling, 'Destroy 'em! Burn 'em out! I, *Ras,* commands you.' You get that, man," he said, " 'I, Ras, commands you — to destroy them to the last piece of rotten fish!' And 'bout that time some joker with a big ole Georgia voice sticks his head out of the window and yells, 'Ride 'em, cowboy. Give 'em hell and bananas.' And man, that crazy sonofabitch up there on that hoss looking like death eating a sandwich, he reaches down and comes up with a forty-five and starts blazing up at that window." [4]

The principal speaker is clearly well, uninvolved, completely relaxed. If he has neuroses they are dormant. He has seen a fine show, and is enjoying it over again as he describes it. Nothing has distorted his vision and his connection with reality is unbroken. From his angle, and at his distance of detachment, Ras and the horse have been richly, satisfyingly funny.

No lesson in how thoroughly perspective determines whether given material appears humorous or grotesque could be more effective. But still more can be learned. Ellison now returns to the perspective of the protagonist, still hidden behind his hedge, "wanting to laugh and yet knowing that Ras was not funny, or not only funny but dangerous as well, wrong but justified, crazy but coldly sane." The difference between him and the man who has been talking, and the difference in their two accounts, measures the psychic effect on him of what he has lived through. In a moment he will resume his flight and then disappear into his coal cellar.

Isolated cases like these of Ellison and Céline may seem more suggestive than conclusive, but committed readers of modern fiction can, I hope, be relied upon to recall other examples of capitalizing on the proximity of humor to the grotesque. If so, I hope also that among such novels will be a few like Grass's *Tin Drum,* in which an ambiguous playing back and forth between possible responses to various episodes becomes a determinant of the structure.

Oskar Matzerath is a peculiarly unreliable narrator. *Is* his grandfather dead or alive? *Is* Matzerath his father or not? *Did* Oskar try to maim himself? *Is* he the father of Maria's child? *Did* Lankes really gun down the nuns on the beach? Conclusions regarding such factual matters must be drawn at the reader's own risk. But uncertainty extends beyond the realm of fact to include Grass's intentions, meaning his motive for inserting certain episodes in the story and for assigning them the places where they appear.

Few of Grass's interpreters fail to study the chapter in which

4. *Ibid.,* pp. 424–425.

little Oskar disrupts an open-air Nazi rally. His three-foot height makes it easy for him to slip under the speakers' stand with his drum. From there, when the crowd has assembled, he beats out the rhythm of "The Beautiful Blue Danube." The rhythm becomes compulsive and the audience begins to waltz. The atmosphere changes from brown haze to blue. Oskar shifts to a charleston, compulsion becomes irresistible, and while speakers and officials on the platform writhe and storm in frustration, their audience skips and twists away from them across the meadow.[5]

One would be blind, of course, not to see in this episode a satire on National Socialism and the herds it recruited, or not to see the inherent humor. But critics have rarely insisted on its relationship to the episode of the Onion Cellar in the postwar part of the story. This Zwiebelkeller is a specialized nightclub where emotionally paralyzed Rhinelanders flock to drink, listen to music, and have their tears drawn by inhalations of raw onion. One evening the proprietor has a burst of generosity and doubles the dose of onion per customer. Maudlin weeping gets out of hand; the proprietor takes fright and tells Oskar, now adult and playing in the orchestra, to disperse the guests. Oskar beats a rhythm that makes the weepers increasingly docile and childlike; they rise and follow him around the floor, up out into the open air and to an open space where, their infantilism now complete, they form a ring-around-the-rosy, squat . . . and wet their imaginary diapers.

Taken by itself, the episode might pass for nothing more important than another of Oskar's demented phantasies, and perhaps an example of somewhat pointless humor. In the total context, which must include the dispersing of the Nazi rally, humor disappears. These people in the Onion Cellar are not Nazis, but they are Germans, and despite the lesson they might have learned from recent history these Germans are as mindless and easily led as ever the Nazis were. The episode of the rally can seem funny because the danger is in the past. But let the

5. *Die Blechtrommel* (Frankfurt and Hamburg: Fischer Bucherie, 1962), pp. 93–99. For a fuller discussion of the episode see H. C. Hatfield, *Crisis and Continuity in Modern German Fiction* (Ithaca, N.Y.: Cornell University Press, 1969).

perspective be altered to bring the danger into the present and what was funny becomes grim indeed. Thematically, the two episodes take their places in the structure of what can be read only as Grass's statement of his disappointment, if not despair, in what has happened to his country.

Especially in view of Ralph Ellison's intention for the final pages of *The Invisible Man* — but also because, given the pre-occupations of current criticism, the subject would come up in any event — it is proper to ask whether such literary behavior indicates anything more than the survival of European sur-realism. We have recently witnessed a renewal of interest in *l'humour noir,* together with the minor apotheosis of André Breton. Can we be sure that our recent fiction is not living on a legacy from a generation only slightly earlier?

One thing is certain: novelists like Grass, Céline, and Ellison cannot have learned anything from a form that could be called "the surrealist novel." In fact, it is exceedingly difficult to show that such a novel ever existed, because the surrealists — those of the strict observance, anyhow — did not write novels: Breton's *Nadja,* which must be accounted the major prose monu-ment of the movement, reports something that actually hap-pened; Louis Aragon took to writing fiction only after his "ex-communication"; Raymond Roussel's linguistic exercises have stronger affinities with the later Joyce, and with the anagram, than with any novel one can think of. In brief, the late Claude-Edmonde Magny's doubts that surrealism contributed anything at all to the development of prose narrative[6] were surely not without foundation. The most determined attempt to assess what contribution there may have been is obliged to occupy itself with minor, even peripheral, figures.[7] And the few novelists, like Julien Gracq and Georges Limbour, whose writing does re-veal a surrealist affiliation, remained — I believe unjustly — unknown and obscure too long for them to have exercised even local, not to say international, influence.

6. *Histoire du roman français depuis 1918* (Paris: Editions du Seuil, 1950), pp. 33–40. Because of its date this account does not consider the later writing of Julien Gracq.

7. J. H. Matthews, *Surrealism and the Novel* (Ann Arbor: University of Michigan Press, 1966).

Novels like, say, Gracq's *Château d'Argol* are also very different in character from these others that are alleged to reveal a surrealist influence. The people who move through Gracq's Poesque landscapes do not respond to stimuli as we do, or to the same stimuli; cause and effect are not related in the same way, and the motives of conduct are consequently inscrutable; the reader has no way of imagining himself a participant in the action, or of identifying himself, even remotely, with a character. His role becomes one of pure spectatorship. He looks in upon a world that is not the world he lives in.

In contrast, the world of Grass and Céline and Ellison — and even the world of the novelists most often cited as having "rejected realism," like John Hawkes and J-M. G. Le Clézio[8] — remains one recognizable as ours. Its reality, however distorted, is the one we have to deal with. These authors do not share the surrealist's intention of creating a better, more tolerable frame of life.[9]

It is perfectly true, of course, that the sequence in Ellison's novel assembles irrationally disparate materials — asphalt, glass, bones, mannequins — in a manner reminiscent of certain surrealist *montages,* just as the image of the man on the bicycle in Céline suggests Salvador Dali in some of his belligerently paranoid moods. And quite similarly, certain pages of *Die Blechtrommel,* for example those where the action is moved to the pillboxes on the shore of the English Channel, might pass for an imitation of some surrealist master. But the point is that, for all the surrealists delighted in such distortions, they did not invent them. Such materials would have been available even if history

8. That the novel has "retreated" from realism has been taken as axiomatic in many quarters, including the two colloquia recently convoked by *Novel: A Forum of Fiction,* in England and the United States. At a later date I shall yield to the temptation to voice a mild dissent.

9. How literally some critics have intended their remarks on the survival of surrealism is an open question. Albert J. Guerard notes in his Introduction to John Hawkes, *The Cannibal* (Norfolk, Conn.: New Directions, 1949), that the latter's work recalls Kafka and Djuna Barnes, but that Hawkes seems less "surrealistic" than in the earlier *Charivari.* See also Robert Scholes, *The Fabulators* (New York: Oxford University Press), pp. 59–94, where the term appears to designate a recurrent literary "mode" rather than something historical.

had never known surrealism. They are out on loan from the treasury of the perennial grotesque.

They were equally available to Shakespeare, and apparently — according to G. Wilson Knight — he used them well. I have been trying to show that certain modern novelists, endowed less richly than Shakespeare, have contrived to adjust perspectives so as to achieve similar ends. This fact suggests that if Shakespeare had failed to control his grotesque material . . . hoity, toity! then the less Shakespeare he.

ROBERT ALTER

Jewish Humor and the Domestication of Myth

It is an instructive paradox that one of the grimmest stretches in Jewish history — the recent centuries of Yiddish-speaking culture in Eastern Europe — should also prove to be the period in Jewish history that produced the most richly distinctive humor. Especially since popular stereotypes of diaspora Jewish history tend to represent it wholly in the image of the ghettos of Central and Eastern Europe and the townlets of the Pale of Settlement, it is worth stressing that rarely before had Jews been so physically constricted, so continuously depressed economically; and perhaps not since the Crusades and the Black Plague did they feel so repeatedly threatened by physical havoc as in Russia during the last decades under the czars. In such circumstances, it has been suggested, a shrewdly ironic humor became a source of necessary inner strength, a mode of survival. Maurice Samuel, the eloquent expositor of East-European Jewish culture, states the case pointedly:

> There was nothing jolly and hilarious about the destitution that lay like a curse on millions of Jews in the Yiddish-speaking world; and it would be grotesque to speak of Sholom Aleichem's and Mendele's *kaptsonim* [paupers] and *evyonim* [indigents] as

255

"poor and happy." They were miserable, and knew it; but the question that haunts us historically is, why did they not disintegrate intellectually and morally? How were they able, under hideous oppression and corroding privation, under continuous starvation — the tail of a herring was a dish — to keep alive against a better day the spirit originally breathed into man? The answer lies in the self-mockery by which they rose above their condition to see afar off the hope of the future.[1]

This is beautifully apt, but the implications of "self-mockery," and its relation to a sense of the future, deserve exploration. The European cultural tradition, I would suggest, characteristically conceives suffering as a mystery, beginning with and drawing on the cultic or literary formulation of the mystery of suffering in Greek tragedy and in Christ's passion. Affliction is the medium through which man must realize his humanity, or more-than-humanity; accordingly, he must view both himself and his suffering with the utmost seriousness, defining his time, which is the time of human fulfillment, by the internal rhythm of his suffering. Hamlet, Werther, Dmitri Karamazov, Camus's Stranger are paradigmatic figures of this European tradition. Against them, one might usefully set Sholom Aleichem's Tevye, who acts upon the wisdom of the Yiddish proverb "burdens are from God, shoulders, too," never for a moment imagining that it would be appropriate to seek fulfillment through suffering, to create a mythology out of suffering; and who uses his shoulders as much to shrug at adversity as to bear it.

Jewish humor typically drains the charge of cosmic significance from suffering by grounding it in a world of homey practical realities. "If you want to forget all your troubles," runs another Yiddish proverb, "put on a shoe that's too tight." The point is not only in the "message" of the saying, that a present pain puts others out of mind, but also in its formulation: *Weltschmerz* begins to seem preposterous when one is wincing over crushed bunions. If in the tradition of Jewish humor suffering is understandably imagined as inevitable, it is also conceived as incongruous with dignity — thus the sufferer is at least faintly ridiculous, his complementary comic embodiments of *shlemiel*

1. Samuel, *In Praise of Yiddish* (New York: Cowles, 1971), pp. 210–211.

and *shlimazel* become central in the folk tradition and the literature deriving from it. The perception of incongruity implies the
perception of alternate possibilities, humor peeking beyond the
beleaguered present toward another kind of man and another
kind of time; for the very aura of ridicule suggests that it is not,
after all, fitting for a man to be this pitiful creature with a blade
of anguish in his heart and both feet entangled in a clanking
chain of calamities.

As the sense of inner crisis has deepened in modern literature,
one important direction taken by writers beginning with Conrad, Mann, and Eliot has been a conscious re-mythologizing
of literature, usually in order to make it sound the full cultural
resonance of our collective disorders. Against this general drift
of literary modernism, writers significantly touched by the Yiddish heritage have often been de-mythologizers, using the wry-
ness and homey realism of Jewish humor to suggest that a less
melodramatic, less apocalyptic, perspective than that of myth
might be appropriate for viewing even the disquieting state of
affairs of the modern world. I would like to begin with an extreme example — a novel peopled entirely by WASPs and black
Africans, set in the heart of the dark continent, with not a hint
of an *oi* or a *veh* amidst the native ululations — precisely because it may illustrate the persistence of a Jewish modality of
imagination even in the total absence of Jewish realia. The book
I have in mind is of course *Henderson the Rain King,* a novel
that remains one of the most engaging of Saul Bellow's fictions,
despite the flaws of its conclusion. Bellow, it should be observed,
is one of the very few American Jewish writers who has more
than nostalgic misinformation about the Yiddish-speaking ancestral world: from his ghetto childhood in Montreal he retains
enough Hebrew to make proper use of biblical and liturgical
motifs in his fiction, enough genuinely literate Yiddish to have
produced admirable translations of stories by Sholom Aleichem
and I. B. Singer. *Henderson* would seem to be a conscious attempt on the part of a writer who generally uses Jewish milieux
and characters to write for once a thoroughly American novel.
(In this, and little else, it resembles Malamud's *The Natural* and
Philip Roth's *When She Was Good.*) The hero is a strapping
Westchester county millionaire of Protestant descent, first seen

wallowing among pigs on his farm. The plot consists of a spiritual safari to Africa — Henderson's initials, Leslie Fiedler has
observed, are the same as Ernest Hemingway's — in which the
hero eventually tries to prove his manhood and discover wisdom
by staring down a lion in an underground cell.

Henderson's irrepressible innocence suggests a kind of aging
Huck Finn of the Eisenhower years, yet for all his exuberant
Americanism, one is also strongly tempted to apply to him
some of the rubrics of Yiddish characterology. An inveterate
misadventurer, there is a good deal of the self-perceiving
shlemiel in Henderson, tinctured with an admixture of the *klots*
(clumsy oaf) or the eternal *grober yung* (slob, boorish young
man). Following parodistically on the trail of Conrad's Marlow,
Lawrence's Kate Leslie, and other modern questers into dark
regions, Henderson clearly carries along a very different apparatus of imagination, and it is worth observing precisely how
his mind copes with the unspeakable mysteries of the jungle.
His version of a native ceremonial procession is characteristic:
"amazons, wives, children carrying long sheaves of Indian corn,
warriors holding idols and fetishes in their arms which were
freshly smeared with ochre and calcimine and were as ugly as
human conception could make them." So far, this seems a
factual enough evocation of a primitive rite, and might easily
fit into a narrative by Conrad except for its avoidance of those
Conradian adjectives of looming immensity and ominous things
impending. Immediately, however, something peculiar begins
to happen to the exotic scene: "Some were all teeth, and others
all nostrils, while several had tools bigger than their bodies." The
conversational hyperbole ("all teeth," "all nostrils") of course
heightens the grotesqueness of the idols while suggesting a
quality of ironic observation or perhaps even wondering amusement which separates the speaker from the savage rite, and that
quality is reinforced by the use of the familiar-colloquial (but
not obscene) "tool" to describe the carved phalluses. Henderson, who has excruciating difficulties with a broken dental
bridge, who feels the world's beauty through a tingling in the
gums, to whom even the African mountains look as though
they might have bad teeth, is struck first by the apparition of
toothy gods: as with the pinched feet in the proverb, the novel

as a whole tends to shrink suffering and sensitivity to the realistic dimensions of a homey physical detail. Henderson goes on to render his response to the African scene through a rhetorical device that he uses repeatedly elsewhere: "The yard suddenly became very crowded. The sun blasted and blazed. Acetylene does not peel paint more than this sun did the doors of my heart. Foolishly, I told myself that I was feeling faint. (It was owing to my size and strength that this appeared foolish.) And I thought that this was like a summer's day in New York. I had taken the wrong subway and instead of reaching upper Broadway I had gone to Lenox Avenue and 125th Street, struggling up to the sidewalk." [2]

The energy of the style makes Henderson's experience seem very "real," but in a way that violently assimilates Africa to an American metropolitan landscape. Henderson's narrative is a continual farce of deliberately gross similes: acetylene torches and peeling paint, bubbling percolators, baseball stadiums, limousines to La Guardia Field, the smokestacks of Gary, Indiana, cover the African vistas of the novel. The technique effectively destroys any possibility of using exotic climes as a vehicle for myth. Henderson is in his own way open to new experience, as his friendship with King Dahfu demonstrates, but he remains imaginatively anchored in a world of familiar places, objects, and implements; and he cannot be drawn into a yawning abyss of the unknown because his first mental reflex is to domesticate the unknown with a comparison. (The deflation of mysteries through an attachment to the familiar also operates in his sense of who he is. In whatever bizarre roles circumstances cast him, he knows that Henderson the clumsy clown is no mythic Fisher King. Here, he maintains the comic self-consciousness of a knowing *shlemiel,* which enables him in the midst of his account of a wild ceremony to note how absurd it is that such a hulk of a man as he is should think himself on the point of fainting.) Many a newcomer to New York has undergone the inadvertent *rite de passage* of neglecting to change trains at 96th Street and thus discovering himself in the heart of Harlem instead of at Morningside Heights. Henderson's

2. Bellow, *Henderson the Rain King* (New York: Viking, 1959), p. 166.

invocation of that experience at this point vividly conveys a sense of sudden disorientation in an unfamiliar crowd of Negroes, but there is an underlying congruity in the comic incongruity of the comparison that might best be paraphrased with a Jewish verbal shrug: "Natives, shmatives, there are people everywhere. So maybe someone can tell me where I should go?"

The point of the comedy of similes throughout *Henderson* is to banish from the protagonist's world the possibility of a primordial Other Side of human life. We deceive ourselves, the novel suggests, with the drama of a return to archaic origins. Through Henderson we are led to acknowledge the home-truth that we have only our civilized selves to work with. Appropriately, Dahfu, Henderson's spiritual guide, turns out to be a former medical student with looney theories about the road to inner transformation — more or less, a black cousin germane to the New York Jewish intellectuals (like Bellow's friend Isaac Rosenfeld) who, for example, plunged into Wilhelm Reich and built themselves orgone boxes to hasten a personal redemption.

A similar process of ironic or playful domestication of myth is often observable when Jewish writers deal with heaven, hell, and the realm of fantastic creatures in between. Though it is customary to think of Judaism as a this-worldly faith, Jews in fact have often believed fervently in reward and punishment after death, in ministering angels (invoked by name in the bedtime prayer) and lurking demons. Nevertheless, all these otherworldly paraphernalia never quite attained what would be canonical status in another religion, a fact that has given the folk imagination and writers inspired by it considerable freedom in treating these materials. Thus, the charm of Itzik Manger's *Book of Paradise* (1939) depends upon the completely uninhibited way in which the celestial Eden is recast in the image of the Rumanian *shtetl* that Manger knew as a boy. The first glimpse of the streets of Eden at nightfall is of a piece with everything that follows: "Bearded angels were bent over yellowed holy books. Fat lady angels with triple chins were patching shirts; young mother angels were rocking cradles, lulling the first-born little ones with song," while at the local tavern — named after Noah, the proverbial biblical drunkard — angels of the coarser sort "were sitting at small tables, drinking spirits, smoking cheap tobacco, and continually spitting at the floor through their teeth." [3]

Manger's translation of a spit-covered tavern floor into the fields of paradise has an imaginative affinity with Bellow's conjuring up Lenox Avenue and 125th Street in the supposed heart of darkness, though the emotional effect is rather different: Bellow transports a zest for things familiar into the scary realm of the unknown, while Manger, equally moved by affection for the familiar, introduces into the True World (*di emese velt*) the grossness, the poignancy, and the sadness of things flawed in the world below. In both cases, humor is generated by the disparity between our expectations of an ideal type (the primordial African, the paradisiac soul) and what the writer actually invents for us; but Manger's comedy is tinged with wistfulness, for if indeed we have only our familiar world to imagine with, then wherever there is life schoolboys are whipped, poor tailors starve, parents and children bicker, and the spiritual magnates (*tsadikim*) lord it over the common people.

Something of this mood of soberly realistic humor touched with sadness is present in Bernard Malamud's naturalization of fantasy to the American Jewish immigrant milieu. Malamud has his own vividly humanized angels — the black Jew from Harlem in "Angel Levine" who, trying to earn his wings, comes to the aid of a poor Jewish tailor; and Ginzburg, the ominous Yiddish-accented figure in "Idiots First" who turns out to be the *malekh-hamoves*, the Angel of Death. At the penultimate moment of "Idiots First," Mendel, the distraught father, seizes Ginzburg in anger, crying, "You bastard, don't you understand what it means human?" [4] and a moment later Ginzburg is actually shocked into relenting, despite himself allowing Mendel's idiot son to depart for California. This final turn of the plot could serve as an emblem of how the whole mode of imagination works, wresting a kind of concession from the ultimate powers by the very act of humanizing them, conceiving them in such a way that they will understand what it means human.

A related translation of the fantastic into the familiar is

3. Manger, *The Book of Paradise*, trans. from the Yiddish by Leonard Wolf (New York: Hill and Wang, 1965), p. 8.

4. Malamud, *Idiots First* (New York: Farrar, Straus, 1963), p. 14.

effected, perhaps with more artistic success, in another Malamud story, "The Jewbird." It becomes evident very soon in the story that this remarkable talking bird — "Gevalt, a pogrom" are its first words when the Jewish pater familias takes a swipe at it — is virtually an allegorical figure of the wandering old-world Jew. Its name, after its color, is Schwartz, and in the eyes of its unwilling host it is clearly what is known in the vernacular as a *shvartser yid,* a Jew who is "black" not in the racial sense but in the foul oppressiveness of his crude manner and his religious obscurantism. "The Jewbird," in fact, deals in its peculiar way with essentially the same predicament of identity as Philip Roth's "Eli the Fanatic" — the ambivalence, guilt, and impulse to rejection aroused in an American Jew by the confrontation with a black-garbed survivor of the ancestral world. Without the fantasy of the talking bird, and the muted comedy generated by that incongruity, this would be merely a sour story. As it is, the conclusion is bleak enough, Schwartz finally being cast out and ending in the snow with a twisted neck. Without the grubby realism in which the fantasy is embodied, the bird would be only a contrived symbol and the story would lack conviction. Malamud's invention engages the imagination precisely because the black bird of exile is able to assume so persuasively the habits and accents of a familiar milieu and a familiar type. He has a fondness for herring and schnapps, his breath stinks of garlic, his speech is a chain of wry Yiddish twists only minimally conforming to the prevalent syntactical and lexical requirements of spoken English.

Now, one might be tempted to dismiss all this as a compound of anecdotal affectation passed off as fictional invention were it not for its necessary function in the Jewbird's relation to his host, Harry Cohen. For Cohen, the "Americanized" frozen-food salesman, the bird must embody in all its details the stigmatized stereotype of a kind of Jew that he emphatically wants to leave behind. Cohen is really attacking a part of himself in his hostility toward Schwartz; this becomes clear at the end of the story when, swinging the bird around his head, he enacts a parody of the ceremony of *shlogen kapores,* in which a rooster was whirled in the air before being slaughtered on the eve of the Day of Atonement, while the person holding the bird recited the formula "this is my surrogate, this is my atonement." What the reader quickly realizes is that Cohen is by far the grosser of the two figures, and that by contrast Schwartz, in the very pungency of his garlic-redolent Yiddishisms, possesses a certain quality of nobility.

He is a creature who lives meagerly, but lives nevertheless, by his wit, and even though this resource finally fails him, the impress he makes is of a shrewd, engagingly stubborn survivor. He knows too much of the hardships of surviving to have any grand expectations of future circumstances, but his mental shrugs help him maintain some sort of inner equilibrium through his difficulties by ceding their inevitability while contracting their ruinous nature to imaginable dimensions. The very first words of the story, where the narrator seems to move immediately to a rendering of Schwartz's interior speech, briskly define the use of a kind of acerbic stoicism as a means of coping with adversity: "The window was open so the skinny bird flew in. Flappity-flap with its frazzled black wings. That's how it goes. It's open, you're in. Closed, you're out and that's your fate." [5] As we perceive from the grief to which the Jewbird finally comes, this is hardly a way of overcoming disaster, but it does provide a strength of resolution to go on.

The procedure of amiable domestication to which Manger and Malamud subject their angels is happily applied by Isaac Bashevis Singer to the multitude of demons who variously prance, slink, and amble through his stories. One of the most memorable of all these is the nameless narrator of "The Last Demon," a story in which the immense sadness of matter and the delightfulness of manner constitute a paradigm for the use of comedy as a last defense of the imagination against grim fate. This story is one of the rare attempts anywhere in Singer's work to respond to the horror of the Holocaust, and it is effective precisely because of the brilliant obliquity of its method. The demon briefly alludes to the Holocaust in the opening words of his tale but then promptly drops the subject and seems to forget about it until the last three paragraphs of the story: "I, a demon, bear witness that there are no more demons left. Why demons, when man himself is a demon? Why persuade to evil

5. *Ibid.,* p. 101.

someone who is already convinced? . . . I board in an attic in Tishevitz and draw my sustenance from a Yiddish storybook, a left-over from the days before the great catastrophe." [6] The original is less ambiguous, since *khurben,* the word rendered as "catastrophe," is the accepted term for the Holocaust. In any case, our immediate attention is caught less by the magnitude of the catastrophe than by the amusing, cool-headed logicality of the speaker — "after all, should I go convince someone who's already convinced?" — who at once proceeds to affirm by statement and demonstrate by tone his authenticity as a familiar folk figure: "I don't have to tell you that I'm a Jew. What else, a Gentile? I've heard that there are Gentile demons, but I don't know any, nor do I wish to know them. Jacob and Esau don't become in-laws." Tone, of course, is tied up with language, and so "What else, a Gentile?" catches only part of the homely nuance of *"vos den bin ikh, a goy?"* — while the humor of Jacob and Esau as in-laws is largely lost because there is no English equivalent for the Yiddish *mekhutonim,* which implies an elaborate and dignified sense of social alliance and extended kinship, and is sometimes also used jocularly or sardonically to suggest a dubious or presumptuous relationship.

The demon-narrator is thoroughly engaging not only in his easy command of the comic inflections of the folk, sharpened in the Yiddish by his talmudist's fondness for Hebraisms and Aramaicisms, but also in the way he maintains the jaunty posture of a city slicker (from Lublin) condemned by the infernal powers-that-be to cool his heels among the hayseeds. He has a worldling's contempt for Tishevitz, a one-horse, mud-choked town so small, he claims, that "in the tailors' synagogue a billy goat is the tenth in the quorum." [7] He can only condescend to the resident imp of Tishevitz, a hopeless yokel who "cracks jokes that didn't amuse Enoch" and "drops names from the Haggadah," to whom he charitably proposes the possibility of a devil's position elsewhere: "We have an opening for a mixer

6. Singer, *Short Friday* (New York: Farrar, Straus & Giroux, 1964), p. 119. The original appears in *Gimpel tam un andere dertseylungen* (New York: Central Yiddish Culture Organization, 1963), pp. 237–247.
7. *Ibid.,* p. 120.

of bitter herbs. You only work Passovers." [8] Alongside the breezy urbanity of the demon, the virtuous young rabbi whom he chooses as his target seems a pale figure. The minimal plot of the story consists of the demon's futile effort to tempt the rabbi. The implicit point of that action is its very humanity: this is a world where good and evil are still struggled over and the rules of the game are familiar to both sides, where the rabbi is truly saintly and the demon one of the old school, the sort that can quote Bible and Talmud with the best of them and conjure up for his victim visions of sex and power and even a chance at messiahship, who preens himself on his abilities but is smart enough to know when he has met his match. Then, in a few swift sentences, with no transition and without the hint of an appeal for pathos, this whole world is wiped away:

> The rabbi was martyred on a Friday in the month of Nisan. The community was slaughtered, the holy books burned, the cemetery desecrated. The *Book of Creation* has been returned to the Creator . . . The generation is already guilty seven times over, but Messiah does not come. To whom should he come? Messiah did not come for the Jews, so the Jews went to Messiah. There is no further need for demons. We have also been annihilated. I am the last, a refugee. I can go anywhere I please, but where should a demon like me go? To the murderers? [9]

Tempting though it may be to read the last word of the passage as it appears in English with a throat flooded with outrage, it seems to me that what the whole context of the story calls for is another sardonic shrug, closing the circle of those with which the story began — "what do you think, a self-respecting demon like me should go mix with murderers?" The consideration of tone is essential because the tone suggests that even after genocide — and the entire story, we must recall, is told retrospectivey after that ghastly fact — the demon maintains his humanity (what else, devilishness?) by preserving his

8. *Ibid.*, p. 125. The translation here, though in the jaunty spirit of the original, is a free improvisation on the Yiddish, in which "mixer of bitter herbs" is literally "salad-chef."

9. *Ibid.*, pp. 129–130.

knowing, ironic sense of things, though tinged now with bitterness.

Significantly, the story ends with the narrator's attention wholly absorbed in the Yiddish storybook he alluded to at the beginning. The book is an old-fashioned compilation in the best demonic manner, filled with blasphemies, denials of God's justice, invitations to transgression and despair. "But nevertheless the letters are Jewish," the last demon affirms, and he lingers over them, torturing each one with the traditional *pilpul* of interpretation, drawing nurture from them. In cabalistic lore, the twenty-two letters of the Hebrew alphabet, the letters through which God created the world, remain ontological constituents of reality. Through their combinations and permutations man can tap sources of cosmic power, establish connections with the ultimate ground of being. The Yiddish black book over which the demon pores represents merely a reversed mirror-image of that cabalistic tradition: the narrator concludes with the recitation of a demon's alphabet, from *aleph* to *yod,* in which each sacred letter is made to spell disaster but nevertheless remains a sign in a system of cosmic orthography, a key of meaning, though the meaning is dismal. Humor collapses in the face of utter chaos, and the characteristic Jewish humor of shrewd observation especially needs to assume a realm of meaning accessible to intelligence, even if it suspects that whatever meaning it unearths will be perverse, unconsoling.

Something of the general function of the comic domestication of myth may be revealed by the fact that in Singer's story the surviving demon proves in the end to be a surrogate for the writer — a wry teller of tales in the old way, steeped in the values and traditions of a vanished world, conjuring with the letters of the lost in the sickening vacuum left by their destruction. My description, of course, of the narrator's final predicament is a little misleading because it neglects his engaging buoyancy of tone in all but the three concluding paragraphs of the story: the last demon is not a self-dramatizing Survivor[10] but, almost eerily, an enlivening voice from the old world, demonstrating the peculiar vitality of its values through his own person.

10. The hint of melodramatic tremulo in the title is absent from the Yiddish, in which the story is simply called "A Tale of Tishevitz."

Instructively, writers who draw on this whole mode of folk imagination tend to create fictional events that are not impersonally conveyed but manifestly *narrated,* as though the act of narration and the presence of a narrator sane enough to be funny in a mad world were a way of hanging on to lucidity. If much modern writing, from Rimbaud's attempted *dérèglement de tous les sens* to the jumbled hallucinations of William Burroughs, has conceived radical disorientation as the necessary path to reality, the legacy of Jewish humor, by contrast, seems to encourage a kind of traditionalism in writers, leading them to draw even the realms of the ultimate unknown into a comfortable human space warmed and worn by long usage. This imaginative at-homeness with the experience of a personal and collective past generally implies a stubborn if cautious hopefulness about the future, or perhaps simply the ability to imagine a human future. Thus Singer's demon draws "sustenance" from the letters, knowing that when the letters are gone he will be gone too, and the imaginable world at an end. If disaster, whatever the scale, seems to be our general fate, the persistence of the comic reflex is itself evidence of the perdurability of the stuff of humanity: a shrug is a small and subtle gesture, but, in the face of the harshest history, it may take a world of strength to make.

MATHEW WINSTON

Humour noir and Black Humor

For some two millennia the term "black humor" had a clear and limited meaning: it signified the black bile that was thought to be produced by the brain and to cause melancholy. André Breton changed all that in 1939 when he coined the term anew in his *Anthologie de l'humour noir,* a collection of miscellaneous writings by forty-five authors, with a preface (*Paratonnerre*) and an introduction to each author by Breton. Breton's selections, which include epigrams, letters, essays, poems, and portions of plays and novels, are too short and various to fit comfortably under the rubric of any single literary form. In his highly mannered prose, Breton provides what is less a definition than a subjective impression of *humour noir:*

> Pour prendre part au tournoi noir de l'humour, il faut en effet avoir échappé à de nombreux éliminatoires. L'humour noir est borné par trop de choses, telles que la bêtise, l'ironie sceptique, la plaisanterie sans gravité... (l'énumération serait longue) mais il est par excellence l'ennemi mortel de la sentimentalité à l'air perpétuellement aux abois — la sentimentalité toujours sur fond bleu — et d'une certaine fantaisie à court terme, qui se donne trop souvent pour la poésie, persiste bien vainement à vouloir soumettre l'esprit à ses artifices caducs, et n'en a sans doute

plus pour longtemps à dresser sur le soleil, parmi les autres graines de pavot, sa tête de grue couronnée.[1]

Extrapolating from Breton's remarks and from the evidence of his selections, it is clear that he did not intend *humour noir* to designate a genre. Rather, he presents black humor as an attitude, a stance, or a perspective which exists independently of literature but which may be embodied in writing. It uses an ironic and biting intelligence to attack sentimentality, social convention (including literary convention), and an apparently absurd universe. It is opposed to simplistic thinking, and expresses this opposition by verbally yoking disparate concepts without attempting to reconcile them. It scorns the limitations of rational thought, and therefore favors the fantastic, the surreal, and the grotesque. It wishes to break down complacency and to reveal how a man's unconscious realities belie his harmonious surface, and consequently employs violent images and shock tactics. Although the black humorist often takes a moralist's or satirist's stance, his perception of inseparable complexities and unresolvable antitheses keeps him from advocating or hoping for any reform. Instead, he attempts to bring his audience into the same position he occupies by threatening or horrifying it and then undercutting its fear by some witty or comic turn. This position is seen as a liberating one, as an assertion of human independence, because it acknowledges the pains and fears of life and transcends them.[2] Breton cites with approval a passage from Freud's essay "Der Humor" (1927):

1. "To participate in the black tournament of humor, one must indeed have passed through several stages of elimination. Black humor is circumscribed by too many things, such as stupidity, skeptical irony, jokes without seriousness... (the enumeration would be long), but it is especially the mortal enemy of sentimentality with its perpetually hounded air, sentimentality on a sky-blue background, and of a certain short-term fantasy which too often tries to pass for poetry, which persists vainly in wanting to subject the mind to its collapsing artifices, and which for this reason probably has little time left to raise against the sun, among the other poppy seeds, its head of a crowned crane" (*grue* may also mean "prostitute"). Breton, *Anthologie de l'humour noir* (Paris: J. J. Pauvert, 1966), pp. 21–22. This is the definitive edition of the *Anthologie*.

2. My interpretation of Breton has been shaped in part by Michel Carrouges, *André Breton: et les données fondamentales du surréalisme*

Like jokes and the comic, humour has something liberating about it; but it also has something of grandeur and elevation, which is lacking in the other two ways of obtaining pleasure from intellectual activity. The grandeur in it clearly lies in the triumph of narcissism, the victorious assertion of the ego's invulnerability. The ego refuses to be distressed by the provocations of reality, to let itself be compelled to suffer. It insists that it cannot be affected by the traumas of the external world; it shows, in fact, that such traumas are no more than occasions for it to gain pleasure.[3]

Breton's perspective of *humour noir* is a view from a safe distance; the author stands apart from the hopeless world at which he laughs and brings his audience to the same distance. But he also mocks himself, makes jest of his earnestness, and belittles his own work. These characteristics place Breton's concept within a continental tradition of humor as a kind of Romantic irony which simultaneously perceives all of life as ridiculous and as deadly serious. In 1804, Jean Paul Richter described humor in this fashion in his *Vorschule der Ästhetik*: "I divide my ego into two factors, the finite and the infinite, and I make the latter confront the former. People laugh at that, for they say, 'Impossible! That is much too absurd!' To be sure! Hence in the humorist the ego plays the lead; wherever possible he brings upon his comic stage his personal conditions, but only to annihilate them poetically. For he is himself his own fool and the comic quartet of Italian masks, himself the manager and the director." [4]

(Paris: Gallimard, 1950), pp. 110–114; Claude Mauriac, "Breton et l'humour noir," *Hommes et idées d'aujourd'hui* (Paris: Albin Michel, 1953), pp. 147–160; and J. H. Matthews, "Intelligence at the Service of Surrealism: Breton's *Anthologie de l'humour noir*," *Books Abroad*, 41 (Summer 1967), 267–273.

3. Sigmund Freud, "Humour," *The Standard Edition of the Complete Psychological Works of Sigmund Freud*, vol. XXI (1927–1931), ed. and trans. James Strachey (London: Hogarth, 1961), p. 162. Cited in Breton, pp. 19–20. It is significant that Breton emphasizes with italics "something of grandeur and elevation" (*quelque chose de sublime et d'élevé*).

4. Cited in Alan Reynolds Thompson, *The Dry Mock: A Study of Irony in Drama* (Berkeley and Los Angeles: University of California Press, 1948), pp. 66–67.

One hundred years later, Luigi Pirandello discussed humor in much the same manner in his *L'Umorismo* (1908), defining it as *il sentimento del contrario*.[5] This tradition may have helped Breton's coinage to become popular in France, where his phrase is current, although its meaning is by no means fixed. A recent anthology of *humour noir* emphasizes its satirical aspect;[6] another reading stresses its harshness and potential metaphysical implications.[7] Eugène Ionesco, who has aligned his own work with black humor, incorporates both interpretations in his discussions of *humour noir*.[8]

Humour noir underwent a sea-change when it made its appearance in English and American criticism of the early 1960's as "black humo(u)r" and "black comedy." Given a darker, less affirmative interpretation, it seemed to be the dominant tone of a new generation of writers. By 1961 *Twentieth Century* magazine could claim that "a wide influence is exerted by specialists in nihilistic satire, black literary humour, and the theatre of the absurd."[9] Critics began to feel that black humor was the spirit of the times and often censured the two together. For example, John Gross claimed that "except for odd bursts of euphoria we no longer have the confidence which festive comedy requires . . . Instead, we have learned to take our comedy black, looking to it for additional discords rather than fresh harmonies, demanding of it not light, but rather darkness risible. And black comedy is essentially anti-comedy, resting on a mistrust of all laughter which is neither bitter nor disruptive."[10]

In America, virtually all critics who wrote about black

5. Pirandello, *L'Umorismo*, 2nd ed., rev. (Florence: Luigi Battistelli, 1920). Note also his essays "Immagine del 'Grottesco'" and "Ironia" in *Saggi, poesie e scritti varii*, ed. Manlio lo Vecchio-Musti (Milan: Arnoldo Mondadori, 1960), pp. 990–995.

6. *Le Livre blanc de l'humour noir*, ed. Jean-Paul Lacroix and Michel Chrestien (Paris: Pensée Moderne, 1967), pp. 9–12.

7. "Humour," *Grand Larousse encyclopédique*, vol. V (Paris: Larousse, 1962), p. 994.

8. See the quotation from Ionesco cited in *Le Livre blanc*, p. 13, and his observations on black humor in *Notes and Counter Notes: Writings on the Theatre*, trans. Donald Watson (New York: Grove, 1964), pp. 142–144. Ionesco was labeled a black humorist by Jean Anouilh in "Du chapitre des chaises," *Le Figaro*, 23 April 1956, p. 1.

9. "Comedy," *Twentieth Century*, 170 (July 1961), 4.

10. "Darkness Risible," *Encounter*, 23 (October 1964), 41.

humor ignored its French antecedents, thinking they had dis-covered a new term to fit a new tone in recent American fiction, represented by the works of Joseph Heller, J. P. Donleavy, Wil-liam Burroughs, Terry Southern, Ken Kesey, and Vladimir Na-bokov. The work of these and other novelists was sometimes grouped under the rubric of "the absurd novel," primarily by analogy with the theater of the absurd. However, "black humor" soon became a common, if imprecise, part of the American critical vocabulary. Its currency by 1965 is attested by the pub-lication of an article on "The Black Humorists" in *Time* (12 February 1965, pp. 94–96) and of an anthology entitled *Black Humor*.[11]

It seems unnecessarily provincial to apply the concept of black humor only to American fiction of the past fifteen years, espe-cially since that body of literature shares a common spirit and a similar set of techniques with drama and with European fiction. Rather than operate within such a restricted framework, this essay attempts to define and discuss a concept of black humor which has a broader applicability, a concept partially based on the observations of André Breton and of recent American critics.

Black humor is a tone in drama and fiction which is simul-taneously frightening or threatening and farcical or amusing. It exists as it reverberates within the reader or spectator. Experi-encing it, we feel ourselves caught "between laughter and fear . . . between terror and uncontrollable laughter," to use the words of Witold Gombrowicz's *Ferdydurke*.[12] The violent com-bination of opposing extremes unsettles us so that we do not know how to respond. Our emotional and intellectual reactions become confused; this in turn disturbs our certainty of moral and social values and challenges our sense of a secure norm.

Although black humor is a response within us, we experience it as it emanates from something outside of ourselves. If we are frightened or amused by a person we speak of *him* as frighten-ing or amusing. In the same manner, objects or situations can be seen as terrifying or as ridiculous. We may therefore speak of

11. Ed. Bruce Jay Friedman (New York: Bantam, 1965). This was soon followed by another anthology, *The World of Black Humor: An Introductory Anthology of Selections and Criticism,* ed. Douglas M. Davis (New York: Dutton, 1967).

12. Trans. Eric Mosbacher (New York: Grove, 1968), pp. 13, 16.

black humor residing within a character or episode which elicits from us its responsive mood. The tone may suffuse an entire work, as is indicated by such subtitles as Ghelderode's *tragédie bouffe* (*Fastes d'enfer*) and *vaudeville attristant* (*Pantagleize*) or Ionesco's *farce tragique* (*Les Chaises*). When black humor is the dominant tone it tends to encourage, or to find its home in, a distinctive treatment of character, language, plot, and structure.

The tone of black humor and the characteristics most suited to conveying that tone have become increasingly important in literature since the Second World War. It is significant that many critical studies which have attempted to deal with this phenomenon under such labels as tragicomedy, satire, and irony (often using the same illustrations for all three concepts) have found themselves compelled to posit a "modern" form of these genres which differs radically from the traditional form.[13]

We can understand black humor more thoroughly if we see what it has in common with these forms and how it differs from them. It resembles tragicomedy only insofar as it uses the devices of both comedy and, to a lesser extent, tragedy. But the median nature of tragicomedy, which avoids the extremes of "mirth and killing," [14] is at odds with black humor's violent juxtaposition and combination of just such extremes.

Black humor often reveals life's shabbiness and criticizes in the manner of satire. But unlike satire, it does not assume a set of norms, implicit or explicit, against which one may contrast the mad world depicted by the author. It relies neither on "common sense" as a guide to proportion and decorum, nor on social, religious, or moral convention. This is not to say that the reader of black humor is without norms. He has them, and the writer

13. See, e.g., J. L. Styan, *The Dark Comedy: The Development of Modern Comic Tragedy*, 2nd ed. (Cambridge: Cambridge University Press, 1968); Karl S. Guthke, *Modern Tragicomedy: An Investigation into the Nature of the Genre* (New York: Random House, 1966); Matthew Hodgart, *Satire* (New York: McGraw-Hill, 1969), pp. 155, 202; Patricia Meyer Spacks, "Some Reflections on Satire," *Genre*, 1 (January 1968), 3–30; Leonard Feinberg, *Introduction to Satire* (Ames: Iowa State University Press, 1967); Douglas C. Muecke, *The Compass of Irony* (London: Methuen, 1969)

14. The words are John Fletcher's, describing the genre in his "To the Reader," *The Faithful Shepherdess* (c. 1608–1610).

of black humor exploits them. The reader's sense of decency allows the writer to shock, the reader's humanity allows him to horrify, the reader's sense of verisimilitude enables him to outrage, and the reader's familiarity with dramatic and fictional conventions permits him to parody. But he does not rely on the reader's agreeing with him that a certain norm ought to exist, and he does not attempt to convince the reader of what should be. Moreover, black humor challenges not only the standards of judgment on which the satirist relies, but also the very faculties of judgment. W. H. Auden observes this phenomenon in the works of Nathanael West, one of the most important American black humorists.[15] "Satire presupposes conscience and reason as the judges between the true and the false, the moral and the immoral, to which it appeals, but for West these faculties are themselves the creators of unreality." [16]

The conception of black humor sketched thus far is in general accord with Breton's. It differs in the relation it establishes between the work and its audience. Breton's *humour noir* is ironic. Although it need not be normative, it makes the reader or spectator into a detached onlooker who can savor the incongruities presented to him and unravel the various perspectives contained in the work. Black humor is not ironic in this sense. It disturbs and disorients us. It limits us to the narrow perspective of its characters, does not permit us to feel superior to them, and regularly destroys our secure detachment.

Black humor achieves its distinctive effects by playing with our involvement with the work and shifting our distance from it. It has four main ways of disorienting us. The first is to alternate rapidly between blackness and humor, threat and amusement, horror and farce, or to combine these extremes so that we cannot respond to either one alone.

Second, it may present what appears to be patently impossible and assure us that what we see is true. Its world is often bizarre and surrealistic; motivation and causality are unclear; characters are alienated from us; normality is lost: realistic details, how-

15. The publication of *The Complete Works of Nathanael West* (New York: Farrar, Straus & Giroux) in 1957 may have stimulated the subsequent upsurge of American black humor.
16. Auden, "Interlude: West's Disease," *The Dyer's Hand and Other Essays* (New York: Random House, 1962), pp. 240–241.

ever, are presented with extreme clarity, thereby keeping the work from drifting off into pure fantasy. There is enough veri-similitude for us to feel ourselves in an ordered and familiar world, and enough of the disordered and inexplicable to keep us off balance. As Walter Kerr has observed, "the laughter that greets black comedy is sporadic, uncertain, often ill at ease . . . A laugh begins because we see the contradiction between what is happening on stage and what we hold to be true; then it falters, descends into hollowness, because we cannot be certain that what we hold *is* true and because what is happening on stage has the grim authority of a recorded event." [17] To achieve the same effect, the novel often uses an apparently unreliable nar-rator who matter-of-factly relates fantastic and unbelievable events.

A third technique is continually to change our distance from the characters. Often we are made to laugh at a character, then suddenly to recognize that we share his dilemma and therefore have been laughing at ourselves all along. Our response is like that of the protagonist of West's *Miss Lonelyhearts* as he under-goes this process:

> A man is hired to give advice to the readers of a newspaper. The job is a circulation stunt and the whole staff considers it a joke. He welcomes the job, for it might lead to a gossip column . . . He too considers the job a joke, but after several months at it, the joke begins to escape him. He sees that the majority of the letters are profoundly humble pleas for moral and spiritual ad-vice, that they are inarticulate expressions of genuine suffering. He also discovers that his correspondents take him seriously. For the first time in his life, he is forced to examine the values by which he lives. This examination shows him that he is the victim of the joke and not its perpetrator.
>
> (*Complete Works*, p. 106)

Once this recognition takes place, the laughter has to stop. But black humor keeps shifting the perspective, so that its charac-ters act in a ridiculous fashion when we are prepared to sympa-thize with them and become serious when we wish to laugh.

17. *Tragedy and Comedy* (New York: Simon and Schuster, 1967), p. 320.

Neither we nor the characters are ever on a firm foundation.

Finally, black humor may suddenly distance us from the work and unsettle our responses by reminding us of its own artifice. It is an extremely self-conscious form, which plays with our suspension of disbelief by periodically shattering the illusion of a self-contained fictive world. The drama may do this by direct address to the audience or by allusion to the action on stage as dramatic play. The novel may toy with the format of the printed page, as when Beckett includes in *Watt* footnotes, musical scores, and several pages of "addenda." Either may anticipate and mock our instinctive responses. At a moment of high tension in *Lolita,* Humbert Humbert tells us: "Then I pulled out my automatic — I mean, this is the kind of a fool thing a reader might suppose I did. It never even occurred to me to do it" (pt. II, chap. 29). By breaking the illusion the author calls our attention to himself and to ourselves in the act of reading or watching. This simultaneously distances us from the work and converts our passive participation into an action on the same plane as the deeds we are witnessing. It makes us suspect that we are being made the butt of a joke perpetrated by the author. As Hamlin Hill observes, "the black humorist does not seek the sympathy or alliance of his audience, but deliberately insults and alienates it . . . The tone of black humor — belligerent, pugnacious, nihilistic — underscores that the audience itself becomes its comic foil." [18]

These characteristics are found to varying degrees in all black humor, but it is useful to distinguish two major and different manifestations of black humor. "Absurd black humor" emphasizes the humor in black humor and "grotesque black humor" stresses the blackness; however, the line of demarcation between them is not always apparent.[19]

I refer to the lighter side of black humor as "absurd" because of its close affinities with the theater of the absurd, which Martin Esslin calls "the latest example" "of all the gallows

18. "Black Humor: Its Cause and Cure," *Colorado Quarterly,* 17 (Summer 1968), 59, 62.

19. My division of black humor into absurd and grotesque strata roughly corresponds to Robert Scholes' distinction between "satirical" and "picaresque black humor" in *The Fabulators* (New York: Oxford University Press, 1967), pp. 35–94.

humour and *humour noir* of world literature." [20] According to Esslin, who originated the concept of the theater of the absurd, this theater "strives to express its sense of the senselessness of the human condition and the inadequacy of the rational approach by the open abandonment of rational devices and discursive thought" (p. 6). It expresses itself by "the devaluation or even downright dissolution of language, the disintegration of plot, characterization, and final solution which had hitherto been the hallmark of drama, and the substitution of new elements of form — concrete stage imagery, repetition or intensification, a whole new stage language." [21]

One practitioner of this theater, Eugène Ionesco, describes his own work and the techniques of absurd black humor in a passage that complements Esslin's remarks: "It was not for me to conceal the devices of the theatre, but rather make them still more evident, deliberately obvious, go all-out for caricature and the grotesque, way beyond the pale irony of witty drawing-room comedies. No drawing-room comedies, but farce, the extreme exaggeration of parody. Humor, yes, but using the methods of burlesque. Comic effects that are firm, broad and outrageous. No dramatic comedies either. But back to the unendurable. Everything raised to paroxysm, where the source of tragedy lies. A theatre of violence: violently comic, violently dramatic." [22]

Absurd black humor tends to present characters who seem to belong to the world of comedy. They are ignoble wretches with petty problems, limited responses, and little psychological depth. Such characters do not develop in the course of a work; they are their own dilemma and will forever be so. In most comedy they would be the exceptions to an otherwise healthy and functioning society, but in absurd black humor there is no other kind of character. Without the contrast of "normal" characters, we cannot be certain that the individuals we see are aberrations, and so we do not know what to expect or how to judge.

20. *The Theatre of the Absurd,* rev. ed. (Garden City: Doubleday Anchor, 1969), p. 364.

21. Martin Esslin, "The Theatre of the Absurd Reconsidered," *Reflections: Essays on Modern Theatre* (Garden City: Doubleday, 1969), p. 184.

22. *Notes and Counter Notes,* p. 26.

The typical flat comic character is totally on the surface and therefore completely knowable; his whole character may be summed up by his name. The absurd character, on the other hand, is totally incomprehensible, because we are not given an adequate perspective or standard of judgment by which to evaluate him. His name may be highly suggestive and call out for us to make sense of it: Oedipa Maas, Floristan Mississippi, Nicholas d'Eu. We want to imitate the IBM machine in *Catch-22* which promotes a soldier named Major Major to the rank of major so that all will seem harmonious. But "absurd" means "disharmonious," and the names do not provide us with a key to the characters' natures.

We are distanced from these characters by a comic style which calls attention to its own witty artifice in the novel and by the techniques of farce in the drama. We are further separated from them because they lack motivation and their world is without normal causality. One may apply to all of absurd black humor Martin Esslin's observation about the theater of the absurd: "As the incomprehensibility of the motives, and the often unexplained and mysterious nature of the characters' actions in the Theatre of the Absurd effectively prevent identification, such theatre is a comic theatre in spite of the fact that its subject-matter is sombre, violent, and bitter. That is why the Theatre of the Absurd transcends the categories of comedy and tragedy and combines laughter with horror" (*Theatre of the Absurd,* p. 361).

The characters are unable to communicate; words become cliché, babel, or a refuge from experience. The absurd detaches itself from the language of rational discourse because such language posits a rational world. The resultant breakdown of language is both funny as verbal play and threatening because it indicates an inability to comprehend the world or to control one's life. We do not know whether these characters who lead lives without significance and speak words without meaning are amusing because they are so trivial or frightening because they are so empty.

All of the characters are equally ridiculous and equally pathetic. There is therefore a tendency toward total democratization in which all become interchangeable machine parts.

In Tom Stoppard's *Rosencrantz and Guildenstern Are Dead*
the protagonists are continually mistaken for one another and
do not know themselves which is which; in the original version
of the play their muddled roles are taken over after their
deaths by the two English Ambassadors. Mr. and Mrs. Martin
end Ionesco's *The Bald Soprano* by repeating the roles and
words that had belonged to Mr. and Mrs. Smith at the beginning. In Beckett's *Watt* the household of Mr Knott is successively tended by Vincent, Arsène, Erskine, Watt, Arthur, and
Micks, all equally unworthy, each displacing his predecessor in
turn. Different roles do exist, but they can be exchanged in a
mechanical fashion; the strong and weak characters precisely
reverse their positions in Ionesco's *The Lesson* and in Harold
Pinter's *A Slight Ache*. Joy and misery are also constants; as
Pozzo tells Estragon in *Waiting for Godot,* "the tears of the
world are a constant quantity. For each one who begins to weep
somewhere else another stops. The same is true of the laugh."
Since the lot of humanity is constant, individual differences are
unimportant; Ionesco gives the name Bérenger to three distinct
protagonists (in *Rhinoceros, The Killer,* and *Exit the King*).

Like Everyman, these characters enact constant, recurrent
situations rather than live through unique histories, but their
situations have no message for us. The cyclical nature of absurd
black humor is part of its playing with its own form; a literary
plot repeats itself every time it is acted or read. The cycle is
also a trap for the protagonist; he cannot break out of it because there is no alternative. He is trapped by his own limitations and by the world he inhabits. He may recognize that his
problems are petty and laughable, but he is too close to them
to feel the humor. Like Philip Roth's Alexander Portnoy, he
finds himself living through "terrifyingly laughable situations" [23]
and suspects that he is caught up in a joke:

> Doctor Spielvogel, this is my life, my only life, and I'm living
> it in the middle of a Jewish joke! I am the son in the Jewish
> joke — *only it ain't no joke!*   (pp. 36–37)

23. Philip Roth, *Portnoy's Complaint* (New York: Random House,
1969), p. 257.

I can't live any more in a world given its meaning and dimension by some vulgar nightclub clown. By some — *black humorist!*
Because that's who the black humorists are — of course! — the
Henny Youngmans and the Milton Berles breaking them up
down there in the Fountainebleau, and with what? Stories of
murder and mutilation! . . . The macabre is very funny on the
stage — but not to live it, thank you! [24]   (pp. 111–112)

We laugh at such a character because we are removed from
his ridiculous plight, but, because he takes himself seriously, we
are also made to empathize with him. As David I. Grossvogel
has noted, to the extent that we are forced "to recognize the
identity of the object laughed at, the spectator becomes a self-
conscious part of the negative forces that hem in, and frustrate
the full existence of, a kindred being. [The result is a] bitter
laughter, which stresses the fundamental identity of laugher
and victim." [25] Even though our laughter is bitter, absurd black
humor leaves us with a feeling of pleasure. The humorous
element is prime because the characters fundamentally accept
their lot. However much they may struggle and protest, they
take whatever is handed out to them and make the best of a bad
business.

Both we and the characters are more thoroughly shaken in
grotesque black humor. I use the term "grotesque" because
that category has often been described as comprising the dual
affinities of black humor. Victor Hugo says of the grotesque,
"d'une part, il crée le difforme et l'horrible, de l'autre le comique
et le bouffon." John Ruskin finds in it "two elements, one ludicrous, the other fearful," and therefore divides it into "sportive
grotesque" and "terrible grotesque . . . but," he notes, "there
are hardly any examples which do not in some degree combine

24. Lenny Bruce makes the same observation in *How to Talk Dirty
and Influence People* (Chicago: Playboy Press, 1965), pp. 97–99. Responding to the label "sick comic," he notes how "sick" a number of
supposedly healthy Jewish comedians really are, and mentions Young-
man and Berle by name.
25. *Four Playwrights and a Postscript* (Ithaca: Cornell University
Press, 1962), p. 195. This work appears in paperback with identical
pagination as *The Blasphemers: The Theater of Brecht, Ionesco, Beckett,
Genet* (Ithaca: Cornell University Press, 1965).

both elements." Wolfgang Kayser says that the grotesque may be subdivided into the "fantastic" grotesque and the "comically" grotesque, and Lee Byron Jennings observes that "the grotesque object always displays a *combination of fearsome and ludicrous qualities* — or, to be more precise, it simultaneously arouses reactions of fear and amusement in the observer." [26]

The distinction between grotesque and absurd black humor is not always precise; the two are part of a continuum and so overlap and merge.[27] Grotesque black humor has the characteristics common to all black humor. It manifests the same basic treatment of character, motivation, and plot as the absurd, is similarly concerned with the breakdown of normal communication, and plays with its own form and implicates the reader in a similar fashion. But it emphasizes the blackness, diminishes the humor, treats the protagonist more harshly, and involves the reader's emotional responses to a greater extent.

The grotesque form of black humor is obsessed with the human body, with the ways in which it can be distorted, separated into its component parts, mutilated, and abused. People become animals or objects, or share their traits, or are likened to them. Bodily parts are exaggerated or distorted. The body's inability to keep to its proper confines is comic, as Henri Bergson has shown in *Le Rire,* but it also makes us fear that such horrible distortion could happen to us. The threat becomes

26. Hugo, *Préface de "Cromwell,"* ed. Pierre Grossclaude (Paris: Larousse, 1949), p. 27; Ruskin, "The Stones of Venice," *The Complete Works of John Ruskin,* ed. E. T. Cook and Alexander Wedderburn (London: George Allen, 1904), XI, 151; Kayser, *The Grotesque in Art and Literature,* trans. Ulrich Weisstein (Bloomington: Indiana University Press, 1963), p. 173; Jennings, *The Ludicrous Demon: Aspects of the Grotesque in German Post-Romantic Prose,* University of California Publications in Modern Philology, 71 (Berkeley and Los Angeles: University of California Press, 1963), p. 10.

27. The terminological confusion is illustrated in the writings of Martin Esslin, who calls "grotesque" in German what he refers to as "Theatre of the Absurd" in English. See his two essays "Der Blick in den Abgrund: Das Groteske im Zeitgenössischen Drama in Frankreich" and "Der Common Sense des Nonsense: Das Groteske im modernen angelsächsischen Drama" in *Sinn oder Unsinn? Das Groteske im Modernen Drama,* ed. Martin Esslin et al., (Basel: Basilius, 1962), pp. 95–146. For an attempt to disentangle the two terms, see Arnold Heidsieck, *Das Groteske und das Absurde im modernen Drama* (Stuttgart: W. Kohlhammer, 1969).

stronger when a character is mutilated, but a comic element is added if the character is untroubled by his mishaps or if the mutilation is acted or narrated farcically.

Bodily deformation separates grotesque black humor from the absurd form. Whereas the characters in the absurd have learned to live with, if not necessarily accept, the universe they inhabit, the grotesque contains at least one character who feels terror or to whom things happen which we would regard as horrible if they happened to us. Because the characters suffer so immediately and graphically, the grotesque is apt to present an inflictor of torments, an aggressor in a world of victims, though he may himself be as grotesque as Jarry's Ubu (*Ubu Roi*) or Dürrenmatt's Claire Zachanassian (*The Visit*).

The threat to the body is part of the omnipresent threat of death in grotesque black humor. Death dominates, but it occurs in a ridiculous manner and is never dignified. Death is the final divorce between body and spirit, the ultimate disjunction in a form that dwells on violent incongruities. Often it is reduced to its physical manifestation, the corpse, which is man become thing; *rigor mortis* is the *reductio ad absurdum* of Bergsonian automatism.

The mind also separates from the body (and from the rest of the world) in madness. The madman is a central figure in grotesque black humor; his lack of rational thought and his mannerisms are comical, but his insight into a disjunctive and chaotic world is frightening. He sees a world where nothing has a sharp outline, where one thing continually becomes another through metaphor or metamorphosis. The same perspective prevails in other states that approach madness: delirium, dream, or intoxication. All are conditions in which one's normal certainties and the ability to evaluate rationally break down; in which it is difficult to distinguish between what is funny and what is frightening, and where one may suddenly turn into the other.

The style of grotesque black humor tries to recreate this uncertainty in the reader. Because of the horrible things that happen to the characters in grotesque black humor, we are more emotionally involved, and therefore more threatened, than in absurd black humor. The style must also serve, then, to distance us from the work, to make us laugh one moment at what horrifies us the next, or to keep us uneasily suspended between the two responses. This is a formidable task; but it can be accomplished, as is shown by the following passage from *Lolita,* which incorporates nearly every aspect of grotesque black humor. Humbert Humbert relates how he killed Clare Quilty:

> I fired three or four times in quick succession, wounding him at every blaze; and every time I did it to him, that horrible thing to him, his face would twitch in an absurd clownish manner, as if he were exaggerating the pain; he slowed down, rolled his eyes half closing them and made a feminine "ah!" and he shivered every time a bullet hit him as if I were tickling him, and every time I got him with those slow, clumsy, blind bullets of mine, he would say under his breath, with a phoney British accent — all the while dreadfully twitching, shivering, smirking, but withal talking in a curiously detached and even amiable manner: "Ah, that hurts, sir, enough! Ah, that hurts atrociously, my dear fellow. I pray you, desist. Ah — very painful, very painful, indeed . . . God! Hah! This is abominable, you should really not — "
>
> (pt. II, chap. 35)

Both absurd and grotesque black humor disorient their audience. We do not know how to react to the literary work any more than the characters know how to cope with their world. We find ourselves in the same confused and problematical situation as the characters of black humor. Which is precisely where the author wants us to be.

Contributors

ROBERT ALTER Department of Comparative Literature
University of California, Berkeley

WALTER BLAIR Department of English
University of Chicago

MORTON W. BLOOMFIELD Department of English
Harvard University

JOHN BULLITT Department of English
Harvard University

DANTE DELLA TERZA Department of Romance Languages and Literatures
Harvard University

DONALD FANGER Department of Comparative Literature
Harvard University

W. M. FROHOCK Department of Romance Languages and Literatures
Harvard University

BRUCE JACKSON Department of English
State University of New York, Buffalo

JOHN V. KELLEHER Department of Celtic Languages and Literatures
Harvard University

ROBERT KIELY Department of English
Harvard University

HARRY T. LEVIN Department of Comparative Literature
Harvard University

JEAN-JACQUES MAYOUX Institut d'Etudes Anglaises et Nord-Américaines
University of Paris

JOEL PORTE Department of English
Harvard University

ROGER ROSENBLATT Department of English
Harvard University

ERICH SEGAL Department of Classics
Yale University

MATHEW WINSTON Department of English and Comparative Literature
Columbia University